Mortality and Faith

Mortality and Faith
Reflections on a
Journey through Time

David Horowitz

REGNERY
PUBLISHING
A Division of Salem Media Group

Regnery® is a registered trademark of Salem Communications Holding
Corporation

Cataloging-in-Publication data on file with the Library of Congress

ISBN 978-1-62157-813-0
e-book ISBN 978-1-62157-849-9

Published in the United States by
Regnery Publishing
A Division of Salem Media Group
300 New Jersey Ave NW
Washington, DC 20001
www.RegneryGateway.com

Manufactured in the United States of America

10 9 8 7 6 5 4 3 2 1

Books are available in quantity for promotional or premium use.
For information on discounts and terms, please visit our website:
www.Regnery.com.

"The meaning of life
is that it stops."

—KAFKA

Contents

Preface

Mortality and Faith is the second half of an autobiography whose first installment, *Radical Son,* was published more than twenty years ago. It completes the account of my life from where the first book left off to my seventy-eighth year. In contrast to *Radical Son* whose focus was my political odyssey, *Mortality and Faith* was conceived as a meditation on age, and on our common progress towards an end which is both final and opaque. These primal facts affect all we see and do, and force us to answer the questions as to why we are here and where we are going with conjectures that can only be taken on faith. Consequently, an equally important theme of this work is its exploration of the beliefs we embrace to answer these questions, and how the answers impact our lives.

The first three parts of this text were previously published in separate volumes, without drawing attention to their autobiographical nature. The final part, "Staying Alive," is new. I have put the four parts together as a continuous text to make their autobiographical nature clear, and to underscore themes that contain the principal lessons I have learned in the course of my journey.

Another of my books, *A Cracking of the Heart,* also contains autobiographical reflections and addresses questions of mortality and faith. I did not include it in this volume because it is an elegy for my daughter Sarah and is a portrait of her life, not mine. Nonetheless, it shares with this volume a sensibility and inquiry that make it appropriate to mention.

In preparing this edition, I have changed a word or phrase here or there to improve the original texts.

BOOK I
The End of Time
(1993–2005)

*It is better to go to the house of mourning
than the house of feasting, for that is the end
of all; and the living will lay it to his heart.*

—ECCLESIASTES

1

Going Home

W hen he was alive and I was still young, my father told me his version of the Fall. "We begin to die the day we are born," he said. What I think my father meant by this was that the cells, which are the invisible elements of our being, are constantly churning in nature's cycle. Silently, without our being aware of their agony, they are inexorably aging and taking us with them. Year by year, the skin parches, the sinews slacken, and the bones go brittle, until one day the process stops, and we are gone.

At least that is what I think my father said because that is all that I can remember. And what I can remember is all that is left of the time we spent together long ago, a fading image now like the rest. I can still see the sunlight on the green hedge where we paused on the sidewalk. I can see the mottled sycamores shading the street, and the way my father turned until the tan dome of his forehead caught the glint of the light when he shared his thought.

On this day we were taking our Saturday walk through Sunnyside Gardens, the neighborhood where I grew up. In the yards the spring warmth had pushed the yellow daffodils and purple crocuses through the black earth, creating warm little splashes of color. I remember the feeling of pleasure I had, and always did, being alone with him. Or maybe it is the lingering memory that is the pleasure. Or both. I can no longer tell.

When he didn't go to work, my father took walks every day of his life that I can recall. It was only years afterward that it occurred to me that for him the aim of these walks was not to go somewhere, but to get away. As though the life he had been given was less than the one he wanted, or more than one he could bear.

As my father imparted his reflection, the timbre in his voice gave off no hint of gloom but was detached and clinical as though he was making a scientific observation devoid of human reference. Even now, I cannot guess what his intentions were, or why he decided to share this dark insight with me when I was so innocent of life myself. But he did; and the words have stuck ever since and into the present when age is already on me and has sunk its teeth into my marrow, and feelings of mortality have made themselves as familiar as hello and goodbye.

It is more than half a century since my father and I took our walk. From that time until his death nearly forty years later in the same redbrick row house on the same tree-lined street, we never discussed the subject again. Though I never forgot what he said, I never bothered in all that time to inquire of anyone who might actually know whether it was based on a biological truth, or not. Nor did it ever occur to me that his words might not actually have referred to the objective world, but to his feelings about himself.

My father was a small, well-intentioned man of melancholy humors and roiling regrets. Bleak thoughts enveloped him in a cloud so dense he was rarely able to see the sun behind it. One effect of this rough-weather approach was to make it difficult for him to find pleasure in the opportunities life offered. When good fortune came knocking at his door, he received it more often than not as he would a visitor to the wrong address.

All our days together I wrestled with my father's discontent and tried as best I could to overcome it. But eventually I understood that the well from which he drew his unhappiness was bottomless, and no one could stem its flow. As a result, the lesson he left me was not contained in the earnest lectures he gave, but in the instruction of a life that clung to its defeats like an infant to its mother's breast.

Unlike my father, I do not feel that life is a downhill run. Nor do I think of it as an arc that rises steadily until it reaches its apogee, tapers, and arches back to earth. The fate we choose is inscribed in multiple flights. Some follow the gravity of rise and fall, while others—those of the spirit, for example—may never head downward but climb steadily to the end, where they just drop cliff-like into the dark.

Consequently, there is no right time for last words, no point of demarcation for our *adieux;* no designated moment to set down the summary thoughts of a mind still counting. Whether you begin to die at the beginning—as my father believed—or whether you burn brightly to the end, you can't wait forever to pass to others what you have learned. When the time approaches you could already have a foot in oblivion, or be crippled by a stroke, or so blasted with pain as to lose the ability to reflect at all. In this life, you can be hauled off without warning. You can step onto the wrong plane, or off the wrong curb, or into the wrong conversation, and be gone. A microorganism can stumble into a passage to your heart and douse the lights before you even learn its name. Or the cells of your being—those busy dying since you were born—can go berserk and betray you in a cancer that chokes your last thought.

No matter how young you are or how far you get, you can never know if there will be hours enough to finish the page. Some of us get yanked before our time while others hang on longer than they should. Still others take themselves out when they think they've had enough. But what is enough, particularly if you wise up and eventually master the game? It doesn't matter. The clock is ticking and the buzzer is set. This is an injustice that no reform can repair and no court redress.

When I began these pages I was living in a Mediterranean-style house perched like an eyrie on the palisades high above the Pacific Ocean. I had gravitated to this refuge only two years before in what I realized was an *hommage* to a passion I inherited from my father. It was the only non-political one he ever really allowed himself: his unfulfilled longing for the sea.

On crystal days, which were many, I would look out through picture windows to my only horizon, a panorama of whitecaps and blue water, and miss him. At such moments my father's ghost would sometimes return to haunt me. I could see the face I had both loved and feared approach on the ether of memory until it was only a breath away. An impulse to please would swell like an ocean wave inside me, and I would look out on the roll of dolphins and pelicans, and welcome my lost father to a luxury neither of us could ever have imagined would be ours.

In these reveries his spirit was so palpable I could almost touch it. I would point my fingers towards the apparition and run them down the slope of its brow until I had fully mapped the frown of his rejection. For there was never a chance he would accept my gift or enjoy its pleasures. Not now; not then; not ever. The opportunity rolled away from us like the ebb of an evening tide. It hardly matters why; whether he felt he didn't deserve this happiness, or I didn't, or both. It only matters that it was so. In my father's house there were no mansions.

Because he was unable to get what he wanted in this life, my father frittered away his days in dreams of the next. The metaphor of this longing was the sea, limitless and unattainable. What my father desperately wanted—or so he believed—was a world better than the one he had been given. This was the unrequited romance of his life, the object of the only prayers he ever allowed himself. But the world did not heed his prayers. It ignored him, as it does us all, and went its own way.

In the end, my father's disappointment was the gift he gave me, an irony that still links us beyond the grave. His melancholy taught me the lesson he was unable to learn himself. Don't bury the life you have been given in this world in fantasies of the next; don't betray yourself with impossible dreams.

Are these judgments too harsh? Are they gripes of an ungrateful son? Perhaps the father I think I know was not so helpless after all; perhaps he was even shrewd. Maybe when he shared his thoughts with me on our neighborhood walk, he meant something else entirely. Maybe what he was saying to his son was this: Prepare now for the end.

When the novelist Saul Bellow reached the age of seventy-eight his brain was still kicking like that of a young man. *All Marbles Still Accounted For* was the witty title he devised for a novel he was writing that was still unfinished. In the pages of the books he did send to press, he showed he was still capable of turning out clever prose and was a step ahead in getting things to add up. He remained a master of the game.

In that same year Bellow published an elegiac tale about his dying mother who had been stricken with cancer a lifetime before. The story recounted an embarrassing incident, which its fictional narrator claimed had distracted him from his filial obligation. It happened on a winter's day when his mother lay on a bed of pain, gulping the arduous breaths her family knew would be her last.

While the mother suffered, life continued for everyone else, including her son who went about his job delivering flowers for a local merchant. Late that afternoon, he was bearing an armful of lilies to the funeral of a young girl no older than himself. Entering the room where her coffin lay open, he cast a diffident eye on the lifeless form. After navigating the crowd of mourners and locating the grieving mother, he pressed his bouquet into her arms and fled.

This encounter with death so affected the young man that instead of returning to the shop for more orders or going home, he decided to stop at a nearby office building where his uncle worked. The uncle was out, but as the youth made his way down the hall he passed the open door of a doctor's office and had a chance encounter with a sexual mystery woman. She was lying on a table naked, but failed to react when she caught sight of him spying on her. This seductive behavior planted the idea in his head that she was available for his pleasure. Hot with desire, he allowed her to lure him across town to an apartment, where she induced him to undress.

All the while his flesh was burning, which caused his brain cells to go numb so he didn't see what was coming. When he had completely removed his clothes, the woman grabbed them and fled into the bitter cold of the Chicago night. Ruefully, Bellow's narrator recalls how he put on a dress that he found in a closet, and went out into the freezing air, dreading the humiliation that awaited him, and his father's anger, when he got back.

His money was gone and he had no carfare, so he went into a local bar where his luck improved when the bartender paid him to see a drunken customer home. Afterwards, he boarded the El that would take him back. But sitting in the train car, alone with his shame, he had an unnerving thought. Until then, he had been fearful of facing his father's fury at what he had done. Now he began to hope for it instead. For he remembered what his desire had caused him to forget: his mother was dying. If his father was angry at him when he stepped through the front door, he would know she was still alive.

One lesson of this story concerns animal desire. Sex is a force so powerful that it is the source of endless human embarrassment and considerable personal grief. Lust will frustrate a man's best efforts to elevate himself and make of his life something dignified and worthy. It will induce him to do things that are stupid and humbling. Like shaming one's mother on her deathbed.

Yet desire is only a sub-theme of Bellow's tale, which is built on facts taken from his life. Bellow's fictional narrator dedicates this memoir to his son as a memento for when he is gone, calling it, *Something to Remember Me By.* This is a typical Bellow trope, since it is a story anyone would prefer to forget. Perhaps that is why it took Bellow until his 78th year to write it down.

The main theme of his tale is announced in its opening paragraph, which is constructed around the image of a turntable. The author doesn't identify the turntable he has in mind, whether it is the kind one finds in children's playgrounds or the kind used to play vinyl records and produce musical sounds, gone now like so much else. Instead he writes, "When there is too much going on, more than you can bear, you may choose to assume that nothing in particular is happening, that your life is going round and round like a turntable." Perhaps the denial he is referring to is larger than the moment itself. Perhaps he is hinting that the music of your days can lull you into an illusion that the present will go on and on, and will never go anywhere else. Or perhaps, more simply, that your life is in motion when you think you are just standing still.

Until something happens, that is. Until you get clobbered by an event and wake up to the fact that the stillness is an illusion. That everything is changing about you, and that one day it will come to an end. In Bellow's case the clobbering was his mother's death. Inexplicably and without warning, the cells in her body had run amok and created a malignancy in her breast. Soon, it was choking her, until she was gasping for air and spitting up blood. And then she was gone.

When Bellow's mother had breathed her last and her agonies finally came to an end, the coroner did not know what age to put on the certificate of death. Like many immigrants she had no idea of the date she was born and neither did anyone else. So the coroner did what he could and put on the certificate what he saw. She seemed to be a woman of "about fifty," he wrote. The certificate was like a tag on ancient bones that had been exhumed in an archaeological dig and that no one could identify. Her surviving son was only seventeen.

"One day you are aware that what you took to be a turntable, smooth, flat and even, was in fact a whirlpool, a vortex," Bellow observes. The vortex of his mother's death had sucked some part of him beneath the surface and it never came back. "My life was never the same after my mother died," he noted long afterward. In the story, he wrote: "I knew she was dying, and didn't allow myself to think about it—there's your turntable."

In the business of mothers dying, fate dealt me a better hand than it did Saul Bellow. My mother lived to a ripe age and was vigorous to the end. When she had her first stroke my children were already adults and had given me two grandchildren besides. I was well into the cycle of the generations. This prepared me in a way that the young Bellow could not have been for the cold hand of mortality that a parent's death lays on your heart. When the time arrived for my mother to go, it seemed almost natural that her life should draw to a conclusion. Even though her death was sudden and unannounced, I had time enough to prepare for it, to see the vortex coming.

On the other hand, the months before she died were not unlike the day remembered in Bellow's story. I, too, let myself go round like a turntable, running about the business of my life while the clock on hers ticked mercilessly away. What else could I have done? Can one focus on death like a watched pot, waiting for it to boil? If we concentrated on our dying with an intensity that never let up, everything in our lives would come to a stop, until our days would seem like the grave itself. So usually we don't pay attention to where we are headed but go round on the turntable and pretend we are standing still.

Here's a tip. As you go spinning round, turn one eye to the side every now and then. Look over the edge and focus on a fixed object. Find a way to calculate your progress. Otherwise, life will pass you by before you wake up.

My father—blessed be his memory—was right: Never forget the cells that are dying. Life is not a turntable, and one day the music will stop.

When I think of Saul Bellow's unhappy evening years ago, I am prompted to consider how different we are, and how incommensurable the lives we are given. How, as a result, each of us is an impenetrable enigma to the other: the young Bellow to the mystery woman who made off with his clothes; the mystery woman to him; both to us.

What would it do to your sense of things if your mother had died a cruel and punishing death when you were still a youth of seventeen? How would the memory affect your optimism, your sense of threat in the environment around you? Would it cause you to become a man more quickly? Or would the missing parent make it more difficult to grow up at all? Losing one's mother at such a young age could certainly make the world seem a lonelier and more unforgiving place.

Saul Bellow eventually married five women. Several of his biographers claim to have found a pattern in his choice of wives, identifying them as motherly types. The list includes even the last who was forty years his junior and took care of him in old age. Are these really psychological insights into Bellow's inner life, or merely critical sour grapes? Who can read another's heart?

Our origins create a gravity that controls our ends but also leaves us to our own devices. In every family there is one who has gone this way, while another heads somewhere else. This one surrenders to awful circumstances; that one survives the worst and flourishes. One benefits from benign conditions; another rejects them. This tells us that we have a biblical free will and are finally the gods of what we become.

Bellow's lot may not seem so hard when viewed from others' perspectives. When my friend Christopher Hitchens was twenty-three and living in London, he got a call from one of his friends. The morning paper was reporting that someone with his mother's name had been murdered by her lover in an Athens hotel. "So I went out and got the paper and there it was," he remembers. He called the Athens police and boarded a plane and was led to the apartment where the tragedy had taken place. At first, the police called it a murder because there was blood everywhere. But then they found a suicide note addressed to Christopher that said, "You will understand one day."

Would he? If you are not in Christopher's shoes, it's hard to imagine how this primal scene would not work itself into the inner ear of the soul and tip the balance of a life. Christopher said, "That was sort of the end of family life, really." What does this statement mean to him? We cannot know, any more than we can know the meaning of his mother's final note. What we know is that the individual soul is life's impenetrable mystery. No matter how intense the intimacies we share, no matter how common our humanity, its code cannot be cracked. This creates a silence between every one of us that is as deep and as wide as the ocean floor.

When he was eighty-five and nearing his end, Saul Bellow published another fiction called *Ravelstein,* which is about the death of his friend, the critic Allan Bloom. Towards the story's end, the narrator goes on a Caribbean vacation with his younger wife, where he becomes deathly ill from food poisoning. This is something that happened to Bellow himself.

In his fevers, the narrator has a vision of a past conversation about death with Ravelstein, now gone. "When I said that the pictures would stop he reflected seriously on my answer, came to a full stop, and considered what I might mean by this. No one can give up on the pictures. The pictures must and will continue." Bellow's comment: "This is the involuntary and normal, the secret, esoteric, confidence of the man of flesh and blood. The flesh would shrink and go, the blood would dry, but no one believes in his mind of minds or heart of hearts that the pictures *do* stop."

What else would you expect from a creator of images? Would a lifetime of lonely labors be requited if all that authorial effort crumbled to dust with the pages that recorded it? Art is long and life is short and the technology of preservation is relentlessly advancing. Memories and thoughts were once inscribed on parchments that decayed. Now we can put our writings in vacuum-sealed time capsules that will last for centuries. But in the eye of eternity, this posterity is nothing. Can anybody believe that human artifice will outrun time itself?

It is more plausible that the images come to an end. *All* the images: the images Bloom impressed on others when he was still alive; Bloom's images of them; and the image of Bloom in the figure of Ravelstein so skillfully drawn by his friend. Eventually the vapors of time will dissolve them, and they will disappear into the black hole from which they came. The pictures will stop.

Think of death as a horizon that travels with us, until one day we reach it, and it becomes us. We vanish in an eye-blink, leaving behind only a little vacancy, like the wake of a ship that is lost at sea. Of all the pictures in our minds, this is the one that is hardest to focus. Yet, it is the one that tells us who we are.

Do even the brave souls among us who can look coldly on their exits believe in their heart of hearts that they will disappear? Or do they secretly hope to wake beyond the horizon in a place that feels like home?

Uncertainty about our end is the one fact that links us more than any other. Pitiful ignorance about what matters most is a bond between us, believers and doubters alike. This is our humanity: not to know who we are or what we will become.

I don't believe the pictures continue. Would it be a good idea if they did? Do believers imagine that the immortal soul still *feels* after the vessel is shattered? Can we still love and hate and have regrets beyond the grave? Consider what kind of hell eternity would be like if we had to look forever on the poor lives we have left behind. Or if we had to face ourselves knowing how the story ends without the power to make it different. Do we really want to think for eternity about what we have done and where we have failed? Or does God make it all up to us when we are dead, so that we are forgiven, and forgive others, and forget?

What are "intimations of immortality" but feelings that we *must* live on, that we need the pictures to continue? Yet such intimations cannot be so easily dismissed, since feelings are often about things that are hidden and also true. We rely on such instincts because they are more in the body than abstract thoughts, therefore closer to what is real. The word "sense" expresses this intimacy between feeling and knowledge. When we "sense" something to be true, we mean it has touched us even if we cannot articulate just how. To know through feeling is to know in the heart.

As an agnostic, I have no idea if the universe began with a bang or has existed forever, or is the work of a Creator. But I do know that the biblical book called "Genesis" conveys a central truth about human fate. The First Parents wanted to be like God and could not be satisfied with anything less. Though they were immortal and lived without labor and suffered no pain, they found paradise wanting. What they lacked became their desire. We are defined by negatives; they describe the emptiness we fill. What is good without evil or love without hate? God warned the first couple that death would be the reward for their immodest desire. But they rejected His warning and pursued their ambition anyway, and were punished. Genesis is the story of our beginning and our end. We are creatures of desires that cannot be satisfied and of dreams that will not come true.

Man's longing for God can be understood as the need to be released from the pain of being, even if that pain is paradise itself. To live eternally in paradise without knowledge of what we lacked, even if it was knowledge of evil, even if it *was* evil, was unhappiness to us. To end our unhappiness, we chose to die.

On a shelf in my living room is a rotogravure portrait featuring a spirited teenager in a 19th-century frock, brashly showing her skirt. This is my grandmother Rose who was still a young woman when I was born, and had a fatal stroke when I was in my twenties. Other than this photograph I have no idea what the girl in the picture was like. In my kitchen there is an incomplete set of her wedding crystal and a blue teapot bearing her initials in silver along with the year of her marriage, which was 1898. These are all the pieces of her life that are left, except for a few fading images in the memories of a handful of people who will soon be gone too.

A quarter of a century after my grandmother's death, my mother suffered a series of smaller strokes. The strokes did not kill her at first but damaged an important function in her brain. Afterwards, my mother was still in good physical shape but she could barely remember who she was. Somewhere in the black hole that her memory had become, she had even misplaced my father and could no longer retrieve him. Although they had been married for more than fifty years, the life she had lived with him had slipped into the void and she could no longer recognize his name. The images of my grandmother's life were fading in other heads; my mother's had disappeared in her own. All she could remember was the house on Maple Street in New Haven where she grew up, and the one in Sunnyside where I did.

Because the strokes left her unable to take care of herself, I returned to the Sunnyside row house where she still lived and moved her to my home in Los Angeles, an English Tudor with a redwood in the front yard that offered her more comforts than she had ever known. Though it was a good life for her, she was unhappy. She desired what she lacked. She wanted to go back to the home she remembered and had lost.

My mother could not adjust to the fact that she had become as helpless as a child and was being taken care of by her son. Her persistent melancholy prompted me to search for another home for her, where she would not feel like a burden whom time was passing by. I located a retirement center where she would be surrounded by people her own age, most of whom were even more helpless than she. Even though it was called a "home," the people she lived with had no idea who she was. Although I had qualms about moving her to a strange place, she seemed happier from the day she arrived. The diminished lives she encountered there made her feel more in control and less aware of what she had lost.

The Book of Psalms says that all flesh is grass and that each of us is like a flower in the field that flourishes and dies: "The wind passes over it, and it is gone, and its place knows it no more." Our feeling that we have a place in the world is a deception we practice on ourselves, because we have none. It is this pretense that makes an otherwise unendurable existence bearable and at times even happy. There is really no place in the world that "knows" us in the Psalmist's sense. There is only an illusion sustained by others who love us and who, like us, will soon be gone.

The illusion of home will overcome even the most grotesque scenes of family dysfunction. The feeling is so strong the reality does not matter. We can be battered by a spouse and never want to leave. We can spend our childhood in a household of abuse and fear, but as long as we draw breath our hearts will still want to go home. On this earth our comfort is deception and we can never tell whether we are dreaming, or not.

Sometimes in the night, I wake with an image of my terrified mother in her last moments on earth. It is only an image but to me it is as painful as if it were real. The source of my nightmare is the fact that when the time came for her to go I was not there to help her. Three years earlier I had left the Tudor house, moving twice before settling alone in a tower of apartments in the Los Angeles marina. It was one of more than twenty addresses I have called home. The apartment was only a short drive from the hospital where my mother lay dying, but by the time someone called me and I was able to reach her, she was already gone.

It was this phone call that planted in my mind the suffering image that wakes me in the night. The manager of the home was on the line telling me how my mother had started out of her sleep and summoned one of the strangers to come to her bedside. When the stranger came, my mother said,

"Something is terribly wrong," as though what was wrong might not be happening to her. It was the impersonal voice my mother had used her whole life to hide herself and avoid unnecessary embarrassments. The Angel of Death had come for her, but she called for help in a way that would not draw unnecessary attention to the one who was in need. This is the painful image that harrows my sleep and leaves me with feelings of helplessness and despair. When these nightmares come, I comfort myself with the thought that had I reached her in time, it would only have been to see her off to where I could not follow her, to the horizon each of us must meet alone.

Arriving at the Cedars-Sinai hospital complex, I entered the room where my mother lay on her hospital gurney and where death had already transfigured her. The corpse was twisted in a tangle of tubes, bruised and discolored by the doctors' efforts to bring her back. The figure in front of me was no longer my mother, and I fled into the night to be alone with my loss. In the hospital courtyard, under a luminous black sky, I was enveloped in a wave of feeling that seemed to issue from the night itself. For a moment I was comforted and at peace. And then the wave receded, leaving me to myself again.

In the weeks prior to these events, I was busy with my own life and frequently out of town. On the turntable, as Bellow would have said. Even though my mother's mind was no longer right, I knew that in her heart she was missing me. And I was missing her. But I couldn't get myself off the turntable to see her. Until a day came when despite my busyness, or perhaps because of it, I made a point of taking time out to stop by and visit. There was no way I could have known that this would be her last day on earth.

I drove to the retirement home and came upon her in the common room, where she was waiting. It was early morning and I took a chair beside her. We sat together in the rays of muffled light pouring through the aged curtains and reflected in filaments of microscopic dust, and held each other's hands. I was happy and completely at peace; and I believe she was too. It was as intimate and satisfying as any moment I had ever shared with her.

After she was gone, I thought about her passage and the gratitude I felt for the time with her, and asked myself: *Why was I there? How had I come to her the very morning that was her last?* I have no answer.

More than 350 years ago, in the city of Paris, the scientist Blaise Pascal was deathly ill and approaching his horizon. He was still a young man and, though wracked with pain, was busily taking notes on scraps of paper for what would be his final work. The scraps had been cut with scissors and sewn together with needle and thread. They were found after his death in a disordered state. No one knew how they were meant to be put together. The plan for ordering them was still in Pascal's mind, which was now out of anyone's reach. The little notebooks he had left behind contained the thoughts he had been unable to complete before the end. When he was gone it remained for others to put the scraps in order and identify them with numbers and provide the collection with a name. They called the result Pascal's *Pensées:* "The Thoughts of Monsieur Pascal About Religion and Other Matters, Which Were Discovered Among His Papers After He Died."

Number 205 of Pascal's scraps contains this cry: "When I consider the short duration of my life, swallowed up in the eternity before and after, the space which I fill, and even can see, engulfed in the infinite immensity of spaces of which I am ignorant and which know me not, I am frightened and astonished at being here rather than there; for there is no reason why here rather than there, why now rather than then. Who has put me here?"

It is the unanswered question of every soul in the night surrounding it. We can never know who is the master of this house, or whether it has a master at all. Or who has put us here; or where we are going. Pascal was one of the greatest scientific minds that ever lived. Yet, he looked into the eye of the universe and could not find an answer. Without a Creator to make sense of it, Pascal wrote, a human life is "intolerable."

So what are we to do? Although Pascal was able to unlock the mysteries of the physical universe better than almost any man who ever lived, and although he solved mathematical puzzles for all time, it is his attempt to answer this question that we most remember him by.

As a mathematician, Pascal invented the world's first calculator and was a pioneer of probability theory. Using this theory, he devised formulas for winning games of chance that are still employed today. It was only natural that he should attempt to analyze the spiritual uncertainties that surround us in the same clinical way he went about his scientific studies.

"229. This is what I see and what troubles me. I look on all sides, and I see only darkness everywhere. Nature presents to me nothing, which is not a matter of doubt and concern. If I saw nothing there that revealed a Divinity, I would come to a negative conclusion; if I saw everywhere the signs of a Creator, I would remain peacefully in faith. But seeing too much to deny and too little to be sure, I am in a state to be pitied; ..."

The sadness of our condition flows like an Aeolian melody through Pascal's final papers and makes us recognize in him one of the great poets of the human soul. But the scientist in him could not rest until he had also calculated a way to rescue us from our desperate state. "If there is a God, He is infinitely incomprehensible, since, having neither parts nor limits, He has no relation to us. We are then incapable of knowing either what He is, or if He is." In short, if God does exist, He is a "Hidden God" and unknowable to us.

It is nature's silence about the existence of God that creates the uncertainty that makes us human. We desire a home in this world and the next. This is what we know about ourselves. But we do not know—and can never know—whether we have one in either. Confronting this mystery, Pascal thought that life could be analyzed like a game in which players roll the dice in ignorance of the outcome. Pascal had already made a name for himself throughout Europe by devising mathematical formulas to calculate the odds that governed such entertainments. Now he proposed a mathematical solution to the game of life.

The players in this gamble must calculate the risks of believing that there is a God who will provide us with what we so pitifully desire. They must weigh these risks against the chance that there is no God and that we are alone. Weighing both, they must make their choice. Pascal summed up his solution to this dilemma in the famous fragment 233: "A game is being played at the extremity of this infinite distance where heads or tails will turn up. God is, or He is not ... What will you wager? Weigh the gain and the loss in wagering that God is ... If you gain, you gain all; if you lose, you lose nothing. Wager, then, without hesitation that He is."

This solution to life's riddle is known as "Pascal's Wager." The advice obviously makes sense, but can it make an unbeliever *believe*? Can a mathematical argument inspire a religious faith? Pascal knew it could not. In an even more famous fragment (277), he wrote, "The heart has its reasons, which reason does not know." His scientific head may have been skeptical, but Pascal was not. "Faith," he said, "is God felt by the heart."

As my own end draws near, I weigh the life I have lived against what it might have been. I ask myself: Could I have been wiser, could I have done more? When I look at my life this way I can take satisfaction in the fact that I mostly gave it my all and did what I could. Perhaps I might have achieved greater heights; certainly I could have spent fewer days in pain. But I have no cause to think that given who I was my life could have turned out much better. Considering the bad choices I sometimes made, it might have been a lot worse.

It is the certainty of death that finally makes a life acceptable. When we live as fully as we can, what room is left for regret? The poet Eliot observed that there are no lost causes because there are no won ones. Everything falls to the same imperfection. Eventually, without exception, we will follow the same arc to earth.

These are the thoughts of resignation and acceptance that pass through my head. But in my heart are memories of my mother and father, the home I once had in theirs, the knowledge that they have gone before me, and that soon I will join them. Saul Bellow's mother is there and Christopher's too. I do not have the faith of Pascal, but I know its feeling. While reason tells me the pictures will stop, I will be unafraid when death comes. I will feel my way towards the horizon in front of me, and my heart will take me home.

Blaise Pascal was born in 1623 in the region of Clermont-Ferrand in France. On an open field in this place more than five hundred years earlier, Pope Urban had launched the first Crusade to the Promised Land. Here, Pascal's mother, a pious woman named Antoinette, gave birth to three children and died when her last, Blaise, was only three years old. After his mother's death, Pascal's family moved to Paris and his father, a learned man, took up the education of his prodigy son. By the time Pascal was twelve years old, he had proved Euclid's 32nd theorem by himself. By the time he was twenty-eight, he had completed most of the scientific work for which he is remembered. In that same year, his father died and his beloved sister Jacqueline renounced the world and withdrew to a nunnery.

Three years after his father's death, Pascal had a religious vision which is as famous as his scientific laws. He called it his "night of fire." Between eleven and midnight Pascal encountered "the God of Abraham, Isaac and Jacob and not of the philosophers." No one knows exactly what he meant by this, but it has been assumed that he was referring to the actual presence of God and not just the idea of Him. After this experience Pascal became even more remote, and wrote of his "extreme aversion for the beguilements of the world." Unlike his sister, he did not completely retreat from the company of others but began to focus his genius more and more on religious questions and, in particular, the problem of last things.

Pascal's body was as weak as his mind was strong. Since infancy, he had been afflicted by poor health and as an adult experienced stomach disorders and migraines that blurred his vision and made it difficult for him to work. By the time he reached his thirty-fifth year, he was in such pain that he had to suspend his intellectual effort. In the midst of this agony, he wrote another literary fragment, which he called, *A Prayer to Ask God to Make Good Use of Sickness,* and returned to work.

To distract himself from his physical pain, Pascal took up the problem of the cycloid, and wrote a hundred-page paper that made significant contributions to the theory of integral calculus. But his main effort was a book of religious philosophy in which he intended to justify the Christian faith. While pain made him so pitiable that his sister Gilberte wondered if his existence could be truly called a life, he went about jotting down his thoughts on scraps of paper, cutting them with scissors and binding them with thread.

As the days progressed, neither his failing condition nor his spiritual intensity showed any signs of abating, while his life became steadily more stoic and austere. He gave away his possessions to the poor, and gradually withdrew from the friends who loved him. "It is unjust that men should attach themselves to me," he wrote in fragment number 471, "even though they do it with pleasure and voluntarily. I should deceive those in whom I had created this desire. For I am not the end of any, and I have not the wherewithal to satisfy them. Am I not about to die?"

He was. In June 1662 Pascal took in a family that was homeless. Soon after their arrival, its members developed symptoms that revealed they had smallpox. But rather than put them back on the street, Pascal left his own house and moved in with his brother. Shortly after the move, Pascal was seized with a violent illness, and on August 19 he died. He was thirty-nine years old.

The last words that Blaise Pascal uttered were these: "May God never abandon me." They reflect how helpless, uncertain and alone this passionate and brilliant and famous man felt as he passed to his own horizon.

I understand Pascal's judgment that since we are born to die it is an injustice that others should love us. But what did he propose to do with their affections? When I had more years than Pascal, I fell in love with a woman who was twenty years younger than I. Our age difference was a matter of concern to me, but not from Pascal's perspective—the view from the end. Undoubtedly I should also have had generous thoughts about the effect my leaving might have on her life, since I was bound to make her a widow. But selfishly I didn't; and since she also loved me, what could I have done if I had such thoughts? In my passion, I didn't even think about the end, but drew strength from her youth and saw only the life in front of me. That was my turntable.

Pascal is right that death is many injustices in one. But what can we do about this fact except learn to live with our fate, and make use of what we have learned?

Life Is a Hospital

I was 62 years old when I began these reflections in the spring of 2001, a time fixed in my mind by the events that followed. It was a period when my work required me to travel frequently. In the solitude of planes, high above the clouds, I began to think about the summary lessons of my life, and how I might structure a text in which to set them down. It was undoubtedly the setting that inspired the project. Although air travel has been around long enough to be normal, it still feels like an unnatural exercise of human powers and makes us think of death every time we climb aloft. I jotted the first notes of this book on a yellow notepad in an airport lounge, waiting for the flight to take me home.

The idea was this: If you stick around long enough to become familiar with the routines, you get a chance to see around the edges of what's going on. The passage of time allows you to weigh what people say against what they do; to see through the poses they strike and the alibis they make; and to appreciate how the inattention of others makes all this deviousness work. This is no small matter, because if you look long and hard enough you will find that a lie is at the root of most human wrong.

If you last a long time and get to look over collective shoulders and measure the consequences, eventually you achieve life's most irreversible result, which is the loss of innocence, the illusion that anything can happen and the hope that it will. This is a particularly destructive mistake. For if anything is possible, then nothing is necessary, and no conclusion follows. Consequently, no consideration can become a caution and no principle a restraint. The desire for more than is possible is the cause of greater human miseries than any other.

Recognition of consequences is the beginning of wisdom. In *Ravelstein*, Bellow summarizes in a single image the importance of death in making us wise. "Death is the dark backing a mirror needs if we are to see anything," he wrote. The idea I had in the airport was to view it all from the vantage of the end.

The 18th-century lexicographer Samuel Johnson is remembered, in part, for a famous observation he made about executions: "When a man knows he is to be hanged in a fortnight, it concentrates his mind wonderfully." The timeline is what sets the mark and focuses the attention. Who doesn't know that death is waiting? But who plans their day with the end in mind? Eventually you may get far enough along that it is a prudence to greet each morning as though it were your last. But until then, the end is only a distant horizon silently drawing near. It approaches so slowly that you can hardly see movement. Then, a day comes, perhaps when you have already reached middle age, when its shadow enters the corner of your eye and remains there, and for a dreadful beat shuts everything down.

To measure the time I had left, I began to develop the habit of looking back over twenty-year patches to see how much living had been packed into the interval. When I turned forty, this twenty-year retrospect fixed me as a young man just out of college and newly married. It was 1959 and I had loaded my first car with books and clothes and household belongings, and set out for California. Sitting beside me was my bride who would bear me four children in the course of the next decade, and before us a horizon of uncharted distances and adventures unknown.

Twenty years does not seem like a long time from some perspectives, but from others it can seem ample. I was only forty, but the road I had traveled included a life derailed by tragedy, a marriage failed, a family grown and a career undone. It was enough to approximate an existence in full. The young groom in the picture was as strange to me now as the toddler of twenty years before would have seemed to him. If my first two intervals had encom-passed so much, I reasoned, there was still a lifetime ahead before I reached sixty. So why think about the end at all?

I remember the precise moment I started this clock: in a London townhouse, in the autumn of 1964. I had become restless in California, where we set up our first household, and wanted more of the world than I had seen until then. In 1962 I moved our little family of three to Europe and eventually to England where we settled in a basement flat near Hampstead Heath, on a street lined with sycamores like the neighborhood in Sunnyside.

One afternoon when the leaves had already fallen, we were enjoying a social chat in the living room of another American couple who lived on the block. The husband was not ten years older than I, but already suffused with a sadness that hinted at battles irretrievably lost. His name was Goodheart, and later he became a minor literary critic and the author of a book, *Desire and Its Discontents,* which was a title that seemed apt for his disposition. In the middle of the conversation, and without connecting his comment to any of its threads, he said, "We're all going to die." Then as if to retrieve the moment, he added, "I guess I've spoiled the party," which he certainly had.

I only saw Goodheart once again after that. It was more than thirty years later at an academic conference in Boston, where we sat down in a cafeteria to reminisce about the past. He had aged much as I expected he would, his shoulders slightly stooped and with the same vague despondency shadowing his eyes. I noticed that all the time we talked a smile never crossed his lips. The tracks of age, wrinkled brow and wisps of hair whitening at the temples, only deepened the impression of defeat.

For many years, the timekeeping I began in the Goodhearts' living room allowed me to recover a certain degree of innocence—time without an endpoint. But the deception remained imperfect. Though I was comfortable on my turntable, I could never again completely free myself from the knowledge that I was not standing still. The effort was not helped by the signs that had begun to mark my own temporal vessel. Small physical irritations that kept me awake—an unfamiliar ache, stiffness in the joints, elusive light the eyes could no longer absorb—all served to remind me of the horizon ahead.

Still, it was not all slippage. The longer I lasted, the more flexible some faculties became. There was a cunning in age that kept the interest awake. Even as light failed, the interior eye gained depth of perception. All arcs, it turned out, were not equal, and some sinews are strengthened by what they endure. In my case, the arduous labors of the written word had gradually transformed themselves into a kind of pleasure. The mastery through artifice of worldly incoherence began to provide comforts that approached a religious consolation.

Among the discoveries of time, on the other hand, was the revelation that the spirit ages too. It gets used to what it has seen, and it sees the wall coming. Even this prospect doesn't slow us down all at once. As creatures we are endlessly devious and resourceful, prodigies in the art of self-delusion. To beat the odds, we hoodwink ourselves into idylls of recaptured youth, dallying with the young and indulging their daydreams. But inevitably a point comes when all devices fail, and we wake to the fact that the past is irretrievable and there is no way back.

In my sixth decade, I watched my children having children of their own. The new families were entirely familiar, the miracle of immanence in the flesh and the fierce bond of a filial connection. Yet nothing was the same. The mark of parenthood was the responsibility it thrust on you for another life. But this responsibility was no longer mine. My children were accountable for their own lives now, and for my grandchildren's too. It was a microcosm of how the world itself was passing me by. All around, others were stepping up. Swifter souls on the make, quicker minds addressing the tasks I once set for myself. It would all go on without me.

In my new household, a similar sea-change had taken place. A second family was, to be sure, a kind of beginning again. There was the seductive, risk-scented encounter with a stranger, new intimacy discovered and the comforts it brought. There were the expectations that flow from unknown futures, and the energies such hopes inspire. But "beginning again" is an oxymoron. You can't really go back to where you have been before and pretend it is new. This time you can see around the corners of the story you are creating and get a good idea of where it will end.

While I pushed forward in denial as though time didn't matter, my younger wife took note of my progress and calculated the odds. As love deepened and entangled us, our shared joys became a cause of concern. She began to worry about a future without me, and how she might fare when I was gone. In the anxious moments these thoughts inspired, she made me promise to live to the age of Methusaleh, to which I happily agreed. But she also insisted on knowing the practical arrangements I might make for her in the event of my demise. Even this pragmatism, I noted, was a form of denial. What security could I give her for her life after ours? Was not Pascal right about this too? The love of someone will change you forever.

We had recently moved into the eyrie on the palisades with a mortgage significantly higher than that of our previous residence. To make the purchase I had undertaken a risk so large that at times it seemed I had a fingernail grip on the cliff itself. It was my wife, still full of the future who had been looking for a new place and located the house. But my calculations showed that to buy the property would be imprudent. We might make the down payment and meet the mortgage for perhaps a year. But to live in the house longer would require me to double my income. As we drove to the site I braced myself to resist her desire, repeating silently the mantra I had prepared. "It's not the time for us to buy; we can't really afford this; the answer is no." But the instant I crossed the threshold and saw the face of the ocean pressing through a wall of windows in our new living room, I blurted *yes*.

I thought: *I am sixty-one years old, and this is my only life. If I don't seize the opportunity and attempt to make it work, I will die without ever having another chance to live this way. I am not going to miss it.* I did not want the buzzer to ring without taking the shot.

We bought the house and it immediately became a spur to late ambitions, the skeleton of a life on which I would be forced to put new flesh. I explored new avenues for my talents and sought rewards for my efforts where I would not have done so before. I had been given a new way to think about the possibilities ahead.

The mortgage for the eyrie was nearly twice that of the house we sold. As a result, the life insurance I had to pay off the old place in the event of my death was about half what the new one would require. For the first year I pushed this deficit to the back of my mind. But in the second, when my insurance agent asked if I wanted to extend our coverage, I told him to submit a proposal. Even as I did, it occurred to me that the phrase "life insurance" was itself a monument to human futility, one more gesture of impotence in our lost battles against time. Nonetheless, the policy would be immediately useful in calming my wife's unease.

A week after I signed the documents, a casually dressed and slightly overweight woman appeared at our door. She was a peripatetic physician representing a company called "Porta-Doctor," a name that fitted form to function. She came carrying her laboratory with her—a small white scale, a laptop to run electrocardiograms, a blood pressure cuff and meter, and a cluster of disposable syringes. With my father's ocean as our backdrop, the Porta-Doctor administered the tests required by the company actuaries to establish that I had enough time ahead of me to make a good return on their investment.

I was reasonably certain I would be around for a while, because four months earlier I had passed my annual checkup with decent marks. Although the test numbers were as obscure to me as the Eleusinian mysteries, I took the good news on my doctor's word. The annual ritual had become a lesson in the arcane religion of modern science. There were good lipids and bad, and cholesterol levels that one should not exceed. I learned about "prostate- specific antigens" or "psa's," which were the telltale indicators of a prostate cancer, a condition so common in men that it was almost a sign of age. When my tests came back, my psa was 4.2, only marginally higher than the bar considered normal, and no different from the year before. It was well below those of my two closest friends, Peter Collier and Wally Nunn, whose levels were twice as high.

Wally had been a helicopter gunner in Vietnam and was a stoic optimist. He didn't expect more out of life than he was likely to get, and had made it through three biopsies on his prostate. This was a discomfiting process that was akin to having a gun barrel shoved up your colon and needles shot into its interior walls. Each time Wally went in for the procedure, his view was that he probably didn't have a malignancy, but if he did he would deal with it. It would be no different from surviving the war. It was still the territory, only this time of age.

Peter followed an opposite approach, expecting bad news with every outcome. His mind ran quickly to the negative and often to its extreme. Each time he went to see the urologist, he was sure he had cancer. It was his form of insurance. He would feel his way into the danger and prepare for the worst. It was a strategy based on family reality. He had lost his father to the disease and his mother was dead from it as well. Long before Peter's levels rose he concluded that he was destined to follow them. But he didn't. His was the reverse of Pascal's Wager. Low expectations allowed him to be surprised every time he was wrong and survived.

The architecture of human character sorts us into pessimists like Peter, and optimists like Wally and me. We don't choose these dispositions so much as they choose us. The interesting question is this: If the option were yours, which would it be? Would you rather expect the good and be surprised when it didn't happen, or be ready for the bad and surprised when things turned out well? Studies showed that optimists actually had a better time of it and led more successful lives. This result is predictable since optimists focus on opportunities and the future, while pessimists dwell on problems and the past. Yet the studies don't account for individual differences, or the occasions when optimism takes a cockeyed turn and sets you up for a fall.

According to the medical numerology, I was a little overweight and my cholesterol level was on the borderline of concern. But the electrocardiogram revealed a heart in good shape. This was reassuring since the cells of the heart follow my father's prescription and do not regenerate but wear steadily down to the end.

Weeks passed after the Porta-Doctor's visit and the insurance company had still not notified me that the policy was in effect, so I called the agent about the delay. Apologetically, he told me that the tests had shown a spike in my psa level. It was now 6.0, exceeding the bar the company had set to exclude risky cases. They had rejected my application. Instead of being concerned by the news, however, the optimist in me was irritated, even indignant. I explained to the agent that his results could not be accurate because a specialist, and not just a Porta-Doctor with her office in a bag, had recently given me a clean bill of health. I needed the insurance and demanded a second test.

The Porta-Doctor returned and we repeated the routine. This time my psa had dropped two-tenths of a point. The decline appeared reassuring, although I had no real understanding of what the numbers meant. When I called my doctor for his opinion he was not so sanguine. The thirty percent increase over a four-month stretch, even from a relatively low level, set off an alarm and he sent me back to the urologist for another round. The urologist ordered a biopsy and reserved a place for me in an outpatient facility.

I had begun the tests in June and now it was the end of summer. Through all of this, I still barely knew where my prostate was located or what its function was. I have no particular excuse for this ignorance or the lack of concern that lay behind it. As with our approaches to the future, each of us deals with these matters differently. Some of us make our bodies the focus of lavish interest; others concentrate on feeding the soul, ignoring the flesh as an unworthy vessel. Why are we so different in matters that are so fundamental? Why is it so difficult for us to change our habits even when we recognize how they affect our fate?

Inertias like these are the gravities that define us, their subterranean pulls more powerful than reason. How can utopians dream of changing the world, I have often asked myself, when it is so difficult to lose an inch from one's waistline? Who really knows where such attitudes come from or why they persist? Why some of us are driven and others are not? Why one person devours emptiness and another is full? Why some are drawn to sorrow, while others can't wait to get up and dance?

As for myself, I expend little energy speculating on distant outcomes and lack a morbid interest in others' misfortunes. I have learned to live with disappointment but still expect good things to be put on my table, however implausibly. A prostate cancer was as remote from the possibilities I imagined for myself as a trip to the moon. This complacency was not entirely ungrounded. I had inherited my mother's genes, and could not remember a day she was ill until her first stroke at eighty. Consequently, when I imagined my own future, I was always in her good health. But my mistake over the Porta-Doctor's test results had torn away the outer skin of confidence that had insulated me, and I could not suppress an uneasy feeling that this picture was about to change.

The biopsy was conducted on September 9, 2001. Five days later, April and I headed for the urologist's office to get the doctor's report. The wait had been wearing on April, who was already testing what it might mean to share the remaining days of a terminal case, but I was glad the uncertainty would be over. When we arrived, the building was almost entirely deserted, having been evacuated earlier in the day because of a bomb threat. The office was open but the urologist was at the hospital, completing an operation that had been delayed for hours because of the scare. We were informed by the office nurse that he would not be available for appointments that day.

Three days earlier, Islamic radicals had rammed commercial jets into the Pentagon and the World Trade Center. Three thousand people had been killed in the attacks, including our friend Barbara Olson, who was in the plane that hit the Pentagon. Millions of ordinary lives had been disrupted.

Why should ours be unaffected? We rescheduled our appointment and drove home.

In the days following, I watched the news and carried on my routines. Attempting to assemble a map of what might lie ahead, I took time to read some medical literature about the disease that might be spreading inside me. A *New Yorker* article provided me with a retrospect on the "war on cancer" that the government and the medical profession had launched fifty years before. I was still in my adolescence then and remembered how the first campaigns had begun with great fanfare and an abundance of hope. Massive public resources had been channeled into the crusade, and in the intervening years scientists had doubled the sum of human knowledge more than once. Yet for all the effort and intelligence expended, the causes of the disease were still not understood and no cure had been found. Apparently there were limits to what the human mind could accomplish in the span of a lifetime, if at all. There was a positive side, however, in that many new treatments had been developed, which were effective when the cancer was identified early.

One of the books I read was *How We Die* by a physician named Sherwin Nuland. He described how in a cancer the cells rebel against nature's cycle, as though refusing to grow up. Like marauding slackers, they embark on an orgy of creation and destruction, multiplying without restraint and devouring everything in sight. The cancer's first cells, Nuland wrote, are "the bastard offspring of unsuspecting parents who ultimately reject them because they are ugly, deformed, and unruly. In the community of living tissues, the uncontrolled mob of misfits that is cancer behaves like a gang of perpetually wilding adolescents. They are the juvenile delinquents of cellular society."

From reading *How We Die*, I discovered that my father was not quite on the mark. The cells do not simply age and decay, but are born over and over again. It is true that they are continually dying, but they are also "constantly being replenished as they die, not only by the reproduction of their younger survivors, but also by an actively reproducing group of progenitors." As normal cells mature, they assume their appointed functions in the body and lose their ability to procreate. Whether their job is to secrete hormones or absorb nutrients, the more fully they perform their appointed tasks the less they reproduce. But when cells fail to mature fully, they retain some of this reproductive power and a cellular mass or tumor is formed. If the process goes awry early, and dramatically enough, the reproductive energy is almost infinite and the tumor will be a cancer.

These cancers behave like revolutionaries in society. Instead of serving the body and performing the functions that keep the organism alive, in a narcissistic fury the problem cells focus on the uncontrolled reproduction of themselves, feeding on the healthy cells around them. As Dr. Nuland colorfully describes this process, they embark on "a continuous, uninhibited, circumferential, barn-burning expedition of destructiveness," strangling and consuming everything in their path. Nothing escapes them, and nothing can stop them. Defying nature's order, they do not age or even have "the decency to die when they should." The orgy of creation and destruction continues until the cancer kills the host body, and itself in the process.

Having failed to refute my blood tests, I was forced to respect them. When April and I returned to the urologist's office on September 19 and were told that I had a prostate cancer, the news did not surprise or alarm me. I was prepared for the diagnosis. When I thought about it, this was really part of the long process of dying that was my life, and indeed all our lives. Since that autumn day in the Goodhearts' living room, I had never been unaware of the steadily shrinking prospect in front of me.

Perhaps the fact that I had cancer should have caused me a bigger lurch than it did. But I had come to a point in my life, as I have already noted, where I felt I had done pretty much what was in me to do—although this certainty turned out to be another illusion—and had come to know what to expect. I found satisfaction in that. After the first fear, there is no other. Consequently, at the most vulnerable point of my life, I actually felt quite strong.

But April, who was sitting beside me as the doctor described my condition, had the wind taken out of her. When I turned in her direction, her eyes had a stricken look and her voice was stumbling over questions, giving the impression she was ducking the answers even before they came back. She was clearly off balance and my heart reached out to her, though there was nothing I could do to relieve her suffering.

In the time I had known her, I had grown to love this woman of my twilight years with an abandon I would not previously have thought possible.

I had logged so much time in what seemed now like other lives that such a renewal of passion should have been unlikely. But there we were, deep in, and I was sorry to see her enduring such pain.

Shuffling the medical reports on his desk, the urologist unveiled a new aspect of the numerology, explaining that the biopsy slides revealed a "Gleason 6," which he explained was a formula for quantifying the density and mass of the cancer and calculating its rate of growth. My ranking turned out to be not so bad. It indicated that the tumor was contained in the prostate sac and could be removed by surgery. In other cases, where the cancer had escaped into the bones or the lymph system, the odds grew longer.

The doctor checked off these details along with my medical options in a formulaic drone that was irritating. When I tried to ask a question, he brushed it aside with schoolmaster severity. I would have to wait, he admonished, until he completed his list. His formality was a full disclosure mode, the product of the malpractice torts that had become a kind of exoskeleton of the medical profession. I listened as my treatment options were put on the table. Radiation might remove the cancer or it might not. But if it did not work, the treatments would damage the tissues so severely as to make an operation impossible. There were hormone therapies available too.

My attention wandered as he described these choices. Altering hormones seemed to be playing with the very structures of feeling and being, and, like radiation didn't have the certainty of a cure. Besides, April had already decided that if the diagnosis was cancer we were going to cut. "We're not going to take a chance with your life," she said. "I can't lose you." I was sufficiently touched by her concern that I hardly noticed she was making a crucial decision for me. Her passion made it feel as if the choice had been mine.

The drone continued. The surgical operation was called a "radical prostatectomy." It would require four-and-a-half hours and would involve "a lot of blood." He would schedule the operation for the following month. He wanted me to come into the office each of the three weeks prior to the date to donate blood. Impotency was an expected result for about half the patients. The incontinency rate was lower and I thoughtlessly discounted it. Even with all the bloodletting and the downside possibilities, he cautioned, there was still no guarantee that the cancer would be entirely removed. "If we don't get it this way, we can follow up with radiation afterwards, and hope that works."

As we were driving home, April turned to me, her eyes red with worry, and said, "I never thought you would get sick. I thought if you were not going to die of old age, you would die in a car accident or someone would shoot you." Dramatic as these fears sounded, they had a basis. I was a controversial public figure, sometimes inspiring passionate threats. Even if I wasn't going to be the target of a deranged opponent I was at risk on other counts. I was a distracted pedestrian and driver, often drifting mentally and forgetting where I was. It was not a lack of focus so much as a focus misplaced. My thoughts sometimes caused me to be drawn so far into interior space that the environment outside faded to black.

"I never thought you would get cancer," she continued her regrets. "You were always so healthy." As she said this, I thought I detected in her tone a false hope that the diagnosis would prove mistaken. I, myself, didn't doubt it was correct. Perhaps because I had been so healthy throughout my life and had seen so many others suffer, it occurred to me that it would only be fair if my time had come. As if this were a consideration in nature's court.

Even after we left the office, I was unable to think of myself as a victim. My father had warned me that life was terminal and mine had not been so bad, better from where he stood than I had a right to expect. If not nine lives, I felt I had been granted more than one man's share. I was not a young man and had lived longer than Pascal.

After we left the urologist's office, April and I compared notes and agreed to seek a second opinion. This course had been urged on me by my friend Peter, who seemed at times more worried about my health than I was. He wanted me to consult a doctor with a residency in a teaching hospital to be sure of benefiting from the latest knowledge and the most skilled surgical hands. My friend Wally also chipped in with advice. He told me to read Patrick Walsh's *Guide to Surviving Prostate Cancer.* A surgeon at Johns Hopkins, Walsh was famous for the percentage of his patients who emerged from surgery with their sexual and bladder functions intact. From Walsh's book I learned that a majority of men have a prostate cancer embedded in their soma, which is one of the many seeds of mortality waiting in ambush in the landscape of the flesh. I also learned that the name "prostate" derives from the Greek word for "protector," an irony since the gland seemed anything but.

The location of the prostate creates significant problems if anything should go wrong, particularly if the remedy involves cutting. "Although it's only as big as a walnut, the prostate is a miniature Grand Central Station, a busy hub at the crossroads of a man's urinary and reproductive tracts.... It is tucked away deep within the pelvis, surrounded by vulnerable structures—the bladder, the rectum, the sphincters responsible for urinary control, major arteries and veins, and a host of delicate nerves, some of them so tiny that we've only recently discovered them." In other words, anyone planning to prune this area with a knife had better have a clear idea of what is to be cut and where it is, along with the dexterity to do only that.

In selecting a surgeon, Walsh advised patients to look for someone with "nerves of steel," since a radical prostatectomy is "one of the most difficult in medicine" and could include "tremendous, sometimes life-threatening blood loss." This was hardly reassuring. Professional grit, he further explained, was necessary to prevent a surgical panic in the event the incision produced a "sea of blood" obscuring the tissues to be cut. Among those that should not be cut were the neurovascular bundles that produced erections. The distance separating the targeted prostate from these bundles was a mere five millimeters, making impotence a hair away if the scalpel slipped. Walsh had pioneered in anatomical discoveries that reduced the blood flow dramatically. This enabled him to perform the first prostate operation that preserved the filaments. In April 1982, the operation was performed on a fifty-two-year-old patient who recovered his potency within a year.

What I took away from Walsh's book was that the most important service a patient could provide for himself was to find a surgeon who knew what he was doing. Walsh had concrete suggestions as to how a layman could make this assessment. The simplest and most direct was to ask how much time the doctor estimated the operation would take. A skilled surgeon who had mastered the anatomy could perform the task in two hours. This was half the time the Cedars-Sinai urologist was proposing to me.

As Walsh described it, a radical prostatectomy had three goals: "First is removing the cancer, then preserving urinary continence, and then preserving sexual function. In that order." To underscore the point he added: "The primary goal is not to preserve potency. It is to get rid of the cancer..." Why did men need the underscoring? Why did we fear the loss of potency even before we feared death? When faced with the alternatives, April had not hesitated before opting for the surgical cut. "Your life is more important than sex," she said. I had reached a point in my journey, where I felt ready to accept this outcome. It was just part of the leaving, which had begun long ago.

It was not that drastic a concession, moreover, since an orgasm was a nerve response in the brain. Removal of the prostate only eliminated the ability to ejaculate—not inconsequential, but not the end of the world. The tremors, the release, the elation would still be there, although never quite the same. But then nothing was quite the same. I had lost more than a few abilities already. I was confident I could handle this.

April and I made an appointment with a new surgeon named Donald Skinner, head of the Urology Department at the University of Southern California and a noted figure in the field. I had come to him through the good graces of my friend Helene Galen, who was able to get me to the head of a three-month wait list. Helene was all too familiar with hospitals. Her husband Lou, a curmudgeonly, lovable fellow, had spent nearly a year in intensive care, semi-comatose with complications of the heart, before miraculously coming through. Life was just that precarious.

During one of my visits to see Skinner, a young doctor in the building informed me that the university had built the eight-story Norris Cancer Clinic around Skinner's practice. While waiting for the examination, I asked his nurse, Steve, how I would go about giving blood for the operation. Steve said, "Oh, Dr. Skinner never takes blood. He wants you to go in on a full tank." My confidence level, already unwarrantedly high, rose with his words.

Adding to this encouragement, Steve noted that my psa level was low. How high could it go, I asked. "Well," he said, "Egypt's foreign minister had a psa of 110. They flew him in from Cairo, but when he arrived here we had to send him back for hormone treatments to bring it down low enough so that he could be operated on." Steve also let me know how fortunate I was to have discovered the cancer early. Telly Savalas, the bald actor who played the television detective "Kojak" had come in with a psa of ten, he recalled. "Dr. Skinner scheduled the biopsy but Savalas had a Christmas Special and cancelled it. Then he needed a vacation. I called him to tell him how important it was, but he never came back. Four years later he was gone." Perhaps Kojak was afraid to face a life of diminished returns.

A silver-haired gentleman now entered the room to tower over me. His smile was accented by a mild jut of the jaw and a manner that was almost jovial. Before putting on white surgical gloves, he made a sexual quip about those he had passed up in their box on the counter, which were an uncommon purple. I didn't feel trivialized by the humor so much as relieved. When he discussed the impending procedure, his tone conveyed the impression that the carving of my flesh would be no more problematic than preparing a roast.

"How long will he be on the operating table?" my wife asked.

"An hour and a half."

"Should he donate blood?"

"No, there won't be any need."

Like the Cedars-Sinai doctor, Skinner went over my options point by point. He had taken a look at the biopsy and concluded that it was a Gleason 7—one grade higher than I had been told. Evidently, there was more a surgeon had to get right than the angle of the cut. The new Gleason standard suggested there might be leakage in my case and the operation would not remove all the cancer. If this proved correct, I would have to undergo radiation with no certainty about the outcome. On the other hand, Skinner was as confident that I shouldn't worry about this, as he was that the surgery would be routine.

Before we left, I mentioned the Walsh book. Aware that I was nearly sixty-three, he said, "Walsh doesn't take patients over sixty." I picked up the cue: "That's because Walsh wants to keep his percentages high."

My only regret was that I couldn't share the confidence I was now feeling with April, who was moving quietly beside me, her eyes still wounded. Instead of lifting her spirits, the new details had only sharpened our reality and deepened her distress. When I glanced her way, I would catch her looking off into the distance, turning her head from me as if to hide her thoughts. Periodically she would come back from these private spaces, protective as ever, to entertain me with flirtatious daydreams she spun out of the very darkness of her fears. Now she was my nurse, pushing me around in my wheelchair, conjuring the sensual pleasures of our invalid life together on the other side of the ordeal. Her marital solidarity was an even greater reassurance than Skinner's expertise and made me love her all the more.

How did she love me? When you have passed beyond a first marriage, the conjugal mystery inevitably deepens. You have stepped off a coastal shelf into waters where the past works relentlessly against you. Alien corners of the human personality have become familiar. You have met the mercurial elements of the human soul and know how they can turn on you and break your heart. Beset by these thoughts, watching my wife grieve for me while I was still alive, I felt almost grateful for my condition.

April was a little over twenty years younger than I. By my private calendar the equivalence of a lifetime. Her lineage, which was an uncommon blend of Cherokee and Gaelic, had graced her with green eyes set off by high cheekbones and sensuous lips. A regal carriage lent her an aristocratic air. When we stepped out in public together I sensed how others were unable to pass without turning their heads to take her in. I knew she could have her pick of suitors if she so cared; instead she was fearful of a life without me. There she was, attending my crippled future, spinning through her tears the tapestries of joys we would share in my convalescence. I realized that through my illness I had been given a rare gift, the knowledge of my wife's heart.

I didn't spend any time thinking about the cut Skinner was preparing, which I understood from Walsh's text would stretch from the navel to the groin. Nor did I try to picture myself anaesthetized and splayed like a laboratory specimen on his operating table. It was the rule I followed in life generally, not to waste time worrying about what I could not control. Once the anesthesia was in the tube, I was removed from my own fate. It was left to April to soldier it through.

My memories of coming back afterwards are fogged and disjointed. A cup of ice chips, a frenzy at the bedside as my blood pressure rose, an anxious team scrambling to bring it down, a code blue called over the public address system, and somewhere down the hall a family keening when the rescue failed. But I remember clearly the warm lips of my life mate and her comforting words through the darkness, at my side, carrying me through.

On the third day, the hospital released me. April had hired a male nurse named Sam to help her through the first day of my convalescence at home. I was hooked up to a catheter and drain, and had a ten-inch oozing wound in my abdomen, which had to be regularly swabbed with betadine to protect it from infection. I was disoriented and groggy from the anesthetic and irritated with the well-meaning nurse, who had become the symbol of my helpless state. The irritation I now displayed was one of the less admirable traits I had inherited from my father. Painfully self-conscious, he suffered intensely from the indignities his maladies forced on him in age. He had made many trips to the hospital for hip replacements and repairs. As a patient he was ferocious, venting his frustration on the nurses who ministered to him, as though they were the instigators of his distress. I was almost no better. When Sam approached my bedside I looked away and demanded my wife instead, disliking myself as I did so.

When April came, it was a balm to my wounded body and soul. Within days of her ministrations I was feeling well enough to resume work and, improbable though it might seem, actually did so. April had bought me a bed desk, which straddled my legs and allowed me to use a laptop from my prone position so I could continue the text I had been writing. Although my mind was still foggy from the anesthetic and my body was inert, I was in unusually good spirits and resumed my narrative. Perhaps it was just a way of averting my attention from present trials, but I was feeling revived and free.

After a week of convalescence I was up and about, and then out as well. Diapered and dragging my catheter and bag concealed under my suit, I appeared on a national radio show to the consternation of its host and gave a speech at a formal dinner, though by the end of the three-hour evening I was so drained that April thought the guests were probably counting the days I had left. On her advice, I deferred further appearances until I was in better shape and could do them without the medical appliances.

Three weeks after the operation, I returned to the hospital for their removal. The first device to be extracted was the one technically known as an "indwelling Foley catheter." The almost spiritual name identified a tube rudely inserted through the urinary tract into the bladder. At the inner end of the tube was a balloon, inflated with liquid to keep the whole apparatus from slipping out. It had been inserted while I was under the anesthetic. I was not so lucky for the extraction, which proved to be physically discomfiting although not the most brutal part of the process. As I stood at attention, Skinner cradled my organ in a sanitary napkin, turned to April and said, "Did you bring the mustard?" "Mustard?" she asked as he yanked, and it was out.

After that, came the drainage tube whose withdrawal was as painful a procedure as I had endured. When the device was pulled forcefully from my abdomen, I was left sweating and shaking. Still a bit wobbly after putting on my clothes, I bumped into the doorframe trying to exit the room. "Are you all right?" my wife voiced a serious concern. "I'm just trying to make Skinner laugh," I said.

With the catheter gone, I was ready to gauge how skillful his knife had been. In my readings of the literature, I had come across cases of post-operative men whose incontinence caused them to go through eighteen diapers a day, a nightmare to contemplate. Fortunately, Skinner had not failed me. Within a few days I was able to get by with two or three, and within a week had resumed my work schedule and was traveling across the country making speeches to large audiences. By the end of one speech I was so drained that halfway through the question period I didn't have the energy to vocalize my thought, even after I had managed to get it from the top of my brain to the tip of my tongue.

The operation caused me to reflect how vital aspects of our being hang by slender corporal threads. A nerve bundle millimeters in diameter, a slice of tissue almost invisible to the human eye could change you forever. As it was, my sexual function also returned, so I could consider myself, in a manner of speaking, restored. Months after the first post-op check, I wrote a note of thanks to Skinner. I began by observing that his bedside manner had so disarmed me during my previous visit that it made the occasion seem perfectly routine. As a result, I had failed to adequately express my gratitude: "I have read enough now to know that my return to almost normal life is as close to a miracle as most of us are likely to get. Before the operation I had set my mind to accept what might come, which I expected would probably include radical changes in my life. Now, as I realize how familiar my body feels and how intact I am, I wonder how I would be feeling if you and your skills had not made that possible. Would I have been able to be as stoic and as strong as I had hoped? I am grateful I don't have to know the answer to that question."

It hardly seemed sufficient. What could words express in such cases? When I mentioned my good fortune to another surgeon at the cancer center, she said, "Dr. Skinner is as close as you can get to the hands of God."

I was not out of the woods yet. When Skinner examined the gland he had removed, he noted a stickiness in the walls, indicating the cancer could have leaked from the prostate sac into the bones or possibly the lymph. He ordered treatments and sent me to see his colleague, a radiologist named Oscar Streeter, a likeable man even larger physically than Skinner, and as dark of complexion as Skinner was light. April, who had a talent for photography, visualized a dramatic shot of the two of them towering over me in their white smocks with my diminutive self framed between.

The contrast went below the surface. Where Skinner was understated and reserved, Streeter was voluble and engaging. Both were aggressively good-natured. Conversing with them, I could almost forget I was in a cancer ward surrounded by cruelties that not even their skills could meliorate. Perhaps that was the point. Perhaps their good humor was also a shield they had developed against the occasions when their imperfect science was bound to fail.

Streeter scheduled a series of treatments over the next three months. Every weekday morning, April and I would get into her blue Pathfinder and she would drive us along the Santa Monica freeway to the radiation center at Norris. On route, I would force down a quart of water as Streeter had instructed. The object was to fill the bladder so that it would push aside some of my internal parts and provide a better target for the x-rays. Once we arrived, April would wait in the parking lot outside, feeding carrot sticks to our caramel Shih-Tzu, Molly, astride her lap, while I sat in the waiting room studying the faces of my new community until I was called in for the five-minute session.

In the center of the treatment room was a table engulfed by an x-ray machine, whose giant arm rotated a beam vertically around the patient. A bank of computers guided the beam to the site in my groin area whose latitudes a technician had marked with tattoo points. The ceiling of the room had been painted with clouds as in a child's nursery, a graphic fantasy of heaven. Recessed speakers piped in popular tunes, and an irritating buzzer was set off when the beam was activated. I felt nothing, but then I had not felt the cancer either.

I could not say the same for the after effects. Coming out into the southern California sun, I was overcome by a wooziness that lasted most of the day. The nausea reminded me of the anesthetic gas I had been given at the dentist's office when I was a youngster, before the discovery of Novocain. I had recurring images of my childhood dentist, dead now thirty or forty years but, like my new doctors, an inveterate kidder.

As we drove back through the haze of late morning traffic, life was going on in its normal rush. Lines of commuters were headed towards their appointments in a way that I no longer was. Like my fellow patients, I had entered a state of suspended animation, and was bound by the knowledge that freedom was a gift and not forever.

Day in and day out, my wife prayed for my health and for my continued presence on this earth. Her brother Joe and his wife Martha, who attended a Catholic church, St. John's of Vianney, had organized thirty Hispanic men, women and children, including my nieces, to pray for me too. There were others. Every morning these relatives and strangers whispered my name in their intimate conversations with God, and implored Him to spare me. I was touched and strengthened by their love and by their answered prayers. I was saved—at least for the moment—and was grateful for that. I would be able to share life with April again, to be with my children and grandchildren, to rise in the morning and greet the sea.

Was God really behind this good fortune? Had he intervened to rescue an agnostic soul as a reward to the believers? Thankful as I was for their concern, I didn't like to think so. For if He had saved me to answer their prayers, then I would also have to hold Him responsible for the others whose prayers went unheard. One of the patients who came regularly at my appointed time was a young woman who seemed to be in her twenties. She did not come in from the parking lot where her husband might be waiting for her as my wife did for me. She came in a wheelchair accompanied by a sad woman who appeared to be her mother and who had wheeled her to the radiation clinic from one of the recesses of the vast hospital complex we were in. She had barely begun life, but her eyes had already traveled to a distant space, displaying a vacancy that could have been equally the result of medications or resignation. I could not help thinking, each time I saw her, of the many lives I had been privileged to live in my span, and those she would not.

I was acutely conscious of the inhabitants of the cancer ward whose prospects were worse than mine. They had endured multiple operations, multiple setbacks, years of a crippled existence, and a fate on hold. "Life is a hospital," the poet Eliot wrote. I could appreciate the metaphorical truth in the image, but it still felt like a violence to the reality before me. Not all life's hospitals were equal, and not all God's children were saved.

All my life, wherever I have been, in whatever places I have found myself, I have felt like an outsider. And who hasn't? Every home is temporary and we are only transients. But I was not prepared for the irony I encountered now—that even as a patient in a cancer ward I would feel myself an outsider too. I looked at the women in their kerchiefs and wigs, and the men in the watch caps they donned to hide their baldness; I took in their gray pallor and the dark looks of the family members who came to support them, and felt, "I am not one of them."

It was the false consciousness that had accompanied me my entire life. These tragedies happen to others. *I am not one of them.* Even as I entertained these thoughts, I recognized how self-denying and ultimately absurd they were. None of us are outsiders. We are all headed in the same direction. Though my recent ordeal was over and I could walk back into the sunlight and resume my interrupted life, I was not really free. I had been lucky but had not been given a pardon, only a reprieve. My father was right. Life is a cancer ward, and death is in our cells metastasizing every day.

On Earth As It Is in Heaven 3

*L*ove death. This is the improbable instruction that the founder of an Egyptian sect called the Muslim Brotherhood imparted to his followers in the 1920's. A disciple named Mohammed Atta copied this instruction into his journal just before leading the attack on the World Trade Center three days before my biopsy. Was it a coincidence that this dark creed took root in a country of monuments to the human quest for life beyond the grave? The sentence Mohammed Atta actually jotted down was this: "Prepare for holy war and be lovers of death."

How can one love death? This is a question that is incomprehensible to us unless we are overwhelmed by personal defeats. But it is the enigma at the heart of human history, which is a narrative moved by war between men. For how can men go to war unless they love death, or a cause that is worth more than life itself?

The Muslim Brotherhood was founded in 1928, but the summons to holy war had been planted in Arab hearts more than a thousand years before. The Muslim faith was created by the prophet Mohammed who claimed he was fulfilling the gospel of Christ. But Mohammed was a warrior, while Jesus was a man of peace who instructed his followers to shun the path of history and separate the sacred from the profane. His kingdom was not of this world: *Render unto Caesar that which is Caesar's, and unto God that which*

43

is God's. By contrast, Mohammed summoned his followers to make the world a place for God, which meant conquering Caesar himself.

Sayyid Qutb, an Egyptian who was executed for treason in 1966, is recognized as the intellectual father of the modern Islamic jihad or holy war. His brother was a teacher of the jihadist Osama Bin Laden, and his texts are read by would-be martyrs in madrassas across the Muslim world. The goal that consumed Sayyid Qutb's life was to establish the rule of Islam globally and make the world a holy place. Qutb regarded Christianity as a threat to this Islamic redemption. He condemned Christians for their separation of the sacred from the profane, of God's world from Ceasar's. He called this division a "hideous schizophrenia," which reflected the very corruption he set out to correct. Christians had created liberal societies, Qutb said, in which "God's existence is not denied, but His domain is restricted to the heavens and His rule on earth is suspended." Islam's task was "to unite the world and the faith." Qutb wrote this prescription in one of his most famous texts, which he called Social Justice in Islam. The mission of Islam, he explained, was "to unite heaven and earth in a single system." To make the world one.

This is the totalitarian idea. When the wave of redemption is complete, nothing will remain untransformed, nothing unholy or unjust. Total transformation is the goal of all radical jihads, including the flight that burned the "towers of evil" in Manhattan. It is the cause that Mohammed Atta served. Like all revolutionary passions, the totalitarian hope of radical Islam is to redeem the world. It is the desire to put order into our lives and to heal the wound in creation. But there is no earthly doctor who can cure us.

The practical consequence of all radical dreams is a permanent holy *war.* Inevitably and invariably, the effort to redeem the world begins by dividing it into opposing camps. In order to conduct the work of salvation, redeemers must separate the light from the darkness, the just from the unjust, the believers from the damned. For Islamists this division is the line separating *Dar al-Islam* from *Dar al-Harb,* the "House of *Islam*" from the "House of War," the realm of the faithful from the world of heretics and infidels —the impure of heart who must be converted or destroyed.

A thousand years before Mohammed Atta set off on his fatal mission, a Shi'ite named Hassan al-Sabbah began a holy war to overthrow the Muslim state. In Hassan's eyes, the Sunni caliphate that the Prophet Mohammed had established to govern Islam, had already fallen into a state of corruption. It was no longer holy; it was no longer God's. To cleanse Islam and restore the faith, Hassan created a martyr vanguard whom others referred to as the "Assassins," and whose deeds have bequeathed to us the word itself. The mission of the Assassins was to kill the apostate rulers of the false Islamic state, and purify the realm.

Because their mission was a service to God, it was considered a dishonor to return alive, and none did. The Koran assured the Assassins that the reward for the life they gave was paradise itself. "So let them fight in the way of God who sell the present life for the world to come. Whosoever fights in the way of God and is slain, conquers. We shall bring him a mighty wage." When the Assassins' first victim, the vizier of Quhistan, was slain, Hassan al-Sabbah said, "The killing of this devil is the beginning of bliss." Revolutionaries love death because it is the gate of heaven and the beginning of bliss.

Four years before 9/11, Mohammed Atta traveled to Afghanistan to join the International Islamic Front for the Holy War against Jews and Crusaders, whose leader was Osama bin Laden. Atta was a small, wiry man, the humorless son of a demanding father. After his team of modern Assassins had turned the towers in Manhattan into a smoking ruin, his father told reporters, "My son is a very sensitive man. He is soft and was extremely attached to his mother."

Before the hour of his *jihad,* on the very page where he had copied the summons to love death, Mohammed Atta acknowledged that it was a call to perform acts unnatural to men. "Everybody hates death, fears death," he wrote, but then explained why men should love it nonetheless. "Only the believers who know the life after death and the reward after death, will be the ones seeking death." Mohammed Atta had found a cause that was greater than life itself.

But was Mohammed Atta right? Did his martyrs sign up for death to gain a greater return? This presumes that the only reason people would seek to end their lives in this world is the hope of reward in another. Do they not also run towards what they fear? When we have guilty secrets to hide, do we not find ways to end the awful wait before judgment by leaving the clues that betray us? Especially if we are withholding secrets from those we fear and love. Are we not all guilty in the eyes of God, and did not Mohammed Atta fear and love Him?

What if martyrs hate life more than they love death? If we look at the scanty record of Mohammed Atta's time on this earth, it suggests that escape was always on his mind. "Purify your heart and clean it of all earthly matters," he wrote in his instructions to his martyr team. "The time of fun and waste has gone. The time of judgment has arrived."

In his short life, Mohammed Atta does not seem to have had much room for pleasure. His father was a successful lawyer, who was ambitious and austere. The family had two residences but lived frugally and apart from others. "They didn't visit and weren't visited," said a neighbor later. The father agreed: "We are people who keep to ourselves." An adolescent friend of Mohammed's described the Atta household: "It was a house of study. No playing, no entertainment. Just study." Even as an adolescent, Mohammed would leave the room when Egyptian television featured belly-dancing programs, as it frequently did.

According to those who knew him as a young adult, Mohammed Atta was insular, religiously strict and psychologically intense. The death of an insect made him emotional; the modern world repelled him. A fellow urban planning student remembered how the usually reserved Mohammed became enraged by a hotel construction near the ancient market of Aleppo, which he viewed as the desecration of Islam's heritage. "Disney World," he sneered, the Crusaders' revenge. Mohammed continued to avoid sensual images whether from television screens or wall posters. He hated and feared the female gender, averting his eyes from women who so much as neglected to cover their arms.

Others testified that he could not take pleasure in so basic and social a human act as eating. A roommate recalled that he sustained himself by spooning lumps from a heap of cold potatoes he would mash and leave on a plate in the communal refrigerator for a week at a time. A German convert, who hung out with members of the terrorist cell that Mohammed headed, thought it was his morbid seriousness that allowed him to lead others but dismissed him derisively as a "harmless, intelligent, nut." The people he lived with longed for him to leave. A girlfriend of one of them said, "A good day was when Mohammed was not home."

Five years before his appointment with death, Mohammed Atta drew up a will in which he admonished his mourners to die as good Muslims. "I don't want a pregnant woman or a person who is not clean to come and say good-bye to me because I don't approve it," he stressed. "The people who will clean my body should be good Muslims ... The person who will wash my body near my genitals must wear gloves on his hands so he won't touch my genitals ... I don't want any women to go to my grave at all during my funeral or on any occasion thereafter."

In life, Mohammed Atta despised women; but on his way to death he promised his martyrs many, citing the Koranic verse: "Know that the gardens of paradise are waiting for you in all their beauty and the women of paradise are waiting, calling out, 'Come hither, friend of God.' They have dressed in their most beautiful clothing." Mohammed also wrote down these instructions for the mission ahead: "When the confrontation begins, strike like champions who do not want to go back to this world. Shout, 'Allahu Akbar [God is great],' because this strikes fear in the hearts of the unbelievers." Whoever neglected his will or did not follow Islam, Mohammed warned, "that person will be held responsible in the end."

Like Mohammed Atta we long for the judgment that will make right what is not. We want to see virtue rewarded and the wicked rebuked. We yearn for release from the frustrations and disappointments of an imperfect life. Consequently, every God of love is also a God of justice, and therefore a God of punishment and death. If this were not so, if God did not care to sort out good from evil, what would His love be worth? The emotions of fear and hope spring from the love of self, and therefore make our motives suspect. Are those who claim to be God's warriors pure of heart and above doubt? Can men serve God if they are really serving themselves? Do martyrdoms like Mohammed Atta's represent noble aspirations, or are they merely desperate remedies for personal defeats?

Mohammed Atta was a withdrawn and ineffectual man who died without achieving his worldly ambitions. He never realized his goal of becoming an architect or urban planner, never married or had a family. Apart from his jihad, Mohammed Atta never made a mark in life. But in death he was a god, bringing judgment to 3,000 innocent souls.

If Allah is the maker of life, as Mohammed Atta believed, could He desire the destruction of what he had created? What is suicide but rage at the living, and contempt for the life left behind? Mohammed Atta offered his deed of destruction as a gift to God. In his eyes, his martyrdom was unselfish and the strangers he killed were not innocent. His mission was to purge the world of wasteful pleasures, to vanquish the guilty and to implement God's grace. But if God wanted to cleanse His creation, why would He need Mohammed Atta to accomplish His will?

These are the questions of an agnostic who has no business saying what God desires or does not. Nonetheless, an agnostic can appreciate believers like Pascal whose humility is transparent, and who is attempting to make sense of the incomprehensible through faith. Why are we born? Why are we here? Why do we die?

An agnostic can respect the faith of a skeptic who confronts our misery and refuses to concede defeat. He can admire a faith that provides consolation for the inconsolable, and in a heartless world finds reason to live a moral life. But murder is not moral and the desire to redeem the world requires it. Because redemption requires the defeat and damnation of those who refuse to be saved.

My father was an atheist who embraced the secular beliefs of the social redeemers. Along with all who think they have practical answers to the absurd cruelties of our human lot, my father felt superior to those who do not, especially those who take solace in a religious faith. In this prejudice, my father had impressive company. The psychologist Sigmund Freud regarded religion as an illusion without a future. But like all revolutionaries, Freud could not live without his own reservoir of belief, which was science. Progress was his human faith.

Whether they are secularists like my father and Freud, or religious zealots like Mohammed Atta, those who believe we can become masters of our fates think they know more than Pascal. But in their search for truth, where do they imagine they have gone that he did not go before them? What do they think they know that Pascal did not? Their bravado is only a mask for the inevitable defeat that is our common lot, an inverse mirror of their human need.

Like Mohammed Atta, my father was an ineffectual man thwarted in his earthly desires. When he was still young, he gave up his ambitions, and resigned himself to a life without them. But in his imagination he knew no such limits. The hope he no longer had for himself he invested in others. Even though my father prided himself on being a practical man without illusions, he shared with Mohammed Atta and his believers an impossible dream. Their dream was to change the world. What Mohammed Atta and my father wanted was an escape from this life.

If his views had been described to him this way, my father would have rejected the link to theological illusions. He felt as superior to the religious revolutionaries who shared his dreams, as they did to secular radicals like him. But while he disdained their God and their paradise in heaven, he never gave up their belief in miracles of faith. My father's prophet was Karl Marx, who was himself descended from a long line of rabbis. Like my father, Marx disdained the religions of his ancestors, regarding them as the comforting myths of weak-minded men. But the icon he chose for his secular faith was a mythical figure all the same. His hero was Prometheus, the pagan who stole fire from the gods and brought a piece of heaven to earth.

Like Freud, Marx regarded the belief in an other-worldly heaven as a cry of impotence, a memory from the childhood of the race when men were tormented by forces of nature they could not understand. To cope with their predicament they conjured powers that were divine to look after them and keep them safe. Marx regarded the divinities they worshipped as reflections of themselves on whom they projected powers that might one day be theirs. Marx's revolutionary message to humanity was this: You shall be as gods.

For Marx, religious belief was not a consolation for human unhappiness but its cause. The God men worshipped appeared to them as the embodiment of their hopes. But Marx was confident that their deity was only a tribal totem whose worship made them passive and denied them their due. There were no unanswerable questions or unattainable powers that determined human fate. Marx was so confident of this truth that he summed up his conclusion in a single sentence: "All mysteries, which lead to mysticism, find their rational solution in human practice." Marx's revelation was this: The fire is not in heaven; it is in you. Human beings could achieve their liberation by worshiping themselves instead of gods. This was a flattery so great that it changed the world, leaving boundless carnage in its wake.

In Marx's telling, religious faith was not a passage to heaven but a passion of the condemned. "Religion is the sigh of the oppressed creature, the heart of a heartless world," he wrote; "it is the opium of the oppressed."

Thus Marx inverted the martyr's hope. In Marx's gospel, the dream of a heavenly paradise is no longer the aspiration to transcend human fate. It is the snare that seduces us into accepting our unhappy condition. The dream of heaven is a pitiful perversion of humanity's desire to liberate itself and make the world one. Marx's call to revolution is this: Give up the dream of a paradise in heaven in order to create a heaven on earth. In the book he mockingly called *The Holy Family*, he declared, "The abolition of religion as the illusory happiness of the people is required for their real happiness."

These words stand Marx's proclamation on its proverbial head and show how pathetically human his prophecy was. Having dismissed religion and fantastic dreams, he succumbed to them himself. Having claimed that the world could not be saved by religion, he insisted it would be saved by abolishing religion. In place of the old redemption through the grace of God, the revolutionary offers a secular salvation. In place of the Final Judgment and a world made holy through divine intervention, the revolutionary promises Social Justice, a world redeemed through the actions of ordinary men and women.

Like Islamic radicals pursuing their goal of God's law on earth, Marx drew a line between the House of Faith and the House of War; between those who were chosen for the progressive mission and the reactionaries whose removal was necessary to transform the world. My father was a decent man who was not prepared to harm others, even in the service of his radical faith, let alone murder innocents as Mohammed Atta did. But along with millions of decent progressive souls, my father abetted those who did just that. Progressives looked the other way and then endorsed the murder of untold innocents for the same reason that Mohammed Atta and the Islamic martyrs did: to make a new world possible. Their desire for Judgment in this life was so strong that it inspired them to believe that if enough of the guilty were punished and removed, they could actually produce a world redeemed.

I understand Pascal's religion. I understand his anxious bewilderment at a life of no consequence. I understand his hope for a personal redemption, and his search for an answer. But I no longer understand my father's faith—his belief that men alone, without divine intervention, can transform the world in which they find themselves and create a paradise on earth.

Some may regard these speculations as unreasonable. How can a man invoke his father in the same sentence as Mohammed Atta? My answer is,

How not? Was Mohammed Atta not flesh and blood? If you pricked him did he not bleed? What did Mohammed Atta hope for but a better world? And what progressive soul does not wish for that?

Like my father, I once thought I knew the answers to unanswerable questions, and allowed myself to dream impossible dreams. But one day these dreams brought tragedy to my door, and I put away the illusion for good. Whoever asks how Mohammed Atta's awful deed can be linked to decent people has not understood the deed, or who they themselves are. Ask yourself this: Up to the last act of Mohammed Atta's life, would he have been judged an evil person? No one who actually knew him thinks so. The act that ended Mohammed Atta's life and thousands of innocent others was surely evil. But except for the terrible deed itself, there is not an inconsiderate gesture attached to his memory. He appears to have been an ordinary man who was seduced into committing a great crime in the name of a greater good. Is this not the most common theme of the human tragedies of our time?

Ordinary lives will encompass selfishness and greed and the occasional ability to inflict harm without compunction. But the capacity for dedicated evil is a rarer quality. The Pharaonic masters of our suffering are a small current in the human sea. Decent multitudes must swell behind them to create history's monstrous tides. Many historic crimes have been supported by common fear, but more are driven by desperate hope. What the worshippers of history's murderers seek is justification for a life. And for a life that is not this one.

Martin Amis is one of Saul Bellow's literary disciples. In a book he called *Koba the Dread*, Amis cast a novelist's eye on Joseph Stalin, the Marxist liberator and my father's hero, who attempted to engineer the future on an epic scale. Amis's portrait of the great man draws on the witness of Stalin's contemporaries, among whom we find this instructive note: "[Stalin] is unhappy at not being able to convince everyone that he is greater than everyone." This is the diary comment of Nikolai Bukharin, a Bolshevik leader and intimate of Stalin's, and imminent victim of the great man's dementia. In happier days before his fall, Bukharin had romped with Stalin on *dacha* lawns and had once even carried the nation's savior on his back.

Bukharin jotted down this diary entry during the blood-soaked days that history knows as the Great Purge, which was Stalin's campaign to eradicate enemies of the revolution and rivals to himself. In a two-year period beginning in 1936, Bukharin's playful friend ordered the executions of a million citizens of the Soviet state, mostly members of his own party, often his closest associates and friends. Among the dead were acolytes who had promoted him as the "Father of the Peoples" and a "genius of mankind," and artists who had praised him as a human god. The victims of his terror included family intimates, their wives and children. His own wife committed suicide in horror at what he had done.

As the procession of executions accelerated, the pathetic Bukharin was desperate to explain why Stalin would destroy those so near to him, fearing correctly that he would be next. Even as he contemplated his doom at the hands of a maniac, Bukharin felt a tug of sympathy for the man whose intentions he had shared. "This unhappiness of his may be his most human trait, perhaps the only human trait in him. But what is rather not human, but something of the devil, is that because of this unhappiness he cannot help taking revenge on people, on all people, but especially on those who are in any way better or higher than he."

Of course, Bukharin was wrong. It was this very envy and the cruel desire for revenge that accompanied it that were Joseph Stalin's most human traits. These are the passions that produced the great leveling called "socialism," which until his moment of truth had been Bukharin's own.

Amis notes that Stalin, who murdered forty million people to create the workers' paradise and make himself immortal, had two famous comments about the mortality of others. The first was this: "Death solves all problems—no man, no problem." The second: "The death of one man is a tragedy, the death of millions a statistic."

Not all the plans that men devise to find a way out of history turn on the elimination of social classes or the establishment of religious law. Hitler's idea was to get rid of the Jews and other "mongrel" races. As a result of his plan, most of my family lineages end in 1939, the year I was born. I can trace my origins back through my father's father and my mother's grandfather, but the trail stops there. The communities of Eastern Europe, of Moravia and Ukraine from which my ancestors came, ended up in the gas chambers and are now erased.

Even if Hitler had not launched his Final Solution, I still would probably have a hard time tracing my family's steps. This is because well before Hitler my forbears had found a way—or so they hoped—to escape their Jewish fate. Instead of embracing the congregation of Abraham, they abandoned both tribe and faith and became progressive "internationalists" instead. As progressives they joined a movement that also proposed to "solve the Jewish problem," but benevolently, by turning humanity into one happy family and making the Jews "like everyone else." As socialists, they set out to eradicate the very sources of human division and conflict—property, classes and national identities—as though history could be abolished by human decree.

My father was one of the millions of decent souls who believed in Stalin as the peoples' leader, and counted on him to rescue them from their benighted state. But if you were to ask them, not a single one of these enlightened souls would concede any connection between their personal anxieties and their social agendas. They would be repelled by the idea that the progressive fantasy is really the expression of a religious desire.

To the faithful, the source of human misery cannot be located in a deficiency of self, let alone the wish to escape it. That would diminish the suffering and make human beings responsible for themselves. To the revolutionary, the source of this misery can only be a corruption in "society," a fault in the world that others have made. The revolutionary mission is to cleanse the world of this corruption and its agents, and reverse the human Fall. The secular purification of the world has a name: *social justice*. It is the *sharia* of political faith.

Marx explained the difference between the revolutionary desire for social justice and all other attempts at social reform: "[The revolutionary class] claims no particular right, because it claims no particular wrong, since wrong in general is perpetrated against it." In other words, injustice is not a specific dysfunction, or crime. The very order of the world is criminal and the revolutionary's task is to make it right. The language is secular, but the aim is no less comprehensive than forcing infidels to submit or purging them from the face of the earth. For believers the creation of a just world is the end of history, and therefore its beginning. Their vision is total, and nothing escapes it. Because it is both the beginning and the end, the mission to create a new world justifies anything. And everything.

In his book about the hell that progressives like Bukharin had constructed in Russia, Amis included the diary entry of a factory-school worker named Stepan Podlubny. For his loyalty to the cause, Stepan had been made a "Sentinel of the Revolution." His task was to inform on workers who failed to observe the revolutionary code. The year was 1932, and the collectivization of agriculture had already begun. In his diary, Stepan recorded feelings he could not reveal without putting his own life in danger.

He was concerned about his mother who had been sentenced to eight years in a concentration camp for concealing information. The incriminating information was the fact that she was a *kulak*, a peasant who owned some land. She had been a *kulak* whose family property was confiscated to make way for the liberated future. Her son could not believe the judgment the socialist authorities had pronounced on his mother. "They consider her a danger to society. You'd think they caught a bandit, but even bandits get lighter sentences than that," he wrote. "Is this the end of justice on earth?"

With this question, Stepan had come face to face with the revolutionary truth. Consider how the effort to redeem the future begins by making identity a crime. Who was Stepan's mother? How did she acquire the status that condemned her? This was the question that Stepan could not answer, and it was one the court could not ask. The court's mission was revolutionary; its mandate was not to understand the past but to condemn it.

We come into this world unequal and each follows a unique path to the seat of judgment. What is justice if it cannot recognize our human uniqueness? How can there be a *social* justice that is not an offense to who and what we are?

The revolution has no time to pause over the individual and his truth, nor could it do so without losing its way. To become socially just, the world must obey the revolutionary rule. Because revolutionaries cannot respect what lies outside the rule and remain revolutionaries, they are led to statements like this: "We must rid ourselves once and for all of the Quaker-Papist babble about the sanctity of human life." These are the words of the Bolshevik Trotsky who, along with his son and his friends and comrades, was eventually murdered in the revolution's name.

In another passage, Amis cites the testimony of a Nazi doctor who was inter- viewed in the aftermath of World War II. The doctor had participated in Hitler's attempt at a final solution to the problem of the Jews, experimenting on the condemned and assisting the radicals in their genocidal campaign to purify the race. The interview with the doctor was conducted in sight of the ovens in which his victims' corpses had been disposed. Pointing to the chimneys that were now smokeless, the interviewer asked, "How can you reconcile *that* with your oath as a doctor? The Nazi answered: 'Of course, I am a doctor and I want to preserve life. And out of respect for human life I would remove a gangrenous appendix from a diseased body. The Jew is the gangrenous appendix in the body of mankind.'"

This is the paradox of all dreams of a redeemed future. The more beau- tiful the dream, the more necessary and more total the crime.

Pascal understood the human pain from which epic ambitions arise: "Man would be great and sees that he is little; would be happy and sees that he is miserable; would be perfect and sees that he is full of imperfections; would be the object of the love and esteem of men, and sees that his faults merit only their aversion and contempt. The embarrassment wherein he finds himself produces in him the most unjust and criminal passions imaginable, for he conceives a mortal hatred against that truth which blames him and convinces him of his faults."

Self-loathing is the secret revolutionary passion. Every transformer of mankind is inspired to destroy a world that condemns or perhaps only ignores him. Every revolutionary despises the other who tells him who he is. It is the unbeliever who provides the mirror in which the truth confronts him: the peasant who wants a piece of the earth; the Jew who triumphs despite an alien heritage; the infidel who finds pleasure in a world that is dust. To the radical soul, it is this that is finally unbearable.

While Pascal was an agnostic of the intellect, he was a believer of the heart. Pascal recognized that his condition was hopeless and that only a divinity could heal his mortal sickness and make him whole. Because science afforded no answers to his questions, he trusted in the God of Abraham to provide what no mortal can. Pascal was a realist of faith. He drew a sharp line between the sacred and the profane, respecting the gulf that separates this world from the next. Therefore, he did not presume to achieve his own salvation in this world, or anyone else's.

Not so the redeemers. They cannot live with themselves or the fault in creation, and therefore are at war with both. Because they are miserable themselves, they cannot abide the happiness of others. To escape their suffering they seek Judgment on all, the rectification that will take them home. If they do not believe in God, they summon others to act as gods. If they believe in God, they do not trust His justice but arrange their own. In either case, the consequence of their passion is the same catastrophe. This is because the devil they hate is in themselves, and their sword of vengeance is wielded by inhabitants of the very hell they wish to escape.

There is no redemption in this life. Generation after generation, we transmit our faults and pass on our sins. From parents to children, we create the world in our own image. And no power can stop us. Every life is an injustice. And no one can fix it. We are born and we die. If there is no God to rescue us, we are nothing.

Being Here

⁴

At innumerable points in the trajectory my life has taken there have been turns where my fate would have been irrevocably altered had I but changed the simplest decision and set my foot on a different path. It is a fact I reflect on often, but like everyone else can't do anything about.

One July day in the summer of 1993, I set out to meet a woman I didn't know in a place I had never been, with intentions that were incompletely disclosed. At the time I was living in the marina apartment and working on the manuscript of my autobiography *Radical Son*. The encounter came unexpectedly through a friend who asked me to provide advice on a medical matter to someone she knew. As an afterthought, or perhaps to pique my interest, the friend had also mentioned that the patient, whose name was April, was "gorgeous."

The counsel I was being asked to provide concerned a virus-induced ailment known as chronic fatigue syndrome, a malady I had been stricken with years before. The condition was one normally diagnosed as "incurable" and, if you thought about it, was almost a metaphor for middle age. A poignant aspect of this case was the youth of the victim, who was in her early thirties.

The symptoms of the illness were a brain perpetually fogged and an immense tiredness that hooded the eyes and suffused the limbs with a languorous indolence from which I felt I would never wake up. I went through a summer in this state and then a winter, and then another, shuffling along

sunlit sidewalks like a sea tortoise encrusted with time, until I began to wonder if this was what I had finally become.

Frustrated with the prognoses of doctors who prepared me for a permanently reduced existence, I consulted New Age practitioners of the healing arts who assured me that treatment was possible. Eventually I came
under the care of a Belgian doctor who had a license in acupuncture, and a
reputation for achieving cures. He stuck me with needles, injected a Chi-
nese serum into my "acupoints," pumped me with amino acids and adjusted
my diet. He also encouraged the only exercise I could manage, which were
the long walks I took at a reptilian pace.

The virus was affected by heat and dampness, and on days that were
overcast and muggy I surrendered to its superior force. In time the syndrome established its own rhythm of ebb and flow, allowing me to work in
the intervals when its virulence receded. In those hours, I resumed my half-
life and doggedly followed the regimen the doctor prescribed, dragging my
shell along glacial miles while awaiting a miracle that would return the
spring to my step.

My recovery was slow and the setbacks recurrent, but it did come.
When I finally revived I was unable to determine whether it was the remedies that had succeeded or whether I owed my return to the healing powers
of the body itself. Nonetheless, I routinely praised the man who had looked
after me when I needed encouragement and help. This was how, on a hot
summer's day, I found myself headed for Brea, California to see a woman I
had never met.

The pretext for the trip was an appointment I had at a venue in Costa
Mesa, which was twenty-five miles to the west. In our phone conversation
I had mentioned I would be "in the neighborhood," which might be a con-
venient time to drop by with an armful of medical texts. On route, I lost my
way and became so frustrated with the effort to get back on course that I
began to think seriously about turning around and going home. Why was
I pursuing a strange woman like this at *my* age?

The work address she had given me was a plastic surgeon's office
where she provided skin care for patients who came to have their faces
redone. This odd but very modern idea became the subject of my
thoughts during the boredom of the drive, and led to some familiar
reflections. How much of our selves is finally in our bodies? What is reality and what appearance?

These were ancient questions that I had first encountered as a young man. Plato and his followers believed the flesh was incidental to our being and that ideas were the only reality. The eyes, he thought, were the windows to the soul, as though in the darkness behind retina and iris lay the goodness, beauty and truth of who we are. It was an interesting suggestion, but unconvincing. How much do we see of others when we see them? Especially for the first time.

When I arrived at the medical office, April appeared (gloriously, I thought) in her white smock, more blonde than I had imagined. She welcomed me with a generous smile, and I felt my head lower in unaccustomed shyness. As we slipped into a patter of introductions, I was struck by the thought that the romantic angle I had devised for the plot was not going to work. I thought: this woman's life is so different from mine we could have been different species.

In an attempt to collect myself, I began thumbing the pages of one of the tracts my doctor had written as guides through the bog of chronic fatigue. Nervously, I began to read aloud, selecting choice advice from the open text. I was encouraged when she seemed more intrigued by my fluster than by the doctor's good counsel. But when I asked her to dinner she begged off, saying she wasn't feeling well and didn't have the energy for an evening. Had my intentions been purer, her explanation would have seemed perfectly reasonable. As it was, I thought: *that is the end of that.*

However, as is often the case when we try to predict our futures, I was mistaken. From our first steps continuing to our last we see through the glass darkly; our lives are a series of blind encounters, and no surgeon, no matter how expert in his craft, can alter that. We can never know where the paths we follow may lead, and yet we cannot take a single step back. And no power available to us can change this fact.

I don't know why April responded to the calls I made to her after I left, or why she agreed to see me again; or why, when we had become familiar and my lips reached for hers, she wanted to receive them. Or how an improbable romance bloomed as it did. But then I am not alone in my ignorance of such important things. "God knows," Saul Bellow observed late in his life, "why we are drawn to others and become attached to them." As if to provide an answer (or to illustrate there was none), Bellow recalled how Proust, the novelist of love, once said that he was "often attracted to people who had something in them of a hawthorn hedge in bloom." Was April, then, an iris blonder than spring, as she seemed to me now? Perhaps Proust would have understood the attraction.

As I continued to reflect on how alien we were to each other, the idea became increasingly attractive. Perhaps there was an advantage for us in the strangeness itself. Experience had taught me that one of the chief obstacles to maintaining a bond between two people lay in taking the other for granted. It occurred to me that our distances would prompt us to be mindful of the gap and encourage us to keep the other in sight.

Our trysts took place on my turf in the marina. Several days a week she would travel the forty-mile distance along the freeways to have dinner with me and spend the night. I didn't think much about this pattern of our meetings, because the arrangement suited me. But whenever I did, I assumed it was somehow for her convenience. Perhaps she found my apartment, which fronted the water, more congenial than her subdivision with its thick summer heat. Our romance was well into its fourth month before she revealed the reason behind the routine. This was the fact that she was the mother of a boy of eight, whose name was Jon, and whose existence she had hidden. By design, she had kept our romance at my end of the woods, so to speak, in order to conceal our relationship from him and theirs from me.

As she told me this, I noted her hesitation and read into it several folds of concern. Our mutual passion had grown unexpectedly and she now realized that the penalty for her deception might be more serious than she had bargained. It was possible that a man of my years might not want the burdens of a second family so late in life. She could have saved herself the worry. Even before she began explaining, I understood that hiding her son was a way to keep from me an intimate and vulnerable part of herself when our relationship was still fresh. Far from alarming me, her secret was reassuring. The lengths she had gone to protect her child's love told me how careful she would be with mine. I had already given her my own hostage, for who can hurt you more than someone who has your heart?

Sigmund Freud was bent on returning us to the animal kingdom. To account for my attraction to April, Freud would have reached for a biological function and explained it as my plot to stay alive. "The union of numerous cells into one vital connection is a means to the prolongation of their span of life," he asserted in a famous text. "Conjugation, the temporary mingling of two unicellular entities, has a preservative and rejuvenating effect on both." April, then, was my rejuvenating mate. *Beyond the Pleasure Principle,* which contains these observations is Freud's effort to understand what he called the "death wish," a concept he based on the idea that we are drawn to what we fear. According to Freud's text, organic instincts are conservative and regressive, seeking to reinstate a previous condition. From the beginning of life, we instinctively long for the end. This read like a commentary on my father's observation about the cells dying from the day we are born.

But why *instinctively*? Why not logically? If life is a meaningless ripple of empty space, why not get it over with, and sooner rather than later? Isn't it the will to survive that requires an instinct and explanation? This question itself reveals what a mystery life is, even to those who believe we are no more than bodies and imagine it is a puzzle that science can solve.

In thinking that we are no more than the cells that compose us, contemporary materialists display an arrogance even greater than Freud's. The tissue of the human brain has a hundred billion neurons connected by a hundred trillion synapses, but evolutionary psychologists are convinced they can figure out what makes us tick. "Every emotion and thought gives off physical signals," writes one, "and the new technologies for detecting them are so accurate that they can literally read a person's mind. . . . Neural network modelers have begun to show how the building blocks of mental computation, such as storing and retrieving a pattern, can be implemented in neural circuitry. And when the brain dies, the person goes out of existence."

And how, exactly, would he know?

No scientific argument, no matter how persuasive, could convince me that the love I feel is simply a case of biological pulls. At my age the electrical pulses don't account for nearly as much as when I was twenty. They have been overtaken by the impulses of the soul which, no matter how old you get can still grab you and make you take notice. When April and I had been together for ten years, she said this: "When you die, I tell myself I'll be seeing you spiritually some day again. I don't know how I would live with the thought of you gone, if I didn't believe that. I don't know how people who have no belief in God manage. It's a sad way to carry your heart through life."

But she knew I did just that. She said, "You need to respect God more. He's been good to you. When you came out of the operating room you were so handsome and your skin was magical. There was a glow on you. I knew that someone, maybe your Grandma Rose or your mom was looking out for you." And then she said, "You have a mission. Most people are like me and don't. But you have a mission. God is protecting you."

It is a privilege to be loved. It can almost make you a believer, even if believing is not in you from the beginning. You give, and if you are fortunate what you give comes back, and it comes back in ways you would never have imagined.

I could not easily dismiss this idea of a grace unseen. I knew I had taken risks others avoided and escaped unharmed. I had been felled by a cancer and was still around to talk about it. But what was the mission that might cause God to look out for me? Why would the God of the Jews take a hand in the affairs of one of His creatures in any case? The Biblical point was that the Creator gave his children free will to determine their fates. Why would He intervene to change mine?

I did have a mission at one time that tragedy overwhelmed and brought to an end. As a result, I no longer shared my father's dream of an earthly redemption. I had come to see such dreams as a vortex of destruction and had become an adversary of those who kept them alive. It was my way of atoning for what I had done. This was the mission to which April referred.

But while I took pleasure in her romance I could not flatter myself to think a providential eye was looking out for me and shaping my ends. This was the very illusion I had escaped. The personal dream of every revolutionary is to be at the center of creation and the renewal of the world. What I had learned in my life was that we are not at the center of anything except our own insignificance. There was nothing indispensable about me, or anyone.

The wars of the social redeemers were as old as Babel and would go on forever. The dreamers would go on building towers to heaven, and just as inexorably they would come crashing to earth. Some would take to heart the lessons of the Fall, but most would fail to notice them, or care. Inspired by those who preceded them and innocent of their crimes, an unending cycle of generations would repeat what they had done. The terrible suffering of guilty and innocent alike would continue without end. The prophet Mohammed would beget the disciple Atta; the prophet Marx, my father. Others would follow them, and nothing I could do or say would change it.

The summons I answered was modest. It was to bear witness to what I had learned. Perhaps hearing my story, another as innocent as I had been would take heed. For myself I needed to remember what I had learned through pain, and to honor my debt. My mission was as much for myself as for anyone else. It was about wrestling with the most powerful and pernicious of all human follies, which is the desire to stifle truth in the name of hope.

Here is why you cannot change the world: Because we —all six billion of us—create it. We do so individually and relentlessly and in every generation. We shape it as monarchs in our homes and beyond, when we cannot even master ourselves. Every breeder of new generations is a stranger to his mate and a mystery to himself. Every offspring is a self-creator who learns through rebellion and contrition, through injury and error, and frequently not at all. This is the root cause that makes us who and what we are—the good, the bad, the demented, the wise, the benevolent and the brute. We are creatures blind and ignorant, stumbling helplessly through a puff of time.

The future is a work of prejudice and malice inextricably bound with generosity and hope. It is carried out now and forever under the terrible anarchy of freedom that God has imposed on his children and will not take back. This world is created every day by us at odds with each other, and over and over. It is irrevocably broken into billions of fragments, bits of human unhappiness and earthly frustration. And no one can fix it.

In my life's journey I have acquired a public persona. As a result, strangers sometimes approach me bearing images of a self lost long ago. In a recent spring, I spoke at a university in Connecticut whose name I have forgotten. When my talk was over, a compact man with Irish curls and a snow-white beard came up to introduce himself. "It's me, Johnny O'Brien," he volun-teered, foreseeing that I would not be able to recognize him. All at once, the eye of memory began daubing color into place, rusting the locks and deepening the freckles that time had faded, until I was able to identify the youth who had stood in front of me in the lines arranged by size place at the elementary school we both attended half a century before.

With the recognition came old feelings that reminded me of the fond-ness and frustration with which I had approached him when we were both so young. I recalled my desire to reach out to him and be his friend, and also how we never did become close. When we had talked for a while, I asked him how he had regarded me then. "You were frightening," he answered. "I was twelve and just trying to figure out who I was and what it was all about. But you already knew." Of course I did; I was already embarked on my father's mission. "You had a certainty and a purpose," John continued, "that was daunting in someone so inexperienced and young. It was as though you already knew what to think about everything, about who you were and where you were going. I sensed in you an indefinable con-tempt for those who were too ignorant to see these truths. It became clear to me that someone unanointed with such knowledge could never get near you. So I gave up trying."

John's father was a New York fireman with an eighth-grade education, an immigrant who wanted his son to make good in a country where making good was a possible dream. John was able to fulfill his father's ambition, becoming a classics professor and writing a noted book about Alexander the Great, with sources in seven languages. The life of his subject even res-onated with his own, since Alexander was a man driven by the ambition to surpass his father. While able to dominate others, however, Alexander lost the battle with his own demon, alcohol. In John's view, the god Dionysius was the "invisible enemy" who eventually brought down the greatest war-rior of the classical age. As John told it, Alexander's story was that of a man who had conquered the world but in the end could not conquer himself.

The certainty that had frightened John when he saw it in me was my Dionysian nemesis, my wine of denial fermented in the vineyard of my father's dreams. At twelve I was already intoxicated by my father's mission, pursuing his hope and earnestly recruiting others to follow. In my memoir *Radical Son* I related how this fantasy undid me, and how tragedy had finally bled its arrogant presence from my soul.

Small as I was compared to Alexander, I had made a conquest of self that he could not. The advantage I had over the undefeated hero was failure; the fall I had taken was my saving grace. In my memoir I wrote: "The disorder of my life—which I understood to be a disorder of myself—allowed me to see for the first time. I began asking questions I had never thought to ask. *Why am I doing this? What do I want? What do I need?* As the life I had so carefully and purposefully constructed disintegrated before my eyes, I realized that I didn't really know. The chaos I found myself in had shifted my vision. The very sense of failure, of bottomless defeat, proved a grace. For the first time in my life, I could not address others from a moral high ground. I was no longer busy bringing them the good news. It was I who needed help. For the first time in my life, I wanted to listen." Discussing fathers and sons with a professor of classics, and also the intimacy between suffering and knowledge, made my conversation with John O'Brien seem very old. What could be more Oedipal or more obvious than that we must be humbled in order to see?

A few months after our first encounter, April and I traveled to Santa Fe— the City of Holy Faith—to pay a visit to the doctor who had helped me through my illness and to see if he could help her with hers. The air is thinner in the high desert and the light whiter and more intense than anywhere else. It is a combination that creates weightlessness in the head and soul. The result is an environment not recommended for heart cases, but seductive for artists and lovers. I had planned the trip in the hope that my doctor could improve April's health but when we got there he failed to inspire her faith in his homeopathic remedies, and the medical agenda of our trip was thus concluded.

The first night in Santa Fe we bedded down in a motel designed like a Spanish inn with rooms furnished in dark oak. Soon after falling asleep we were roused by a banging at the door and the noise of human voices. It was April who lurched to consciousness first. "Someone's breaking in," she said, her voice a blade of panic in the dark. I was on my feet instantly, grabbing one of the heavy Spanish chairs and brandishing it lance-like, my knight to her damsel in distress. *Who's there?* I barked menacingly, still leaden with sleep.

Just then April flicked on the light. Its glare exposed my nakedness and revealed that I was facing a blank wall. The noise we had taken for intruders at the door was a drunken party in the neighboring suite; and my chair, still risibly aloft, was fending off phantoms. Seeing me so preposterously poised, she burst into laughter, rendering my situation immediately worse. But just as quickly she relented. "How romantic," she said without a trace of irony. This was the first of many light-hearted interludes of our intimacy together, which I already hoped would carry us to the end of time.

In the next days, we planned to visit friends and explore the desert landscapes. Driving north past cactus plains and red-earth mesas, we arrived in the city of Taos, a luminous place where the painter Georgia O'Keefe had made canvases bloom and D. H. Lawrence had written a story about a woman who fell in love with the sun. We stopped there to tour an adobe church, which seemed haunted by the spirits of dead padres and conquistadors, and then continued our drive. The road took us up through the *Sangre de Cristo* mountains, where the escarpments were a deep hunter's green and the crests haloed in blue mists that made the range appear as sanctified as its name.

My friends had built a lovers' retreat in the high country, but—as we were soon to discover—had become ensnared in the web of a doomed marriage instead. The wife had hoped to find respite in the mountains from the turmoil of her life in California's Silicon Valley, where her wealthy husband was a corporate leader. She was restless there—as indeed wherever she was—and had persuaded him to buy the isolated nook in the *Cristo* range to create their mountain idyll. It was a location she had selected long before she met him, when she was a student without means and could hardly have dreamed of the house she eventually built. With funds he provided, she had overseen the construction of a two-story villa fitted with great wooden beams and fieldstone carapaces. The imposing edifice made a fitting crown to the romance that had failed. "I placed each stone in that wall and designed every room in the house," the wife told me bitterly when it was no longer hers.

Alongside the main structure was a stream which they had blocked, dredging the bed to form an artificial lake that rippled gracefully in the mountain wind. A canopy of clouds drifted listlessly overhead, and in the pale light the unquiet surface of the water acquired a metallic sheen and a serenity that seemed otherworldly. Long before her marriage, my friend had adopted the Hindu faith in an effort to calm her unsatisfied desires and lift the veil of unhappiness that had shrouded her from youth. When the knot was tied, she led her husband onto her spiritual path, encouraging him to invest millions in his adopted creed. On the verge of the lake, she had built a meditation room out of redwood planks and fitted it with a window facing the water, where the melancholy light could inspire her reflections. When it was finished, her Hindu guru came to visit and bless the site. Daily, beside the magical tide, the wife meditated on Maya, the illusion of the world she had created. But its loss devastated her all the same.

It is our common lot to share our joys but be alone in our sorrows whose labyrinths no other can enter. April and I took in my friends' misery, considered it, and returned to our private delights. In the rooms that had been decorated with elaborate care, in the gardens cultivated with affection, we reveled in our own Maya, exploring the life we had begun together and relishing the wonder at where we would go next. I already knew I loved April and hoped that her feelings were as tender towards me.

When our Santa Fe trip was over, we headed back to Los Angeles and to our solitary homes, a constant separation I looked forward to ending. But I kept my counsel and did not reveal in so many words the feelings I harbored. It would be months before I would be able to do so, and more than a year before I would ask her to share a house with me so that we would return always to the same address. Another would pass before I felt free to ask her to be my wife.

It was April, skeptical of verbal commitments, who imposed this discipline, making clear that too bold a declaration would be suspect if it were based on experience too slight to trust. She was as cautious in these matters as I frequently was not. I yielded to her restraints, keeping my desire to marry her secret until patience had earned it a gravity she would respect. Was this deception? Only if her reasons for requiring the caution were identical to mine in resisting it. Only if the judgments each of us makes proceeds along similar axes to similar results. But the experiences that shape our judgments are never the same. We are alone in our choices. No matter how intimately we know each other, or for how long, we will always be strangers in this.

It has been ten years now that we have been together, but I will never know whether the wait she imposed was necessary to achieve the desired result. It is the same for all the decisions that define us. We do not get to retrace our steps or test the choices we make, or see where others would have led.

As the marriage day approached, I searched for some ceremonial words to say to my bride and was reminded of a phrase from a play I had seen as a young man. I have remembered this line for nearly half a century. It is a comment made by one of the characters on how the strange and uncertain circumstances of our lives cause us to grope in the dark and to feel ourselves lucky when we actually find our way. "Sometimes," the character remarks, "you have to go a long way out of the way to come a short way correctly."

Perhaps I was impressed by this sentiment because it seemed to justify the mistakes I made along the way that had deflected me from my intended paths. This is a rationale familiar to everyone. We are constantly telling ourselves that something we regret and cannot explain "happened for a reason." But did it? Do we not use this phrase, rather, to comfort ourselves for the mistakes made or opportunities missed, or for tragedies we cannot comprehend? There is a reason that we yearn to make sense of lost time. We are looking for reassurance that God is taking care of us, and that it is death finally, and not life, that is the dream.

It occurred to me that in counseling patience, April had become my tutor in a lesson that had eluded me all my life. Her caution was the reason it was her first marriage and my impulsiveness why it was not mine. I knew she was anxious about the fact that she was not my first wife and decided to let her know during the ceremony that it was actually a bond—however implausible—that connected us. At the altar on our wedding day I said, "We pay for our sins, but we are not always rewarded for what we do right. Today I am rewarded. Unexpectedly, undeservedly, but rewarded all the same. I am grateful to have been given this day a woman with so good a heart and so generous a soul. In this moment I see that my whole life has been a long going out of the way to come a short way to you."

Saul Bellow had five marriages. In his novel, *Humboldt's Gift,* he created an alter ego with similar bad luck named Charlie Citrine, whose wife had left him for another man and filed a ruinous lawsuit against him. While telling a friend about his marital trials Citrine makes the following observation about his case: "It keeps me in touch with the facts of life. It's been positively enlightening."

"How so?"

"Well, I realize how universal the desire to injure your fellow man is."

It is tempting to dismiss this judgment as the self-serving cynicism of a habitual defendant. But an honest reader will recognize in it a theme of all our divorces, marital and otherwise. Each time an intimacy comes to an end and ardor turns to revenge, we are given a glimpse of the abyss that lies under the surface of all our peace. Our innocence is amazed that someone who has loved us can want to destroy us. But why should this be remarkable? We are rootless and alone and threatened with extinction. In this circumstance, the quest for survival is our consummate narcissism, denial our first defense. Is there a limit to what human beings will do to save themselves when they believe their backs are to the wall? Will they not lie, steal, cheat, even kill? When we think we have no alternative—a conclusion reached easily enough—what is unfair and injurious to me will seem like perfect justice to you.

A rabbi named Joseph Telushkin has written a popular text called *The Ten Commandments of Character* whose aim is to offer readers "essential advice for living an honorable, ethical and honest life." The Rabbi's Third Commandment tells us to "Treat All People With Kindness and With The Understanding That They, Like You, Are 'Made in God's Image.'" To prove the wisdom of this commandment, Rabbi Telushkin asks, "Would terrorists plant bombs in public places if they had not first blinded themselves to the fact that the people they kill and maim are, like themselves and their families, created in God's image?" The rabbi answers: "All instances of evil—from the Holocaust to the humiliation of a single person—have in common the perpetrator's unwillingness to see the image of God in each human being." In other words, understand that God is in every one of His children and you will harm none.

But is this so? Is it possible that when Mohammed Atta drove his plane into the Trade Center Towers he did not believe with his whole heart that Allah had created each and every one of his victims? Of course he did. He killed them to fulfill God's plan. Was not Mohammed Atta himself created in God's image? If Atta had survived his own atrocity, should he then have been treated with kindness and respect? Was not Satan created in God's image? The Prince of Evil was God's favorite angel before his fall from grace. And what are we if not fallen ourselves?

It is folly to imagine that terror can be exorcised by saccharine bromides like Rabbi Telushkin's. You could invert the meaning of his commandment and do better: *Do not aspire to see God in yourself for pride goeth before a fall.* The fall of Satan, as of Adam, sprang from his dissatisfaction with the world as it is, from his desire to be *like* God. The evil of this world is not caused by ignorance of the good, or failure to appreciate the holiness of human life. It is caused by the black hole that lies at the bottom of every human soul.

What I had learned through the most painful experiences of my life was to pay attention to the differences. It was a lesson at odds with the moral teachings that have come down to us across the millennia. All the prophets—Moses, Jesus, Buddha, the Hindu gurus—have taught an opposite truth: that however different we may look and act, we are one. High and low, strong and weak, virtuous and sinful, we are all incarnations of the same divine spirit. Underneath our various skins, all are kin. *There but for the grace of God go I.*

But are we? And do we?

"Treat a stranger as you would be treated. Love thy neighbor as thyself." These commandments are said to sum up the moral law. But is it really prudent to put our trust in strangers, or to love our enemies as ourselves? Would we counsel our children to do so?

Do we really regard ourselves as one with rapists and murderers? Or should we? It is true that the capacity for evil is in our nature, and this makes us kin. But I can feel no kinship with those who can cut a human life short without remorse; with terrorists who target the innocent for death; or with adults who torment children for sexual thrills. I suspect I am not alone in this.

In the realm of the spirit, it is easier to slide a mile back than to advance a single step. One lesson I had learned through all my trials was to note, and never forget, that some have fallen farther than others, and will not come back. To my own children I would say: Do not take the sympathy of others for granted. Do not presume they will respond as you do, or that they share your human compassion. To act without caution on such assumptions is to invite consequences that can be as severe as death.

The lack of respect for immutable difference is the cause of endless human grief, and is why my father's dreams have failed.

After our descent from the mountains, April and I stopped in Santa Fe to visit my oldest childhood friend, Danny Wolfman. Danny and I were born a month apart in 1939 and had been passengers in the same baby carriage pushed alternately by our mothers who were also best friends. As infants we attended the same nursery school and remained close to each other until we left for colleges in distant cities. Now that our parents were gone, Danny was the person I had known the longest who was still with me on this earth.

When I set up my first household in California, and before I had any children, Danny and his wife Marianne stayed with us, spending the night in sleeping bags on the living room floor in our one bedroom apartment. It was 1960 and we were graduate students, all anticipating an endless horizon. I was studying literature, while Danny had entered the field of archaeology, tunneling through time to retrieve the shards of lost civilizations. Over morning coffee he and Marianne talked enthusiastically about a dig they were headed for in Mesa Verde, where they intended to search the ruins of a cliff dwelling tribe called the Anasazi, which was a Navajo word that meant "ancient people." More than a thousand years before, the Anasazi had carved stone pueblos out of the side of a plateau rising out of Colorado's Montezuma Valley. Three hundred years after arriving, they abandoned the villages they had built and disappeared. Nobody knows where they went or why; only their artifacts remain. Danny and Marianne were going to look for them.

Even in my imagination I had a hard time following their path. The very image of glacial time zones in which whole worlds were submerged was something I found oppressive. Perhaps I saw my own dreams swallowed up in mountains of indifferent earth alongside the Anasazi. While Danny and Marianne were looking backward in time, I was eagerly anticipating the revolutionary future. I couldn't begin to understand their romance with the long-buried past.

I lost touch with Danny for a long time after that, as we went our separate professional ways. For a time I lived in Europe, then returned to Berkeley to write. He got into the driver's seat of his Ford van, which was to be his transportation for the next thirty years, and took off on exotic travels into the heart of Mesoamerica. In Mexico and then in Peru, where he went to visit Machu Picchu, the lost city of the Incas, he would park his van and continue on horseback along wilderness trails, pursuing the lives of the ancient dead. Once, near Oaxaca, bandits posing as policemen kidnapped him and took his money and archaeological samples before they set him free.

Eventually, Danny and Marianne settled in the state of Arkansas with their daughter, a beautiful child they named Lauren. He had been hired as the state's archaeologist, where one of his projects was to take an inventory of the Buffalo National River. A generous teacher, Danny encouraged one of his students to develop a tree-ring chronology for the state and the entire southeast, which had a significant influence on archaeological dating in the region.

When we were both in our forties, we met up again in our old neighborhood in New York. The physical change in him was noticeable, and not only because his brown hair had acquired flecks of gray. There was an urgent appeal in his eyes and his complexion had turned a bright, worrying red. Always a bear of a man, he had blown up to where the envelope of his body seemed about to explode; when he spoke, his voice was pinched as though his lungs were under pressure. I kept wanting to tell him to breathe.

The alarming appearance conveyed an equally disquieting reality. His doctors had detected an irregularity in his heart, and his blood pressure was so high it had caused him to lose consciousness twice. He was just then recovering from a blow to the head suffered when he blacked out in the street and fell backwards onto the pavement. Afterwards his doctors warned him to make changes in the way he conducted his life, or face an early death. But it was evident that even under a sentence so dire he could not do it. My old friend Danny is going to die soon, I thought. We are only in our forties and in another ten years he won't be around.

I tried to talk to him and bring him back. With a feeling of immense futility, I urged him to stop what he was doing and change. Take deep breaths, I said helplessly. *Slow down.* "But I can't," he replied. "There are things I *have* to do." I marveled at how a man who inhabited time zones measured in eons could be so ensnared by the imperatives of a few weeks in the present. But he was. He had scientific rivals to respond to and positions he needed to defend. "I'm scheduled to give two important papers at a conference next month. I can't afford to miss the deadlines."

Danny was a pioneer in the specialized field of chronometrics, and was working on a specific technique for dating artifacts, called archaeo-magnetism. The earth whirling through space shifts its axis over the course of time and thus its magnetic pole. The shifts have been mapped. A hearth built by the Anasazi contains traces of iron in its clay floor. These traces are magnetized in a pattern that parallels the shifting positions of the earth's field. When the Anasazi fired the hearth more than a thousand years earlier, the pattern froze. By matching the magnetic lines in the ancient clay to the time map of the polar shifts, Danny could date the hearth.

Measuring these samples required a magnetometer and other lab equipment to which Danny had no access for most of his career. To secure lab time he had to travel to California, which added to his pressures, but also made it possible for me to see him. Recently he had obtained a job at the Museum of New Mexico in Santa Fe. He moved into a small adobe house in town, where he resided alone. Marianne had left along the way, and now lived a thousand miles distant on the west coast, where their daughter Lauren was attending college.

Danny's new museum position came with the promise of a new archaeo-magnetic laboratory, which had been completed the year before April and I went to see him. On the road to Santa Fe, I looked forward to our meeting with anticipation. I was happy that I had been wrong and that he was still alive more than ten years after our encounter in New York.

At his suggestion, we met in a local café with oak tables that were warm from the autumn sun. The conversation over breakfast was bathed in the nostalgias of our own lost time. As we talked about his life in Santa Fe, I began to feel a pang of discomfort at having brought April with me, who was the very image of my own late-achieved happiness. It made me acutely conscious that he was alone and his health problems were still with him. He was overweight and his face was flushed. When I asked about his health, he said he was scheduled to go into the hospital the next month to have his heart defibrillated. There was no particular incident that made the medical procedure necessary, he added. It was just something his doctors ordered to be safe. Santa Fe was not a backwater, I reassured myself, and it would be a good hospital with doctors who knew what they were doing. I felt a deep affection for this man I had known longer than any other, and whom I could not help.

Near the end of the meal, I had occasion to go to the men's room and left April and Danny at the table. "When you were gone," she told me later, "he leaned over and asked me, 'How old are you?'" I told her I didn't think he intended disapproval by this question. I thought it was more like an encouragement to himself. April was thirty-three, which was twenty-two years younger than either of us.

April and I said our goodbyes to Danny and went back to California to resume our lives. A month later he went into the hospital where they hooked him up to the defibrillator for the routine procedure. Soon after, I received a call from Marianne whom I hadn't seen or heard from in the thirty-four years since she and Danny were students bedded down on my living room floor. "Dan is dead," she said. "He went into the hospital for the procedure and they lost him."

Into the 5 *Future*

Ten years later, I am still pushing on. The world we inhabit remains a mystery but I go on living and writing nonetheless, as though there were a reason for both. I have survived long enough to see my chronometer run in reverse. The future is now a dwindling proposition. If there are only ten years in front of me, it will be enough to consider myself lucky.

Almost every day I create an order on the page that reflects the order I see in the world. What matters is that the search moves me forward as though I am headed somewhere, an illusion that rescues me from the despair that would overwhelm me if I were not. In any case, I am so far along in my journey that there are projects I am reluctant to begin now, because I do not know whether there will be time enough to finish the page. If I did not believe there was actually an order in the world, I suppose I would not be able to pursue goals at all. The quests I pursue are my comfort and my personal line of faith. They put oxygen into the air around me and allow me to breathe.

At the halfway mark of the last century, which to me does not seem so long ago, the gifted American writer William Faulkner won the Nobel Prize for Literature, an award, like every other human vanity, bestowed on the undeserving and the deserving alike. Faulkner titled his most famous novel, *The Sound and the Fury,* after a Shakespearean tragedy. Shakespeare's story concerns a nobleman, Macbeth, who in pursuit of worldly gain betrays every human value and relationship that is meaningful to him. In the process he is stripped of all human companionship and respect, until he is only an empty and embittered shell. "My life has fallen into the sere, the yellow leaf," he reflects. Having emptied his own life of its spiritual supports, he turns against life itself, which he describes as "a tale told by an idiot, full of sound and fury, signifying nothing." When Faulkner mounted the podium in Oslo to receive his Nobel Prize and felt as though he was speaking to the world, he struck a very different note. The year was 1950, the dawn of the nuclear era. Faulkner looked into the eye of its darkest prospect and declared, "I refuse to accept this. I believe that ... when the last ding-dong of doom has clanged and faded ... in the last dying red evening ... man will not merely endure: he will prevail." Others criticized this pronouncement as empty bravado. What basis could Faulkner have to make such a claim? But the claim was not something he knew. It was his faith. It was the oxygen he needed to breathe.

April and I had acquired a little Mexican dog with black and white markings, whose improbable name is Jacob and whose brain is smaller than my fist. When Jacob wags his tail to signal his happiness, he does not hide his pleasure as we, who are burdened with self-consciousness, often do. Instead, his whole frame is swept into the motion as though life had no reality but this. Jacob is one of the myriad creatures on this earth, ridiculous and also beautiful, whose origin is a mystery and who do not worry the significance of who, or why, or what they are. In the morning when I step out of my shower, this little self comes to me unbidden to lick the glistening drops from my feet. This is not a ritual of submission. It does not have any meaning for him at all. It is merely his pleasure. What is interesting is that I, a creature who lives by meanings, am also affected by this action. When he does not come, I feel the absence and miss him. This is a microcosm of all the visits and vacancies that bring joy and misery to our lives. Our choice is to embrace them or not. These are decisions we freely make that determine whether life will hollow us out and embitter us, or provide us oxygen to breathe.

Two years after my tumor was discovered, I went back to the Norris Cancer Center for an annual checkup. My first checkup six months after the operation had revealed a psa level of one tenth of a point—low for someone who still had a prostate, but apparently twice that for someone without one.

I say "apparently" because like so much human knowledge this too was uncertain. From a strictly scientific angle my fate remained a mystery. For the next six months I lived with the possibility that some of the wilding cells might have leaked through the wall before the prostate was removed and then resisted the radiation afterwards. When I took the second test, the level had dropped to where it was undetectable, indicating that I was disease-free. But now the number was up again, albeit only one-half of one-tenth of a point, enough to be still tracking what might be a cancer or not.

When I went in to consult Dr. Skinner about the result, he was his usual sanguine self. "We'll watch you. Even if it grows, the pace will be slow enough that more than likely you'll die of old age first. If it gets to a five or a six, I'll order a bone scan. If it gets to twenty, we'll probably give you some hormones to slow it down. But there's nothing to worry about. You'll probably die of natural causes before this gets serious." I didn't understand the numbers. How could the six I had registered when I first went to see him be dangerous enough to warrant an evisceration, but a twenty not cause for alarm? What was the secret of renewed life? What was *really* going on? I confronted Skinner: If it's there, can't you just cut it out? I asked him even though I knew the answer. "There's nothing left to cut," he replied. "Come back in six months. We don't even know that this is a cancer. There's a difference of opinion over what such low post-operative levels mean."

He conveyed all his observations with a conviction that did not invite challenge. How would I challenge him anyway? Skinner's expression pre-empted such melodramas. He was a doctor, not a sorcerer. It occurred to me that this man had his own mortality to consider, and was closer to a natural span than I. I had been alive for sixty-four years—not as long as Methusaleh, but twice the age of Alexander. I was far enough along so that the cancer—if it was a cancer—would not make a hair of difference when it was over, just as Skinner said. I did not like the idea of carrying a time bomb inside me. But then who did? I had more symptoms of creeping age than any other malignancy. If I did still have a cancer I had no symptoms at all. I left Skinner's office with a refreshed perspective. Once I accepted my condition, I was in a position to appreciate its positive aspects. The ticking—whether it was cancer or merely age—made it easier to keep vital distinctions in view, never letting me forget the space I occupied was finite, no matter how limitless my desires. "This is the monstruosity in love, lady," Shakespeare's incurable romantic Troilus observed: "that the desire is boundless and the act a slave to limit." He might have made that life. The monstruosity of life.

When I think of Troilus's complaint, the words never fail to bring to mind my romantic father and all those who long for a world made whole and a life that will not let them down. It was the limitless boundaries of my father's desire that took away his freedom. The hunger for redemption swallowed him up, and buried him alive. He was right, of course, that the world is broken—along with its beauty, goodness and truth. What he could not accept is that it cannot be otherwise. He did not understand that the glory is in the brokenness: that we do it despite that, and we do not submit. The poet Wallace Stevens embraced his fate, writing, "Death is the mother of beauty." What he meant was that all our significances—whether love or nobility or art itself—are created by the end towards which we are heading. If there were no end, why would anything matter? If time is infinite, what is the moment? If nothing can be lost, what can be gained? Therefore consider what you have and be grateful for it, and remember to look while your eyes are still open.

Isn't that just like you, to think you can psych out death by treating it as an aesthetic device? This could be my father's voice, but it is my friend Peter's. Years earlier he had become a devout Catholic. When he read this text and made the comment, it was Ash Wednesday, the beginning of Lent, the last suffering days of his Savior's time on earth. My answer to Peter is this: I understand the finality of death, and do not make light of the end. But my journey has led me to these conclusions, which I cannot deny so late in its course. I have no faith in a life hereafter. But I will not be desperate over my own disappearance. If there is nothing further, what of it? Why should I waste the time I have left in misery over what cannot be changed?

The voice I could not answer was April's. "You're so arrogant," she rebuked me. "Think of what God has done for you. Look at the times He has looked after you, how He saved you from cancer. You need to show some gratitude. *I* need you to do this for me. If you don't believe, you won't be there when I come for you and I'll be alone. And I don't want to be without you." I tried to soothe her. "Don't fret," I said. "If there is a God, I am sure He is merciful, and will not condemn me for my lack of faith. Life cannot be merely a test to see if God's children will believe." I thought this reasoning effective, but the pain in her eyes would not quit. She was already missing me. Her distress caused me to reconsider what I had said. In fact, I had no answer. I *was* arrogant. If there was a God, how could I, in my mere mortality, know His plan? Maybe the whole idea *was* to see through the chaos and, through an act of faith, discover the divinity in it all. I had been lucky, and had no explanation why. Once again I was forced to question what I had taken for granted and ask, *Is it I who am blind?* "I'll think about it," I said. "I don't want you to think," my wife replied. "I want you to open your heart."

In the afternoon light, April was golden. She was clutching the string of a heart-shaped party balloon whose metallic surface was painted with brightly colored flowers and the inscription, "I Love You Mom." It had been filled with helium and was straining at its tie.

"It's Mother's Day," April said. "I bought a balloon for your mother."

"My mother is dead."

"That's why I bought the balloon. To send it up to her, to keep her spirit alive. When it goes up to heaven, her spirit will grab hold of it."

I followed my wife onto the deck at the back of the house, facing the ocean. The afternoon sea was cobalt blue, ruffling in the dry wind like goose flesh, as though its skin had come alive. I scrutinized the object she held with the eyes of a skeptic, just as my father would if he were still alive. What am I going to do with this toy, I thought, and these childlike fantasies? But then I allowed myself to breathe and take in the moment. As I did so, I was pulled up into my wife's feeling for my absent mother and for her wounded son. I thought of the long-dead woman who had delivered me into this world in pain and watched over me as long as she was able. I recalled the years when age had overtaken and crippled her, and I had cared for her; I remembered back to when she was young and handsome and had taken time from her own pleasures and plans to look after me and set me on my way. And I missed her.

As I let my dead mother come near, I also let the corniness of the little object go. It seemed to me now a perfect symbol of our helplessness as we struggle to resist inexorable losses. It captured perfectly the feebleness with which we sought to express our hurt and the futility with which we scanned the eternal silence in search of a help for our irreparable woes.

Oh Lord, when I consider the heavens,
the work of your fingers, the moon and the stars
which you have set in their places,
what is man that you are mindful of him,
the son of man that you care for him?

I cut the weight from the end of the string and the heart rose up. As it left my hand, April shouted after it, "We love you Blanche; we'll meet you in heaven." For moments I just stood watching the balloon dance skyward in the breeze, feeling the familiar pain of old memories. Then April turned to me and asked if I thought our little messenger would be able to reach my mother beyond the clouds, which now seemed impossibly high above us.

I had been wondering myself. I reflected how our technological ingenuity had already lifted us over their crest; how I was used to traveling myself at altitudes high above the point where the plastic heart would finally give out and float gently back to earth. I was thinking: we already know too much for heaven. Our ancestors looked skyward and were humbled by its mystery and made reverent by its wonder. But we have been up there, and know what it is, and are convinced of what it is not. If by some chance my mother's spirit was out there, the little craft we had fashioned was not going to reach her.

Even as I thought this, I was aware of how liquid I had become, how the heartache I had suppressed for years had returned to the surface to remind me of the mother I had lost and how powerless I was to get her back. Even if the little heart would never make it to the lowliest cloud, it had already taken me to her, and for a moment her spirit, as April had promised, was alive again.

My children and grandchildren are filling up the spaces I have left. It is through them that life comes to me now. They pull me towards it, and remind me I am leaving. In my grandchildren I see the energies of my childhood and the horizon of expectation stretching endlessly in front of me. In their parents I watch myself gathering the next generation and hustling it forward to futures unknown. These are my rings of time. They remind me of who I was and am no more. Like the lost civilizations they tell me where I am going and where I have been. I feel my ancient-ness in them.

I know how I will leave. When my time comes, I will be engaged at full throttle, or the best I can muster. If I am fortunate I will be alert and April will be beside me, and—if their busy lives permit—my children, and their children, and my stepson as well. Then a beat, and my soul will start ascending like my mother's heart. It will not dance slowly but go like a rocket to a destination unknown, perhaps to nowhere at all. And that doesn't bother me. If I allow myself regrets, it is for the occasions I did not do what I should have, and for those when I failed to do what was right. It is for not being grateful enough.

For a time, my departed spirit will live on in others, especially April and my children and theirs who will remember me and keep me in their hearts, until they too are gone. And then it will be over. But I don't feel cheated. I do not regret a moment that I lived to the full or did what was good. Nor do I regret the love I gave to my family and friends, or the kindnesses to strangers who deserved them. But then it will be done, and it will be left to others to fill the spaces. It will all happen so fast and so finally that one moment I'll be here, and the next I'll be gone.

BOOK II

A Point in Time
(The Search for Redemption in this Life and the Next)
(2006–2013)

Where do we go when we die? he said.
I don't know, the man said.
Where are we now?

—CORMAC MCCARTHY

October 2006

I

As the years recede, as inexorably they must, and my step begins to falter, I have adopted a routine of taking my dogs for a walk up the long and leafy grade in front of my house, and back. It is the way I keep my body moving and my heart in shape, and how I fix an eye on my animal self, which unlike my imagination that could go on forever will not.

There are four of us to keep each other company on these repetitive rounds—myself, two spirited Chihuahuas named Jake and Lucy, and a lumbering Bernese mountain dog whom my wife has named Winnie after the fictional bear. The big dog's colors are black and brown with a white slash at the throat. She limps affably behind us, hobbled by hips displaced from over-breeding, bearing it all without complaint.

As we make our way up the incline, the little ones race ahead spinning out their spooled leashes, weaving as they go like furry kites, their noses pressed to the ground as they follow invisible trails. Jake is a black and white spot who hurries nervously on spindly legs that narrow sharply at the joints, creating a pink translucence where the light pokes through. Lucy, a muscular auburn, is the alpha of our pack, with moves aggressive and hunter-like. This martial presence is undermined, however, by ears that flop at the ends and quizzical brown eyes whose rims are wrinkled like the Progeria children who grow old before they grow up.

Our point of departure at the bottom of the hill is a stucco house with sand-colored walls and a red tile roof. In the front, a realtor's shingle indicates that my wife and I have put the property up for sale. It is the third house we have lived in during a dozen years of a shared life. Our previous home in Malibu was perched like an eyrie on a cliff above the ocean, while this one is inland, overlooking the San Fernando Valley from hills above Calabasas. The realtor has attached a brochure to the "For Sale" sign which promotes the property as a "Tuscan Villa," perhaps because it is set in a glade of the coastal range, or maybe because of the lion-head fountain on the garden wall. The interior is fitted with other details intended to lend it an Old Country look—a wrought-iron chandelier and a built-in ivory-colored cabinet whose surface has been distressed to give the appearance of age. Of all the environments I have lived in during the course of a life now reasonably long, this one has been especially comforting, and I am reluctant to leave it.

Our excursions begin with a procession to the end of the foyer where I have stored the dogs' leashes in a wicker basket and stuffed the brimmed cap I wear now to shade the sun-damaged skin that can no longer repair itself. I have only to reach for the hat to elicit a fanfare of yelps that celebrate the simple evanescent pleasure before us as the high point of the day. And every day. For it is always the same.

I don the cap, sparking their canine cries, and fasten the leashes to their collars, a task made challenging by the frenzy. When the tussle is concluded and the small dogs harnessed, we step through the front door to begin our adventure. The dogs charge at the squirrels and hares foraging on the lawn, causing them to scurry into the meadow by the side of the house or up the embankment across the way where they disappear into labyrinthine burrows, making good their escapes. A pipe corral rises above the warrens, which is home to a sable-coated stallion with a diamond emblazoned on his regal forehead. His name is Clifton, and every day as we approach he subjects us to the same deliberate inspection. Nearby his companion, an aged pony named Robin, stands so still he seems frozen in time. His matted hair hangs like a Spanish moss from his weathered frame and makes him look so ancient I am always relieved to see him still with us.

And every day, without fail, we attack them. It is Lucy who sounds our battle cry, while Jake seconds her alarms prudently from the rear. Jutting her head through the bars of the corral, she finally provokes the majestic creature who turns and thunders towards us. The sight is fearsome to everyone but the instigator who elevates her cries at the stallion's approach, thrusting her body towards him. When Clifton is just above us, I yank her back. This precaution is not simply for her. Once, when I failed to do so, she coiled on her tiny haunches and waited for the noble head to dip, then leapt and airborne bit the stallion on his cheek.

Inside the house, the little dogs do not lead, as they do on our walks, but follow at my heels wherever I go. Whether I am ascending the stairs or descending, whether entering a room or leaving, their patter, like Marvell's chariot, is always hurrying near. I am the keeper of secrets whose mystery they seem to covet. What to do? Where to go? Is it an anthropomorphic folly that I am projecting onto these creatures? Perhaps it is. But such a skepticism also slights their need as kindred souls to keep their master close.

When the battle at Clifton's corral is over, we proceed up the grade to where other diversions await. Approaching a neighbor's yard, Lucy is again ready to summon its residents to arms. Behind these fences are less formidable foes but they still outsize us by daunting margins. Sometimes, if our adversaries are inside the houses or reluctant to leave the shaded overhangs where they lounge, we will wait vainly for our challenge to be answered. But if they do come, a feral fury awaits.

Up and down the length of the fences the antagonists race snout to snout, teeth bared, jowls aquiver. I watch these skirmishes with a worried eye, since a slip too close to an opening would expose my reckless charge to jaws ready to pounce. An occasional passerby displays alarm but it is a misplaced emotion, for the battles are not real. They are martial dances not unlike the ones that engage us in our ordinary lives, which also feature danger and mortality peering about the edges at each turn.

A furrow of autumn wind spins the leaves and unsettles the dogs with intimations of the oncoming weather. The season will indeed grow harsher but in the end will hardly seem a winter in this desert clime. The muffling of nature's cycles creates a sentimental fallacy for our aimless routines: no dramatic change of course, no auguring of brighter worlds to come. Having spent a lifetime avoiding occupations that appear to accomplish nothing, I find myself happy with this arrangement. It teaches me to embrace my circular horizon and accept it.

I am always impressed at how the dogs, familiar with every sight and smell along our way, come at these walks with renewed enthusiasm each time we set out. As though life were an endless horizon always met for the first time. How their excitement, when I put on my cap at the onset of our rituals, never fades. How they do not contend with their fates but devour them as if their days will go on forever. But I, who do not have the luxury of their comity with nature, see the silence coming, and look on the brief turn of their lives with bittersweet regret, and mourn them before they are gone.

These walks are a peace I make with my own fate. Like my dogs, I look forward to a journey where the sights are familiar and nothing is accomplished, where nothing will happen that hasn't already happened before.

II

When I was still young and living in my father's house, there were no dogs to take on our walks or celebrate our returns. It was not something I thought about at the time, or until long after I had animals of my own. But now that I have entered my own autumn, and these dogs with their quirks and affections have become integral to my routines, the omission seems strange.

A recurring pattern of my father's days that he was never able to alter was the difficulty he had in his interactions with others. Social occasions would often end abruptly with him acting badly and feeling misunderstood. By contrast, he was able to approach animals with a confidence and ease that made the encounters pleasurable. Even as a youngster, I appreciated how the playful antics of the neighborhood canines never failed to amuse him; how, encountering them on our walks, his demeanor would change and a rare glow of happiness flush his sallow cheeks.

Whenever I have occasion to reflect on these moments, I am prompted to ask an obvious question. Why would a man who felt at odds with his fellows deny himself the pleasure of these loyal creatures who were unlikely to be put off by his saturnine moods? Confronting this mystery, I am led to wonder whether his true desires were actually the secrets he was most determined to keep from himself.

Whenever the prospect of a pet came up for discussion, my father would camouflage his rejection as a practical matter. The responsibilities of caring for a creature who could not care for itself would distract us from missions that were more important. Or perhaps he was so firmly set in his ways that he was unable to imagine a life that was different.

This conservatism is an inertia that afflicts us all. We roll along tracks that have been laid down early in our journeys and are fearful of leaving them. So we rarely do. My own attitude towards these matters was an inherited disposition to which I hardly gave a second thought. When dogs did enter my life, it was unexpectedly, through the offices of others. It is only now when I have lived with them that they have come to seem indispensable, and I can appreciate the gift I was given.

My father's inattention to primal needs was the other side of his passion for worlds that did not exist. He saw himself as a missionary of a promised future in which a gentle rain of justice would nourish every seed, and never suspected that a fantasy so remote from what was going on directly in front of him might actually be the source of his isolation and gloom. By the time I was old enough to take my father's measure as a man, he was already enveloped in a metaphysical despair so dense he could never break free. Black emotions weighed heavily on him until he could no longer read the books that lined his shelves, a paralysis that piled on even more regrets.

When I was alone in our house, which was often, I would sit on the blue-green living room carpet and study the shelves my mother had unartfully painted in a similar color. My parents had acquired almost all their library, fictions included, from a book club that catered to their progressive tastes. One by one, I would run my fingers over their spines and parse the titles on the faded jackets until I had memorized the placement of every volume. Then I would pull them randomly from the spaces and slowly leaf through the secrets they held.

It was my mother who had acquired the membership, one of the many tasks she performed as the manager of our household affairs. An outgoing, curious, even adventurous woman, her tastes were catholic enough to provoke conflicts with my father when she favored an author who failed to conform to the party line. Her favorite books were not political tracts but biographies, usually of literary figures, and especially of the Russians—Tolstoy, Pushkin, Gorky.

I can still see her propped on the pillows of her bed, holding the open volume of Gorky's Mother, which she read before going to sleep. When she had finished this text, she made her way through the six-volume memoirs of the Communist playwright Sean O'Casey, until she had completed the last one, Sunset and Evening Star. But her unlikely favorite was a social reactionary, the aesthete Marcel Proust, a French Jew who spent the last invalid decade of his life closeted in a Paris bedroom, retrieving memories of lost family and time.

Tucked away on the bottom shelf in my parents' library were a handful of dust-gatherers my father had kept from his college days, mementos of a philosophy course in which he had enrolled. I approached these volumes with a youthful reverence, viewing them as repositories of a proven wisdom I was expected to acquire. It is not clear to me now why I should have had such an attitude. The progressive light that infused our household threw dark shadows across the landscapes of the past, casting the ancients as child-like seekers in a primitive world, groping their way to fragments of knowledge through fogs of religious myth.

Among the relics in my father's unread trove was a volume bound in red covers, which featured a translucent frontispiece that veiled the photograph of a marble bust. It was the likeness of the Roman emperor who had written the book nearly two thousand years before. The Meditations of Marcus Aurelius was a text beyond my youthful ken, but if I had been able to comprehend it I would have seen that the counsels of this long-dead author were a rebuke to everything my father believed.

What my father believed was that a time was coming when history would reward all the sufferings and trials of the past by metamorphosing into a world in which human beings lived in harmony and were guided by justice and reason. Even though he was an atheist, my father's views were like those of a medieval Gnostic. He believed the world was ruled by principles of darkness, and knowledge was a light that would set men free. Consequently, when he read his morning paper it was not to gather tidings of events that actually affected him—prices rising, weather brewing, wars approaching—but to parse the script of a global drama that would one day bring history and its miseries to an end.

While my father's ambitions were grandiose, his actual footprints in the present world were so small as to be practically invisible. When he had finally breathed his last, we held a memorial for him in our living room, attended by a modest group of family friends. In contrast, the long-dead author of the unread book commanded the attention of everyone alive in his time, while the thoughts he jotted down in his private hours are still read by us two millennia after he is gone.

Marcus Aurelius was the nineteenth ruler of Rome—the greatest empire the world had ever seen. But, unlike my father, he did not believe in history or human progress. The former he would have regarded as an illusion and the latter as nothing at all. This is what he wrote:

> He who has seen present things has seen all, both everything that has taken place from all eternity and everything that will be for time without end....

III

Marcus Aurelius was born a hundred and twenty years after the birth of Jesus, and ascended the throne when he was forty years old. He commanded the Roman legions in their campaigns against the northern tribes, and was a warrior through eight winters before he finally succumbed to a fever in Pannonia, where he died in his fifty-eighth year. By all accounts he was an exceptionally good man. The English historian Edward Gibbon, chronicler of Rome's decline and fall, described the reign of Marcus Aurelius as golden—"a period in the history of the world during which the condition of the human race was most happy and prosperous."

Gibbon's comment may be regarded as a reflection of Plato's wish for philosopher- kings who were both powerful and wise. But outside our dreams, no human age is golden, and the reign of Marcus was no exception. His years on the throne were beset by familiar calamities: religious persecutions, plagues, famines, rebellions, and wars. Perhaps Gibbon accepted these sorrows as ordinary aspects of human unhappiness and chose to discount them.

It was said that in his later years Marcus was deceived by his wife, Faustina, who betrayed him in the arms of a Syrian governor named Avidius Cassius. When the emperor's failing health inspired premature rumors of his death, Avidius hatched a plot to seize the throne and proclaim it his own. Before he could act, however, Marcus learned of the design and returned to the capital intending to pardon the usurper and prevent him from doing himself more harm. But as soon as the conspirators realized what had happened, they turned on Avidius and slew him. Hoping to gain favor with the emperor, they brought the traitor's head to court as an offering to the intended victim. But Marcus scorned their gift as dishonorable and refused to see them.

When he died it was said of him that he looked on friend and foe alike with a compassionate heart. The evidence is the text he left behind where no unkind word is recorded against his rival or his wife. His real name was Marcus Verus after his father who died young and his grandfather who raised him. "Of my grandfather Verus," he wrote, "I have learned to be gentle and meek, and to refrain from all anger and passion." And of his parents: "From the fame and memory of him that begot me I have learned both modesty and manliness, and from my mother I have learned to be religious, and bountiful; and to forbear not only to do evil but to intend evil." The emperor Hadrian referred to him as "Verissimus"—more truthful than the name he had been given.

During the German wars Marcus was bivouacked on the Danube River at Carnuntum. There, in his private hours, he secluded himself in his military tent and set down his intimate thoughts in Greek, calling the notes Eis Ta Aon, or "To Himself." The title Meditations, under which they found their way onto my father's shelf, was inserted centuries after his death by Catholic monks who retrieved them, and who found in his writings intimations of their Christian faith.

I had read The Meditations as a younger man, but it was only when I re-read them in my seventh decade that I was finally able to see what he had written. By then I was ten years older than the author when he departed this life, and the volume with the red covers and translucent leaf was long gone, and my father too. The copy I read was part of a set of more than twenty volumes in the "Great Books" series assembled by the Encyclopedia Britannica. The editors' idea was to provide readers with a shelf-long summary of the wisdom humanity had accumulated until then. The volumes belonged to my stepson Jon, who was then in his teens, and had been given to him by his father, who never had the privilege of attending a university and wanted to give his son the opportunity he missed. In acting on this desire he disregarded (as all of us do) the biblical warning of Ecclesiastes: "In much knowledge is much grief, and he that increaseth knowledge increaseth sorrow."

IV

Unlike my father, I do not look down my nose at the ancients but am impressed by their understanding of our case—how they were able to put a finger on the source of our distress: that alone among creatures we know our fate, and learn sooner or later that the world has no interest in it.

Marcus Aurelius was a Stoic, which is the name given to a school of philosophy whose view of our dramas is unfiltered by romance. To ease the heartache of our human plight, the Stoics advised us to accept our lot and refrain from contending against it. The counsel of the unread book on my father's shelf was this: You cannot alter the world, so do not make yourself miserable trying.

It was not simply a counsel of passivity in a situation without hope. Even though you cannot change the world, the Stoics observed, you can change what you make of it, and thus how it affects you. Things outside us "do not touch the soul, for they are external and immoveable," wrote Marcus; "our perturbations come only from our opinion of them, which is within." Therefore look inward, for you are the emperor of your soul. There are no gains or losses, no victories or defeats, but thinking makes them so. "Life is opinion." It is a story we write. This being the case it is wise to construct a narrative that does not multiply unnecessary defeats. Therefore, begin by regarding yourself as part of the natural world and not outside it. Other creatures also come into this life unbidden and leave no trace but do not complain. Emulate them. Make peace with your nature and you will be at peace with yourself.

If my father had read the Stoic's book, would he have been able to take this advice? Would its wisdom have helped to make his days less troubled? I have no reason to think so. By the time my father had reached the middle of his journey, his mind was so freighted with feelings of failure that I do not think he would have been able to recognize that the failure is life itself, and there is no help for that.

V

Two hundred years after Marcus' death, the crypt he was laid in was plundered by vandals so that not even his ashes remain. All that is left of his presence are the thoughts he set down, which live on to haunt us.

Look on times gone by. You will see people marrying, bringing up children; you will see them sick and dying, warring and feasting; doing business and cultivating the ground; you will see them flattering, putting on airs, suspecting, plotting, wishing for some to die, grumbling about the present, loving, heaping up treasure, desiring positions, power. Well, then, the life of these people is gone.

Reading these melancholy words, I am struck by the irony of our lives, how the nearer we approach the end of our journeys the less time is left to benefit from what we have learned; how the opportunities we were once offered appear in a light so different from when we could have taken advantage of them; how, approaching the end of my days, I cannot imagine how my vision altered by age would have affected the decisions I made when I was just starting out; or whether, knowing what I do now, I would have been able to go forward at all.

VI

I was in my sixty-seventh year when I re-read the Roman's words, and could have been reading them for the first time. When I was young, every step forward seemed like the onset of a journey without end, and the morbid reflections of the Roman appeared like a distant commentary on the fates of strangers, unrelated to my own. But the years have worn through my defenses, and I am no longer stepping out on endless highways. Reading his observations now I can hardly regard them as references to a landscape alien and remote, but as a mirror of my own estate.

> One man buries another and is laid out dead, and another buries him. Think how many physicians are gone after knitting their brows over the sick; how many astrologers after predicting with great pretensions the deaths of others; how many philosophers after endless discourses on death or immortality; how many heroes after killing thousands; how many tyrants who rule men's lives with terrible insolence as though they were immortal; how many cities dead and vanished....

> Think of the billions of strangers now present in the world and the lives of which you have no inkling. How every one of them carries a world inside that is opaque to you, as though it never was. How that is exactly the way you are regarded by them. Well, then, what does your striving add up to and where is it headed?

> Consider everyone you have known; how many things you have witnessed, which have already changed and how many people who have ceased to be. Observe how ephemeral and worthless human things are, and what was yesterday a little mucus, tomorrow will be a mummy or ashes.

Consider the emperor Marcus Aurelius and those who revered him, and how they have vanished. How only a handful of them left even the smallest mark, and how even that too will soon be gone. How a thousand-year celebrity is but a flutter in time, and is nothing at all to one who is unable to hear the echoes of his fame.

Be not troubled, for all things are according to nature and in a little while you will be no one and nowhere.

VII

Sometimes in the night, which is an image of this emptiness, I am haunted by reflections of death until I force myself awake to escape them. In the dark which threatens to engulf me, I seek comfort in the familiar kiss of my wife's still-sleeping flesh. Miraculously, I have only to touch her to bring myself back from the empty world to this. If she is settled in her dreams and I am reluctant to rouse her, I can reach for the small bodies curled like furry slippers at my feet who also offer this reprieve.

Sometimes I am roused by the banshee wails of coyotes shrilling over a kill in the canyon nearby. The unlucky prey may be a hare that left its warren to venture into the night. But sometimes the shrieks are from a neighborhood dog that has strayed imprudently from its yard. These awful cries make me fearful for my companions, and I am oppressed by the terrible fate that awaits them should they leave their nest and wander into the wood.

The dogs sleep on beside me oblivious of the danger. Unlike us they do not dream they can live forever, or pretend to be something they are not. Nor do they expend energy attempting to persuade themselves they can be exceptions to a rule. They are scavengers of time, and consume their moments as they come. Consequently they face their trials without protest, and are able to endure their suffering with a dignity that eludes us, and makes them perfect instructors in the stoic idea.

Sometimes when I am unable to retreat into the caverns of unconsciousness, I wander in a purgatory of half sleep and fitful thoughts where I am harassed by images of our common fate. In this interregnum I am often overcome with remorse to think how I have brought four children into the world as hostages of time. And yet I have no more persistent fear than that of losing them.

VIII

Marcus Aurelius commanded an empire that spanned the known world, while his teacher, Epictetus, was a mere slave and master of nothing but his own thoughts. Yet their shared destiny led them to a common conclusion: "Make the best use of what is in your power and take the rest as it happens."

It was a practical wisdom they applied equally to the trials of history and the tribulations of an ordinary life. Every day, Marcus Aurelius advised, you will encounter people who are rude and deceitful. But do not rise to their offense or seek redress for the irritations they cause, for you cannot change them, and the attempt to do so is pointless. "Instead, ask yourself: 'Is it possible that shameless men should not be in the world? It is not possible. Do not, then, require what is impossible.'"

Useful advice if you can follow it. Consider how such an attitude can turn even the grave to advantage. Has someone wronged you? Observe how the event is already past, and how time has begun to erase the circumstances of your hurt. Reflect on the fact that your tormentor will soon be gone. This is nature's way: to come and go. Let it go.

Often think of the rapidity with which things pass by and disappear, both the things that are and the things that are created. For substance is like a river in a continual flow, and there is hardly anything that stands still. Consider that which is near to you, this boundless abyss of the past and of the future into which all things disappear. How is one who is puffed up with earthly things, or plagued about them, or makes himself miserable over them, not a fool? For all these things will vex him only for a short time.

In the Stoic's world, even the prospect of one's own disappearance can seem a minimal inconvenience. A Stoic reflects that the past is already gone and the future yet to come; consequently, neither is yours to lose. It does not really matter, therefore, how much time you have left or how little, since all that can be taken from you is the moment before you. Therefore, it is of no importance whether you are destined to live for one year or a hundred. For if someone were to tell you that you will be dead tomorrow or the day after, what difference would it make? "You would not care much whether it was on the third day or the next; so think it no great thing to die after as many years as you can name."

These are the sober thoughts of the Roman, but of what practical use? They do not tell you how one becomes an emperor. Or how one gets through a single earthly day. Or why one should.

The philosopher is haunted by this ultimate question, but it is one that he cannot answer. "If the universe is only a confused mass of dispersing elements why should I desire to continue any longer in it? Why should I care for anything but how I return to earth again?" Why indeed? It is the question toward which all stoic meditations lead. Yet no answer follows. So, he asks it again: "If there are no gods, or if there are gods but they do not take care of the world, why should I desire to live in such a world?" And then again: "The universe is either a confusion and a dispersion, or it is an order and providence. If it is the former, why do I desire to remaain any longer in a meaningless chaos, destined for oblivion?"

In his heart of hearts, not even this stoic can live with the thought that all his efforts are without meaning and that every trace of him will one day vanish. Nothing I encountered in the pages of the Meditations made as strong or as troubling an impression on me as these passages in which the philosopher wrestles with his dilemma and struggles vainly to extricate himself from it. In the end, he decides to pose the question differently so that it will seem to answer itself: "Either this world is a chaos, or it is a work of beauty, and though seemingly trackless and confused, governed by a certain order."

In other words, our perception of beauty reveals the existence of order—that there is a design to it all within which our lives make sense. But why? Is appearance to be taken as truth? Why should the appearance of beauty be any different than the appearance of meaning? Even an atheist will feel as though his actions are meaningful. But does that mean they are? Do our lives make sense outside the stories we tell ourselves? Can they?

The answer the Roman finally offers is the familiar assertion of a religious faith: "There are certainly gods, and they take care of the world." And that is all he has to say. No evidence is provided for the newfound optimism that appears with these words, and no apologies for the fact that it contradicts his previous advice. For if there are gods who care for us, why must we resign ourselves to a discouraging fate? Why is a stoic wisdom necessary, and why does it lie in the path of acceptance and retreat? What sense can be made of those grim warnings: In a little while you will be no one and will soon be nowhere?

There are still shameless people in the world, but with his new vision, Marcus no longer invites us to reconcile ourselves to what we cannot change. Instead he counsels us to adopt a superior air knowing that there will be justice one day, even if now there appears to be none. "When you rise in the morning, say to yourself, I shall meet today intrusive, ungrateful, arrogant, deceitful, envious and uncharitable men. All these bad qualities in the people we encounter are theirs by reason of their ignorance of what is good and evil. But I who have seen the nature of the good that it is beautiful, and of the bad that it is ugly, and the nature of him who does wrong, that it is akin to me—that it is not only of the same blood or seed, but participates in the same intelligence and the same portion of the divinity—cannot be injured by any of them."

Gone is the stoic's voice, now replaced by the prophet's: "Constantly regard the universe as one living being, having one substance and one soul, for all things are linked and knitted together, and the knot is sacred. For all things there is but one and the same order, and through all things, one and the same God. For all things there is the same substance and the same law. There is one common reason, and one common truth: One perfection."

Obviously, these convictions resonated with the Christian monks who discovered his manuscript. But if a stoic cannot live without a belief in gods who care for him, or a perfection whose order makes sense of our existence, who can? The philosopher who set out to describe how we ought to live inadvertently reveals how we do: by inhabiting stories that have no end.

Credo ergo sum. I believe, therefore I am.

IX

Because my father viewed history as a forward march, many authors were missing from his shelves, among them the Russian writer Fyodor Dostoevsky, who began life as a radical but ended as an unrelenting critic of the romance that absorbed my father's days. As a result Dostoevsky was shunned by progressives as a "social reactionary," an enemy of the redeemed future.

I am struck now by the irony of this parental attitude, which appears to me as an emblem of how irretrievably our lives remain beyond our control. For eventually my father's son left the path on which he hoped to find refuge from this unhappy life. No longer blinded by the utopian light, I discovered in this forbidden author insights that helped to wake me from the dreams that had stifled my father's life.

Fyodor Dostoevsky was born in Moscow's Hospital for the Poor in the year 1821, which by a quirk of the calendar was exactly seventeen centuries after the Roman's birth in 121. A tic of our nature prompts us to seek significance in coincidences like this, but there are none. No chronological links exist outside the stories we tell, and there are no comforting architectures in the movements of time. In the year 18,121 or 181,821 who will remark on the synchronicity of these celebrated births? However impressive to us, the seventeen centuries that separated them will mean nothing to someone born ten or twenty thousand years after we are gone. Who, then, will even read their books, or remember who they were?

Dostoevsky's father was a physician in residence in the Hospital for the Poor, and a person of means. He was also an alcoholic, a man of selfish desires and lecherous drives, who misused both his family and his serfs. When he died under circumstances that were murky and suspicious, his son concluded that he had been murdered by one of his victims seeking revenge. As a writer, Dostoevsky was obsessed with the problem of evil and the human will to pursue it. The killing of an abusive father by a resentful son and a rebellion against God are the dark centers of his greatest work, The Brothers Karamazov, which he completed a few months before he died in his sixtieth year.

At the outset of his career, Dostoevsky had his own brush with oblivion. The chain of circumstances that led to it began when his first book was discovered by the literary critic Vissarion Belinsky, whose praise helped him to gain fame while still a young man in his twenties. Belinsky, a socialist, recruited the young author into a circle of St. Petersburg radicals who were planning a revolution in Russia. Four years after Dostoevsky joined the circle, its members were arrested on charges of plotting to kill the Czar. The accused were brought to trial and convicted, but their sentencing was postponed and they were held in the Peter and Paul Fortress, where they were kept in the dark about their eventual fate.

On a December morning in 1849, Dostoevsky and his cohorts were taken from their cells and led out into the streets of St. Petersburg, which were blanketed in a freshly fallen snow. The prisoners were marched to the Semyonovsky Parade Ground, where a phalanx of soldiers awaited them. In the courtyard three stakes had been planted, which stood out starkly in the winter light. A brisk wind burned the prisoners' faces while an officer read their sentences aloud. For crimes against the state, the guilty were to be executed by firing squad, the sentences to be carried out at once in groups of three. Dostoevsky was assigned to the second group.

Years later, Dostoevsky described the scene in one of his novels: "The first three were led to the posts and tied to them, the death vestments (long white smocks) were put on them, and white caps were drawn over their eyes so that they shouldn't see the rifles.... The priest went to each of them with the cross." The howling of the wind made it difficult for the prisoners to hear each man's name as it was read aloud, before the order was given and the rifles loaded. The firing squad took aim, and everything grew still. Then, just before the first shot was to be fired, a white flag was raised and a soldier read aloud a royal reprieve.

The entire drama had been contrived by the Czar to punish the rebel youth. In his novel, Dostoevsky reported the feelings he had in the moments before his mock execution. These feelings can be taken as a test of the Roman's idea that it should not matter whether our exit comes on this day or the next:

> *Those five minutes seemed to him an infinite time, a vast wealth; he felt that he had so many lives left that there was no need yet to think of the last moment, so much so that he divided his time up. He set aside time to take leave of his comrades, two minutes for that; then he kept another two minutes to think for the last time; and then a minute to look about him for the last time ... He was dying at twenty-seven, strong and healthy ... Nothing was so dreadful at that time as the continual thought, 'What if I were not to die! What if I could go back to life—what eternity! And it would all be mine! I would turn every minute into an age; I would lose nothing. I would count every minute as it passed. I would not waste one!'*

Here Dostoevsky reveals that our last moments matter to us and cannot be separated from our hopes for the future. His response could be interpreted as the flush of a young man's illusion that he will go on forever, or the optimism of a Christian convinced that he is headed for a better world. But from a stoic point of view it doesn't really matter which. Why should the condemned man savor his last moments wherever he is going? Why should he care about farewells? Why thirst for one more draught of a life already lost?

Dostoevsky's actual feelings in his last moments remind us what the Roman forgot: the sensual pull of the tangible world; the hunger for the life we taste, as opposed to the one we merely think about. The desire for this life, regardless of how much we get of it.

X

After his reprieve by the Czar, the prisoner was exiled to a penal camp in Siberia to serve out a four-year sentence. His mock death and subsequent resurrection among criminals changed forever the way he understood the life we did not ask for and are reluctant to give up. Years after his release, he wrote a fiction based on his internment which he called The House of the Dead, and then a series of novels that gave expression to what he had learned. My mother's favorite author, Marcel Proust, said of these works that they could all be contained under a single title: The Story of a Crime. It was a crime committed by men who did not believe in God, but did not therefore believe in nothing. Instead, they believed in themselves as gods.

Dostoevsky understood the dilemma we face if our existence has no meaning. He asked himself whether a human life is possible in such a world, and answered that it was not. "Neither a man nor a nation can live without a 'higher idea,'" he wrote, and added: "there is only one such idea on this earth, that of an immortal human soul; all the other 'higher ideas' by which men live flow from that. . . ."

In the great religious novel he wrote at the end of his life, Dostoevsky put this observation in the mouth of the character Ivan Karamazov, a tormented intellect who resembles the author and struggles to believe against what he knows: "It is only men's belief in the immortality of their own souls that makes it possible for them to love one another, for morality to exist."

This is another way of saying that in order to be moral, men must inhabit stories that have no end. For if we are not immortal, and do not fear a judgment beyond ourselves, what will we not do to satisfy our desires? And of what are we not capable? The life of the world we know is dependent on one we can only guess at, and this invisible world (or our belief in it) is necessary in order for the world we inhabit to continue. Without faith in a God who cares about us, "not only love, but also any living power to continue the life of the world, would at once dry up: nothing would be immoral any longer; everything would be permitted."

The idea that we must be watched in order to behave is unflattering, and atheists find it repugnant. But does that make it false? Atheists may deny that we must fear judgment in order to act morally, but an agnostic can wonder all the same. What assurance is there that we will make virtuous choices in an existence that is brief, and unrequited, and full of temptation? Has there ever been in the history of humanity a community able to maintain order without the threat of punishment, whether here or in the hereafter?

It is true, as atheists will observe, that we often behave well when no one is watching. But will we? Will we do so when our backs are to the wall, and our survival is at stake? If the circumstances are right, who among us can be certain of his limits? On the fields of war where no law exists to keep men in check, it is well known that they will engage in unspeakable depravities. Each of us will want to regard ourselves as exceptions to the rule, and many will refrain from committing the worst of crimes. Perhaps there are even saints who walk among us. But what of it? It is still the rule.

Atheists will also object that religion is no cure for our sins, since those who believe will act as badly as those who don't. But who would deny that a religious faith is no proof against sin? It is a truth the faithful themselves concede and make the focus of their concern. Moreover, the objection does not begin to address the question of whether human beings can be moral without the prospect of a judgment. In our daily lives we can hardly commit a selfish act without fearing discovery. Unless our moral compass is broken we will care what others think, and eyes will peep about in our heads to track what we do. We will even care about others' opinions of us after we are dead. How inexplicable is that?

In the end, the need to be watched is not merely about being good, but about being at all. My father did not believe in a God who numbers the hairs on every head. But he felt the need to be noted all the same. The god he worshipped was History and its eyes were always upon him. The audience of others, real or imagined, is the way we persuade ourselves that our drama has no end, and what we do matters. For if there is only the abyss in front of us and behind, what can matter other than the way in which we bring the curtain down?

XI

W hile Dostoevsky was still a prisoner, a woman he did not know sent him a copy of the New Testament as a charity. He kept the book under his pillow until his sentence was complete. On his release, he wrote the woman a note thanking her for the kindness, and offering this confession: "I tell you that there are moments in which one thirsts for faith like parched grass ... and finds it for the very reason that truth shines more clearly in affliction."

Like Ivan Karamazov, who provided a fictional voice for his doubts, Dostoevsky never did find release. He was a child of his age, as he explained to his benefactor—"a child of unbelief and doubt up to this very moment and (I am certain of it) to the grave. Nevertheless, God sends me moments of complete tranquility. In such moments I love and find that I am loved by others, and in such moments I have nurtured in myself a symbol of truth, in which everything is clear and holy for me. The symbol is very simple. It is the belief that there is nothing finer, profounder, more attractive, more reasonable, more courageous and more perfect than Christ."

A Jew might be expected to be cold to this affirmation, but I am not. It is a devotion we find in all religious faiths. Dostoevsky called the adoration of God a "touching of other worlds" more perfect than ours. From an agnostic's view, it doesn't really matter whether the perfection is imagined or real. If it is embraced, its effect is the same. A modern writer, Cormac McCarthy, has expressed the paradox this way: "In the end we shall all of us only be what we have made of God."

Can we dispense with this reverence for impossible worlds, as atheists insist we must? Dostoevsky's answer is that we cannot. Without belief in the immortality of souls, not only love, but also any living power to continue the life of the world would at once dry up. What can he have meant by this? Perhaps that if we were not inspired by an ideal world we would be reduced to the savagery of this one. Or if we did not look forward to something better, we would not look forward at all.

Perhaps that is why he also wrote: "Even if someone were to prove to me that the truth lay outside Christ, I should prefer to remain with Christ than with the truth."

XII

Dostoevsky's belief in a divine truth set him apart from the other radicals awaiting their execution on that fateful December morning. Standing in the line in front of him was a co-conspirator named Nikolay Speshnev, an atheist whom Dostoevsky later came to regard as the devil incarnate. As the two approached the scaffold area, Dostoevsky whispered to him, "We shall be with Christ." But the condemned man rejected his comfort and, pointing to the ground, said: "a handful of dust."

Because he did not believe in God, however, Speshnev did not therefore believe in nothing. Like Dostoevsky, he too yearned to touch more perfect worlds, and like the other radicals awaiting their sentence he was willing to sacrifice his life for ideals. The future they imagined was a world ordered by harmony and justice. Of their hope, Speshnev said: "[This] is also a religion, only a different one. It makes a divinity out of a new and different object, but there is nothing new about the deification itself."

There was indeed nothing original about this conceit, which was shared by all the prophets of the new creed who regarded socialism as the answer to the religions that had failed. The "God" of traditional faith they viewed as a primitive fantasy born of human ignorance and weakness. Religious belief provided obvious comfort but a false one. Such belief prompted human beings to surrender their birthright, and project onto a Divinity powers that were rightfully theirs—first onto many gods and then onto one. Under the spell of religious belief, they had alienated their human virtues, which were reason and compassion, and then worshipped them as attributes of a Divinity beyond reach. Thus, religion deprived them of the power to change the circumstances of their lives and alter their fates. Religious faith was not a consolation for human unhappiness but its cause.

This radical idea is today the faith of millions of atheists but it makes no sense. Human beings do not project onto God the powers they have but rather the ones they do not have. The love that Dostoevsky associates with Christ is not an attribute of human beings or even something that is possible for them, as he explains: "To love man as oneself ... is impossible; the ego stands in the way."

Dostoevsky inscribed these words on the funeral bier of his first wife, a morbid gesture but a revealing one. "Christ's love for people," he also said, "is in its kind a miracle impossible on earth; he was God, but we are not gods." These words reflect a conservative view of our human lot—the very opposite of the radical faith that we can become as gods and create a new world.

A religious ideal can be useful if properly served. Rather than alienate human beings from their ability to love, the trust in a compassionate God may enhance and even foster it. What of the claim that religious faith breeds ignorance and creates barriers to knowledge? It is certainly the case that ignorant people embrace ignorant forms of faith; and the intolerant have often invoked religion to oppose the advance of science. But the architects of the scientific enlightenment—Copernicus, Pascal and Newton—were all religious believers. It was precisely their faith in a supernatural design that inspired them to search for an order in the cosmos. Spinoza, Locke and Kant, the avatars of the Age of Reason, also drew their inspiration from the lodestar of divinity and the belief in a providential design.

XIII

Speshnev did not think there was much difference between the faith of radical atheists and faith in a supernatural being; between a secular hope that humanity could achieve its own redemption and a religious faith that only a divinity can save us. He asked rhetorically: "Is the difference between a God-man and a man-God really so great?"

Dostoevsky was sure it was. His alarm at the consequences of Speshnev's idea became the principal theme of his art. The centerpiece of his novel Crime and Punishment is the story of a murder. A student deliberately kills an old woman, whom he considers useless and even harmful, to prove to himself that he has the self-possession and will to change the world. The police inspector who tracks him down describes the murder as "a fantastic, gloomy business, a modern case," and identifies its cause as a mind directed by "bookish dreams" and "a heart unhinged by theories."

The murderer has written an academic essay, "On Crime," in which he explains the deed he is about to commit. Humanity, he writes, is divided into two groups. On the one hand, there are the masses who accept a morality that binds them to the existing order. On the other, there are the members of the radical vanguard "who seek in various ways the destruction of the present for the sake of the better." Among these innovators he mentions the imperial conquerors Napoleon and Mohammed, leaders of a secular faith and a religious one.

The quest for salvation breeds a self-righteousness that encourages radicals to commit crimes that are monstrous. "If such a one is forced for the sake of his idea to step over a corpse or wade through blood," Ivan Karamazov warns, "he can find in himself, in his conscience, a sanction for wading through blood." It is the nobility of the idea, the spectacular prospect of a world transformed, that inspires and justifies the spectacular crimes.

Speshnev was hardly alone in identifying the utopian passion as a religious faith. Auguste Comte, who was one of the fathers of European socialism, called it a "religion of humanity." Of his fellow radicals, the anarchist Bakunin said: "They are magnificent, these young fanatics, believers without God...." Of these secular priests, Dostoevsky wrote that they "talk of socialism or anarchism, or the transformation of all humanity on a new model, so that it all comes to the same, the same questions turned inside out." But the same questions turned inside out lead to different answers and results. A God who becomes human and suffers in the flesh to redeem human sins is one thing; ordinary human beings acting as gods to purge others of their sins is quite another.

The radical vision of an earthly redemption requires ordinary mortals, fallible and corrupt, to assume powers that are godlike. Everything is permitted to them because everything can be justified as a service to humanity. "Socialism," Dostoevsky wrote, "is a modern incarnation of godlessness, the tower of Babel built without God, not to raise earth to heaven but to bring heaven down to earth." Of social redeemers like this, he said, "they hope to make a just order for themselves, but having rejected Christ they will end by drenching the earth with blood."

XIV

The ancestors of my little Chihuahuas were called "Tehichi" by the Aztecs, who revered them as gods and coveted them as indispensable guides to the land of the dead. The Aztecs were a people possessed by inordinate fear of their own extinction. The end of an ordinary day made them so anxious they came to believe that only the spilling of blood would cause the sun to rise again. To ensure their future, they held festivals of the sun in the temples of Tenochitlan and cut out the hearts of thousands of virgins as offerings to the gods, hoping this would protect them.

When an Aztec died his survivors cremated him, believing that souls were transported by fire and liberated by the flames. Along with the deceased they placed their dogs on the funeral pyres, convinced that they would help the dead to navigate the nine rivers they believed lay between them and their final destination. Evidently the Aztecs were also impressed by dogs' ability to follow invisible trails.

Canines have been our companions since the Stone Age, surviving the millennia on the kindness of strangers. They were the first animals to be taken into human households, and the only ones to be so included in every society on earth. If you are attentive they will teach you humility, and will accompany you in your journey for a decade or more if you are lucky. Although there are no records to prove it, the Aztecs were obviously as enchanted as we are by the fidelity of these small souls, and their ardent affection for those who show them kindness. Unlike human beings, they will love you to the end, and will not abandon you before you reach it.

XV

The stories we tell ourselves to keep our souls in motion are numerous, but their purpose is the same. Whether we imagine we are creating a family line that will continue forever, or are pursuing missions greater than ourselves whose effects will outlast us, whether we store up our illusions in personal albums or enshrine them in halls of fame, whether we record our days in intimate journals or official annals, every narrative is designed to convince us that what we do is noteworthy and that someone will be there to take it all in.

Every writer tells himself the same story: that someone is listening. A word on the page is one end of a silent conversation, but who is at the other? The English novelist Julian Barnes devoted an entire book to recording the anxieties provoked by the prospect that one day his words would no longer have readers and every trace of him would be gone. His book was an attempt to exorcise a lifelong obsession with his own extinction. He took its title from the advice his friends gave him as a child when he expressed fears about death: Nothing to Be Frightened Of. Barnes wrote the book when he was sixty, and said: "A novelist might hope for another generation of readers, two or three if lucky, which may feel like a scorning of death; but it's really just a scratching on the wall of the condemned cell. We do it to say: I was here too."

But to whom?

November 2008

I

When my wife and I put the house in Calabasas up for sale, it was because we were looking for a property to stable horses. We had recently acquired a young gelding, and rather than board him at a ranch a half hour distant, we wanted him close so that he would become part of our household. The new residence we were seeking would be the seventh I had occupied since April and I met twelve years earlier, and the fourth we had shared together. Although the move was a reflection of her passion rather than mine, this kind of transience was a recurrent theme of my life. Without exactly willing it, the many new residences I acquired and then abandoned had become an almost spiritual practice, preparing me for the day when it would be time to leave.

The new family member was an elegant paint with white flanks and reddish brown markings which were crowned by a fluted mane. Fine in the bone and with a demeanor that was almost feminine, Alvin was the missing piece of a life April wanted and I was determined to help her get. After months of searching we found a suitable location in the Santa Rosa Valley, a green cut of the coastal range thirty miles to the north. Like Calabasas its very name reflected the shifts of time, a landscape memorial to the ghosts of the Spanish past.

The spread we acquired was an acre-and-a-half set on two tiers of land punctuated by a stand of pines. On the lower level there was a ranch-style house with a trellised veranda and wisteria vines covered in purple blooms. On the upper, there was a two-stall barn and pipe corrals for the horses, backed by a large exercise arena. The corrals were shaded by willowy pepper trees and faced by a row of rose bushes, the whole as congenial a setting as I could have hoped for; and I hoped it would be my last.

Because horses are herd animals, it was important that we acquire a companion for Alvin, which we quickly did. The new family member was a caramel draft pony whose name was Diddy, and whose blonde forelock and large brown eyes gave him a particularly endearing look. His breed was Haflinger of which it is said "a prince up front, a peasant behind," a reference to his formidable haunches. These were coupled with a chest so broad you could almost see the cart he was born to pull coming up behind him.

Millennia of attachment to human beings have not bred the wild out of horses. Consequently, they demand discipline and patience until they acquire ground manners to make them safe, in which regard they are not unlike us. A combination of strength and vulnerability makes even the gentlest of these creatures a danger to those who do not understand their nature. Horses are flight animals who have been endlessly hunted through the corridors of time, and are spooked by sights that are unfamiliar and by alien intrusions into their environment. A car engine grinding or a squirrel darting into view can cause a half-ton of flesh to bolt in fear with a velocity that will crush anything in its path.

The muscular beauty of horses has inspired us to regard them as symbols of nobility; and ancient Greeks, like Hippocrates, even affixed the word "hippo" to their names to appropriate an aristocratic aura. But the strength of equines is also deceptive, since they are fragile in their construction. Their intestinal architectures make them prone to digestive disorders that can be fatal, while their massive weight is supported on ankles so narrow as to risk injuries that can bring them down as well.

Two months before we left the Calabasas house, Clifton, the horse across the way, developed a leg infection. It was unclear whether its cause was the steep incline of the hillside or an incompetent farrier who had improperly shoed him. As the days progressed, the infection spread until it brought his majestic frame to ground. To behold so mighty a beast in such helpless agony was a wrenching sight, but it took days for his owner to recognize she was torturing a creature she loved, and finally to call in the vet to put him to rest.

II

Before arriving in our new home, we prepared the building by opening up cathedral ceilings in the master bedroom and living room, laying walnut floors, framing the windows and putting decorative finishes on the interior doors. We hired a crew to cut back the overgrowth on the grounds, paint the barn and tack room red, and put a white fence around the horse arena. It was the fourth home we had remodeled together. We had even gone so far as to renovate the house in Calabasas, which was a new construction when we settled in. Did this reflect a compulsive human need to make the world a better place? Or was it just our scratching on the wall?

Some of the alterations we made to the Calabasas property began with practical agendas, including the pool we built in the back yard. My routines as a writer were sedentary, and except for the walks with the dogs I engaged in no activity calculated to keep my engine running. This lassitude became a problem when I was diagnosed with diabetes and warned by my doctor that I would have to shed weight and exercise or risk troubling complications. Swimming had always been a pleasure for me, and building a pool seemed a happy way to fulfill his prescriptions, although we quickly embellished the plan with superfluous fountains, a garden and artificial rocks crafted to look like granite.

The diabetes that afflicted me was not the inherited kind, and while still a cause for concern was less threatening. A medical website for laymen provided this information: "In Type II diabetes, either the body does not produce enough insulin or the cells ignore the insulin. When you eat food, the body breaks down all of the sugars and starches into glucose, which is the basic fuel for the cells in the body. Insulin takes the sugar from the blood into the cells. When glucose builds up in the blood instead of going into cells, it can cause two problems: 1) Right away, your cells may be starved for energy. 2) Over time, high blood glucose levels may hurt your eyes, kidneys, nerves, or heart." In good bedside fashion, the authors of the website finished these details with a reassuring uplift. "Finding out you have diabetes is scary. But don't panic. Type II diabetes is serious, but people with diabetes can live long, healthy, happy lives."

In other words, my eyes, kidneys, nerves, and heart were under attack, and my energy was in danger of being shut off, but not to worry. And for the most part I did not. I adjusted to the inevitable and put myself on a diet.

I selected the carbohydrates at the supermarket nutritionists said were "complex," lost enough weight to make the routine tests reassuring for my doctor, and used the pool daily. Overall, I considered myself lucky to have no symptoms and went on with my life as before. And what else was I to do?

Diabetes is a condition familiar to Jews. My father suffered from the disease in its more serious version, and required medication to keep it under control. Although the memory has faded, I can still see him standing in the family bathroom, his pants dropped around his ankles, administering an insulin shot to his bared thigh. He conducted this procedure in the clinical manner with which he attended to all medical issues and household emergencies, creating a calm around them so that none of us paid particular notice to his condition.

III

Four years before our move to Calabasas I had received a second, more serious diagnosis when I was told I had a prostate cancer. My maternal grandfather died from a stomach cancer in his seventies, and my father, who was a heavy smoker, had developed a cancer of the tongue in his mid-forties but, after undergoing radium treatments, was able to continue for another forty years. My prostate cancer was unrelated to either case, and consequently I again confronted a medical puzzle when inquiring into its source. It was not until eight years after the operation to remove it that I received a possible answer when my friend Peter sent me an email containing a newspaper report about a virus researchers believed was the cause of chronic fatigue syndrome: "The new suspect is a xenotropic murine leukemia virus-related virus, or XMRV, which probably descended from a group of viruses that cause cancer in mice. How or when XMRV found its way into humans is unknown. But it has also been linked to cancer in people; it was first identified three years ago, in prostate cancer, and later detected in about one-quarter of biopsies from men with that disease; ..."

The illnesses that afflicted me were among many available, and I did not consider myself unfairly singled out. From the cursory research I conducted into my condition, I learned that everyone will develop a cancer if they live long enough. It was one more reminder that we were not built to last, and that age itself is a disease that overtakes us all.

IV

The Santa Rosa Valley where we now resided was cradled between two columns of mountains, which rose from its floor like green waves frozen in space and time. An agricultural plain lay between them, with orange and lemon groves on one side and a warren of horse communities on the other. Ours was gated, and I took my exercise walks with the dogs along the streets at the end of our driveway. The walks were infrequent now because the new property was big enough to provide sufficient space for the dogs to roam without me. Several times a day I let them run loose on the tree-shaded lawn at the back of the house, where they chased horses and dogs passing on the other side of the fence. During their romps I would sit on the veranda and keep a watchful eye out for coyotes and hawks on the hunt for small animals in the neighborhood yards.

I no longer had a pool for a daily swim but made up for the missed exertions with new chores, pitching hay to the horses and lunging them in trots around the arena. April took charge of the paint, and I assumed responsibilities for the draft pony with whom I had developed an affectionate bond. Lunging Diddy was important because he was carrying extra pounds that put him at risk for colic or floundering. He enjoyed the runs and missed them when I was too busy with other tasks. My days now were largely spent with the animals, and in the solitary writing projects that were my principal work. I settled happily into these pleasures, embraced their slower pace and tried not to be concerned about the future.

V

The stories that comfort us are parables of hope. Some are personal and are designed to generate memories that outlive us. Others extend beyond ourselves and promise a transformation of the world we know into one that makes sense. These are the myths of faith, both secular and religious, that shape our histories, and it is no trivial matter whether the future they promise is of this world or the next.

The choice of futures is rooted in our view of origins. Belief in a redemption in the next life can only spring from the conviction that our very nature is corrupt in this one. For if the cause of our suffering lies within us, the only hope we can have of salvation is a divine intervention. By contrast, those who strive for a redemption in this life must believe that the cause of our unhappiness does not lie in our nature but in the world outside us, which we are destined to correct.

Dostoevsky was a man of faith and believed that the source of human misery lay in our corruption. But he also saw that the root of this corruption was the freedom that made us human, and which Saint Augustine described as "original sin." This is the theme of Dostoevsky's most famous fiction, "The Grand Inquisitor," a fable told by Ivan Karamazov to his brother Alyosha. Ivan's tale is set in the 16th century and begins with a prelude in which he observes that more than a millennium has passed since Christ promised to return in his glory. In the story that follows, Christ returns to His creation but with no intention of resolving the uncertainty provoked by His absence, which has left His creatures without answers to the questions that trouble them most. The drama is set when the Grand Inquisitor has Christ arrested, denouncing him as the "worst of heretics" whose very presence threatens the authority of the Church, His ministry on earth.

Ivan's fable is actually the trial of God for the crime of creation. In giving human beings freedom, God is the true source of their unhappiness, for "nothing has ever been more insupportable for a man and a human society than freedom." By refusing to enter history and compel belief, God has condemned His children to live alone and lost, not knowing why they are here or where they are going, or whether what they do or who they are has any significance at all.

Out of compassion for God's abandoned creatures, the Inquisitor informs Christ that the Church of Rome has undertaken the mission of an earthly redemption that He rejected. It has set out to repair the fault in creation and to provide human beings with the earthly happiness and security that have been denied to them. In exercising dominion over worldly things, however, the Church has also entered the realm of corruption, which is the devil's domain. "We are working not with Thee but with him," the Inquisitor tells Christ defiantly. Referring to the temptations the devil offered, as related in the Gospels, which Christ rejected, the Inquisitor says: "We took from him what thou didst reject with scorn, that last gift he offered Thee, when he showed Thee all the kingdoms of the earth. We took from Rome and the sword of Caesar, and proclaimed ourselves sole rulers of the earth.... We shall triumph and shall be Caesars, and then we shall plan the universal happiness of man."

Satan's offer to Christ was made in the desert in the form of three temp-tations: to rule over the kingdoms of the earth; to turn the stones into bread; to cast Himself from a height and thus prove He was immortal. To accept any of the three would prove that He was God, and compel belief. Ivan describes the three temptations as expressing "the whole future of the world and of humanity." The three are really one: to give up freedom for security and happiness.

"You had the power to turn the stones into bread," the Inquisitor scolds Christ, "for which they would have given you their souls. But you refused. What sort of freedom is it, you reasoned, if obedience is bought with loaves of bread?" Christ had rejected this temptation, saying, "Man does not live by bread alone, but by every word that proceeds out of the mouth of the Lord." The Inquisitor agrees. "The secret of man's being is not only to live but to have something to live for; without a stable conception of the object of life, man would not consent to go on living, and would rather destroy himself than remain on earth, though he had bread in abundance." The Church provides its followers with a meaning for their existence through the authority and mystery of its doctrines. All that is required to enter its earthly paradise is submission to its faith.

If God is silent and there are no words from heaven to provide meaning for men's lives, if they are fated to live in uncertainty, what then? Will they believe in nothing? Or is the need to have something to live for so powerful that they will believe in a church that promises them both happiness and bread? This is the Inquisitor's answer: not only will they worship the power that promises them bread and earthly happiness, but they will prefer it to a divinity that would set them free: "You objected that man does not live by bread alone, but do you know that in the name of this very earthly bread, the spirit of the earth will rise against you and fight with you and defeat you, and everyone will follow him exclaiming, 'Who can compare to this beast, for he has given us the fire from heaven?' They will lay their freedom at our feet and say to us, 'Make us your slaves, but feed us.'"

Dostoevsky's Inquisitor is the spokesman for all the tyrannies that have existed from the beginning of time, and that have oppressed mankind in the name of progress. Speaking in a public lecture about his novel, Dosto-evsky described his Inquisitor as an atheist who "distort[s] the truth of Christ by identifying it with the aims of this world." In making the kingdom of heaven the work of human beings, he explained, "the sublime Christian view of mankind is reduced to regarding humanity as if it were an animal herd, and under the guise of a social love of mankind there appears a scarcely masked contempt for it."

The earthly paradise that ordinary mortals create is not the kingdom of freedom but the totalitarian state. For how could the human beings we know become new men and new women without gods to oversee them? How could they live in harmony? "Freedom and bread enough for all are inconceivable together," the Inquisitor admonishes Christ, "for never, never will they be able to share between them!" Without the subservience of those who are to be redeemed, how can the redeemers hope to create new heaven and new earth? Therefore, the church of socialism cannot allow its flock the freedom to oppose its redemption. But this is the one freedom that leads to all others.

Human beings are destined to be unhappy, the Inquisitor explains to Christ, until they "know the value of complete submission." Once they embrace this, "once they are made to submit, we shall give them the quiet, humble happiness of weak creatures such as they are by nature.... We shall have an answer for all. And they will be glad to believe our answer, for it will save them from the great anxiety and terrible agony they endure in making a free decision for themselves."

VI

When we moved to the Santa Rosa Valley, I was already approaching my sixty-ninth year. In a synchronicity of fate, my dogs had reached a similar point along their downward arcs. But while I was only mildly curious about the oldster who looked at me from the bathroom mirror each morning, I was saddened to see the signs of age on them, to note the wrinkled jowls and graying hairs, grim reminders of the destination they would reach before me.

The passing years had instilled in us a greater understanding of each other. At first, Lucy had displayed a feral deference to me as the alpha of her pack, averting her eyes when in proximity to mine, and positioning herself at respectful but frustrating distances when the two of us were alone. However, as the years progressed this diffidence began to fade, and she would often slip up alongside me to allow herself a gaze that was touchingly direct. Out of the corner of my eye I would catch hers, then return her look and be surprised to see her lock into mine and remain. I warmed to this closeness but it also increased the sadness I felt anticipating the end, which only I knew was coming.

Snug inside our stories, we take our worlds for granted and assume they will continue indefinitely. We create our families and plot our bloodlines as though they will go on and on, and when we bury our dead we promise to remember them forever, although it is a promise we know we cannot keep.

When the musical genius Mozart was thirty-one he had created hundreds of works of indescribable beauty, imparting happiness to countless individuals who came after him, including myself. But he was already only four years from the end of his life. While working on his famous "Requiem Mass," he was stricken with a fatal illness that would easily be cured today. His death, which came swiftly, has been rightly called the greatest tragedy in the history of music, depriving us and generations not born of pleasures we can hardly imagine.

In that thirty-first year, Mozart wrote a letter to his father who was then drawing his own last breaths. In the letter he said: "As death (considered precisely) is the real purpose of our life, for several years I have become closely acquainted with this true and best friend of our life, so that his image is not only no longer terrifying to me, but rather something very soothing and comforting!" Then he added: "And I thank my God for affording me, in His grace, the opportunity (you understand me) of realizing that He is the key to our real happiness. I never lie down in bed without thinking that (young as I am) I may not live to see the next day—and yet no one, especially among those who know me, can say that in daily life I am stubborn or sad—and for this happiness I give thanks to my Creator every day and wish every man the same from the bottom of my heart...."

It is a generous thought from a miraculous soul. I wish the faith of this great and gifted young man were mine as well. I wish I could place my trust in the hands of a Creator. I wish I could look on my life and the lives of my children, and all I have loved, and see them as preludes to a better world. But, try as I might, I cannot. And so I am left to ponder the pointlessness of our strivings on this earth and to ask impossible questions, and receive no answers.

VII

O f my four children and their futures, I worried most about my oldest daughter Sarah, who was born with a genetic condition that saddled her with great burdens. These included problems that affected her hearing, her sight, and her heart. An early death was predicted for those born with her condition, but her life was so full that we who loved her forgot the sentence, or pushed it to the backs of our minds. Then, two months after her forty-fourth birthday, I received a call from her sister Anne who said, "Something terrible has happened." And then, "Sarah is gone."

There is nothing more irrevocable than the grave, and no loss ever left me so desolate. With that phone call my life entered a sudden winter from which there would be no release. All that was left to me were the images of times we shared together, which were gone and which I could not get back. My daughter's death inverted nature's order and was a violent rebuke to every parental instinct. Among the afflictions of mourning were the memories of our conversations that had been left unfinished, which I longed to continue. Yet what was this longing, itself so futile, since all our conversations are destined to be unfinished?

My daughter was a writer and an observant Jew, and just before her death she was interviewed by a literary magazine. The interviewer asked whether her religious practice helped her to deal with the recent death of an aunt with whom she was particularly close. "I think it did," she answered, adding that she was "very comfortable" with the idea that Judaism didn't have a highly developed concept of an afterlife. Religion was an effort to find meaning, "and I think at the heart of that pursuit is the fact that we all walk around with the knowledge that we are going to die."

Her words on the page gave me a start. In her father's eyes she was too young to have thought so deeply about such dark matters. But on reflection I realized what should have been obvious—that these thoughts were her birthright. It was her mother and I who had suppressed the warning of an early death. One of the bits of information she provided the interviewer was that, every day over her breakfast coffee, she recited the Jewish prayer of mourning: You resurrect the dead. She did not believe in a literal resurrection, she explained, but in what she called a "rolling of the souls," a reincarnation of the departed spirit in others.

My daughter never married but lived alone in a one-bedroom apartment and left behind piles of manuscripts which she had worked on as a writer, and which with the exception of a single poem had never been published. Her papers included many volumes of a notebook and diary she kept, along with shopping bags full of stories and poems in various states of revision. There were also many versions of a novel, which she had worked on for twenty years and which she called The Carousel of Time, and then The Family of Man. All these scraps represented the uncollected pieces of my daughter's life, the hours she spent by herself day and night to complete works that were now a scattered debris on her apartment floor.

Many would feel sadness at the apparent futility of my daughter's efforts, but I do not. For how different is this than the futility all of us share whether our works are published or not, and whether our efforts are expended alone or in the company of others? How different were the tasks my daughter undertook from those of the most famous authors whose works are read by millions but will one day leave their own debris behind?

When I ask myself why I rise in the morning to write this page and spend the time that time will soon erase, my answer is this: On the days when the words fall into place and an order appears, I am at peace. Thus, it was actually a relief when I saw how my daughter had spent her hours arranging words on a page and transforming her world into one that made sense. I knew then she was happy and at peace.

My daughter was also right about the rolling of the souls. Wherever I go, thoughts of her follow me, and my future takes on a memory and a face.

VIII

It is humbling to look into historical texts and see how images of the past that have been recorded by others are familiar to us, and how little we have learned from their experience. Dostoevsky's Diary of a Writer, which was published more than a hundred years ago, contains this reminiscence: "'Do you know,' Belinsky screeched one evening (sometimes, if he was very excited, he would screech) as he turned to me, 'Do you know that man's sins cannot be counted against him? ... When society is set up in such a mean fashion ... man cannot help but do wrong; economic factors alone lead him to do wrong; and it is absurd and cruel to demand from a man something the very laws of nature make it impossible for him to carry out, even if he wanted to.'"

Belinsky's outburst took place in the course of an evening at the circle of St. Petersburg radicals that Dostoevsky had joined. Thirty years later, Dostoevsky wrote about the incident. He regarded Belinsky's remark that evening as so important that he also incorporated it into the creed of the church of socialism. Ivan's Grand Inquisitor confronts Christ with this prophecy: "Do you know that centuries will pass and mankind will proclaim with the mouth of its wisdom and science that there is no crime, and therefore no sin, but only hungry men? 'Feed them first, then ask virtue of them!' That is what they will write on the banner they raise against you, and by which your temple will be destroyed."

By the time Dostoevsky had reached the end of his days, he was so revered by his countrymen that he had become a national symbol, and was regarded by them as a prophet. Yet no one really listened. In less than an individual's lifetime, socialist radicals seized power in St. Petersburg and renamed it "Leningrad," raising to sainthood the malevolent dictator who decided the fate of millions. Under the rule of Leninists, Russia became the center of a revolution to create a new world and to fashion new human beings to inhabit it. These miracles were to be achieved by transforming Belinsky's "economic factors."

During Russia's bloody upheavals, the Communist playwright Bertolt Brecht took the very words the Inquisitor had spoken—"First comes feeding, then comes morality"—and inserted them into a popular German opera intending to inspire others to join the revolutionary cause. When the destructive energies of the revolution had run their course, they left in their wake a hundred million corpses and blighted the lives of millions more. But the fantasy of a socialist paradise lived on.

There is no secret to Dostoevsky's clairvoyance. He understood that morality was not the product of feeding human beings but was an expression of their humanity and their freedom. The radical view expressed by Belinsky is that we are the products of social engineering and thus constructed by our environment. This is the heart of all schemes for an earthly redemption, and the antithesis of freedom. It is the philosophy, as Dostoevsky, put it, of an anthill. In his Diary he answered Belinsky: "In making the individual dependent on every flaw in the social structure ... the doctrine of the environment reduces the subject to an absolute nonentity, exempting him totally from every personal moral duty and from all independence, reduces him to the lowest form of slavery imaginable."

IX

When criminals are viewed as society's victims, the crimes they commit can be seen as a form of social justice. "Since society is organized in such a vile fashion," Belinsky explained on that memorable evening, "one can only break out of it with a knife in hand." To the social redeemers, criminals are "unfortunates," since the responsibility for their crimes lies with society itself. Dostoevsky described their thinking this way: "Society is vile, and therefore we too are vile; but we are rich, we are secure, and it is only by chance we escaped encountering the things you did. And had we encountered them, we would have acted as you did. Who is to blame? The environment is to blame. And so, there is only a faulty social structure, but there is no crime whatsoever."

From such attitudes it is a small step to regarding those who break the law as social heroes—or to describe them with the term fashionable in Dostoevsky's time as "people's criminals." They break the law to achieve "people's justice." Thus, revolutionaries seeking to change the world do not see the targets of their violence as human beings like themselves but as "enemies of the people" who have earned their fate.

When Dostoevsky came to write a novel about political radicals, he called it The Devils and modeled its central figure on a Russian terrorist named Sergei Nechaev. A colleague of Bakunin's, Nechaev founded an organization called "People's Justice," for which he wrote a "Catechism for Revolutionaries." In the course of his political activities Nechaev induced his small circle of followers to kill a student in their group in order to seal their revolutionary bond in blood. In the "Catechism for Revolutionaries," he elevated expediency to a moral principle. The goal revolutionaries were seeking, a world transformed, justified any means necessary to achieve it: "Poison, the knife, the noose . . . The revolution sanctifies everything."

The creed of the revolutionary divides the world into forces of good and evil; on one side enemies of the people, on the other the social redeemers. The passion to create a new world is really a passion to destroy the old one, transforming the love of humanity into a hatred for the human beings who stand in its way.

X

Nine months after we buried my daughter in a gravesite south of San Francisco, I arranged to have dinner with her rabbi, Alan Lew. We met at the Millennium Restaurant, which was one of Sarah's favorites. Rabbi Lew was a kind and thoughtful man who had written a book about the Jewish days of repentance and awe. In the Jewish calendar these were the days set aside to reflect upon one's life. The rabbi called his book *This Is Real and You Are Completely Unprepared*.

Lew was five years younger than I and had no warning at the time of our dinner that he had only two more weeks to live. Like Sarah, he left behind an unpublished manuscript on which he had been laboring for over thirty years. It was a detailed history of his family, beginning with his great-great-grandparents who had been born in Russia and were the earliest of the Lews that any family member still alive could remember. The Lew children fled the war in Europe to find a better life across the sea, and to bear their children on American soil.

It had taken Rabbi Lew all those thirty years to track down his family survivors and record their stories. At dinner he told me that he had just put the finishing touches on his manuscript and sent it to a publisher. He called his manuscript *The Life That Ran Through Me*.

On my way to meet the rabbi, I had to walk up one of San Francisco's famous hills to the Millennium. This modest effort spiked a pain in the middle of my chest similar to the stitch one feels in the winter cold when the oxygen is thin. The pain recurred the next evening while I was ascending a ramp at a sporting event and again the following day, when I returned to Los Angeles and had to drag my luggage across a parking lot in the Burbank airport. A heartache is not necessarily life-threatening, but the recurrence three times in as many days was a warning I sensed it would be unwise to ignore. While still in the airport parking lot, I pulled my cell phone from the jacket I was wearing and called my doctor who told me to head straight for the emergency room at the local hospital and check myself in.

An angina is a strangling of the heart and can sneak up on you when you least expect it. The cause is often a clogged artery. An episode can be brought on by ordinary events such as a physical exertion, emotional distress, or even a heavy meal, all of which require extra effort from the pump and more fuel than the blocked vessels can supply. After taking my vital signs and listening to my story, the cardiologist assigned to my case ordered an angiogram to see what was there. When his camera located the block, he inserted a stent to open the passage and restore the flow. The blockage was in the left anterior descending artery, which doctors mordantly refer to as "the widow-maker," but there was no damage to the heart, and I was released from the hospital after a day.

I was back home a little over a week when I learned of Rabbi Lew's collapse. He had taken a trip to Baltimore and was jogging to keep his heart healthy when it gave out. The body was flown back to San Francisco, and they buried him in the same cemetery as my daughter, a few feet to the right of her grave. We are here, and we are gone, and everything with us. No more jogs for the heart or books to complete, or dinners with family and friends. The stories simply stop, and all the loose ends are left untied.

XI

I began my rehabilitation on a treadmill I bought as a preventive measure to forestall future attacks. The cardiologist put me on a regimen of blood thinners and beta-blockers and let me know again how fortunate I was to have survived the episode without any damage to the organ itself. Even though I am not one to run to the outer edge of an anxiety and conclude the worst, the attack was not something I could just put behind me. It was a reminder that life is fragile and I was not going to be here forever, which is something that is surprisingly easy to forget.

Once again I was curious about the origins of the disease that had struck me, since there was no history of heart problems in my family. But the doctors had no answers. Scientific research had established that a case of diabetes increased the possibility of heart attacks, but no one knew exactly how. It made me wonder on particularly unsettling days whether my inattention to dietary matters or weakness for desserts was adversely affecting the span I had left. A heart disease is not like a cancer, which moves silently and often slowly in one's bodily depths. The heart is a muscle near the surface making its signals of distress impossible to ignore. Nor can you put out of mind its ability to shut off everything quite suddenly, like the flip of a switch.

When one is entering such uncharted terrain, the tremors of ordinary stress can be difficult to distinguish from a cardiac alarm. This left me for a while in a no-man's-land where I felt each day might produce a final call. Eventually I saw I was not as fragile as the angina had prompted me to feel, and the dilemmas abated. While it lasted, however, the new level of uncertainty led to the thought that I should put my things in order so as not to burden my survivors more than necessary. But I quickly realized there was no chance of achieving even so modest a goal. Whatever I did and whenever I went, there would be a mess left behind.

XII

While Dostoevsky was planning The Devils, he described his ideas for the novel in a letter to a friend. He intended to encapsulate its theme, he said, in an epigraph taken from the gospel of Luke. The passage he chose concerned a man possessed by devils who had come to Jesus seeking release. "Now a large herd of swine was feeding there on the hillside; and the devils begged Jesus to let them enter them. Then the devils came out of the man and entered the swine, and the herd rushed down the steep bank into the lake and were drowned." Dostoevsky explained the connection between this parable and the story he was writing: "The facts have shown us that the sickness that seized civilized Russians was much stronger than we ourselves imagined, and that the matter did not end with Belinsky ... But what occurred here is what was witnessed by the evangelist Luke. Exactly the same thing happened with us: the devils came out of the Russian man and entered into a herd of swine, that is, into the Nechaevs...."

In the novel he eventually wrote, Dostoevsky described how the utopian idea plants itself in the minds of dreamers who are seeking to release the world from its suffering. But it quickly enters the bodies of radical swine who are bent on destruction, and who pursue it until eventually they destroy themselves. Critics of the novel complained that Dostoevsky had maligned Russia's youth by associating them with violence and nihilism, saying that only the uneducated and society's marginal dregs could become Nechaevists, and commit such heinous crimes. Dostoevsky answered: "And why do you suppose that the Nechaevs must absolutely be fanatics? Very often they are simply scoundrels.... These scoundrels are very crafty and have thoroughly studied the magnanimous aspect of the human soul—and most often the soul of youth—so as to be able play on it as on a musical instrument..."

Dostoevsky knew the idealism of radicals and understood its malignant consequences because he had been a radical himself. "I myself am an old Nechaevist; I also stood on the scaffold condemned to death, and I assure you that I stood in the company of educated people." Almost all the members of his radical circle had graduated from institutions of higher learning, and some of them later made distinguished, even noteworthy contributions to fields of knowledge. "No, gentlemen," he warned, "the Nechaevists do not always come only from idlers who have never studied anything.... There was not a single 'monster' or 'scoundrel' among [us] whether we speak of those who stood on the scaffold or those who remain untouched...."

Then Dostoevsky turned to the paradox at the heart of the radical calling: that the noble idea itself is what inspires the passion to destroy. "In my novel *The Devils,* I attempted to depict those diverse and multifarious motives by which even the purest of hearts and the most innocent of people can be drawn into committing such a monstrous offense. And therein lies the real horror: that in Russia one can commit the foulest and most villainous act without being in the least a villain! And this happens not only in Russia but all over the world, and it has happened since time began...."

And was to happen again. Despite Dostoevsky's efforts to warn others, despite the fact that he was a national figure regarded as a prophet, the nihilistic idea that had captured his youth and nearly destroyed him became an inspiration for the next generation to lay waste his country and make it a desert:

> Even in 1846 Belinsky had initiated me into the whole truth of this coming 'reborn world' and into the whole sanctity of the future communist society. All these convictions of the immorality of the very foundations (Christian ones) of contemporary society and of the immorality of religion and the family; of the immorality of the right to private property; of the elimination of nationalities in the name of the universal brotherhood of people and of contempt for one's fatherland as something that only showed universal development, and so on and so forth—all these things were influences we were unable to resist and which, in fact, captured our hearts and minds in the name of something very noble.

Nihilism in the name of something noble. And so it continues to this day, more than a hundred and fifty years later.

XIII

The Communists began their revolution in Russia by killing the Czar and his entire family, down to the last guiltless child. The crime was necessary, they said, to liberate Russia from hereditary monarchy and the tyrannies of the past. To free Russia from religious superstition, they sacked the nation's 75,000 churches. To institute social justice they created a police state. To instill faith in reason they formed a "People's Church" and built it alongside prison camps and execution blocks. The masses now worshipped not God but the Marxist leader who had liberated them from slavery, calling Stalin the "Genius of Humanity" and "The Father of the Peoples." In no time he became a thousandfold more powerful and ruthless than the Czars.

Nothing in Russia's new world was un-foretold, not even this. "So long as man remains free," the Inquisitor had warned, "he strives for nothing so incessantly and so painfully as to find someone to worship." For freedom is a torment and a man who is free experiences "no greater anxiety than to find someone quickly to whom he can hand over that gift of freedom."

When the Soviet nightmare came to an end, the "Great Architect of Communism" who was drenched in rivers of his people's blood, and had brought an entire nation to its knees, was still revered above all others. Stalin had killed and enslaved tens of millions, and reduced his entire country to unimaginable poverty. But without him, his victims felt naked and afraid. Though he had ordered the murder of virtually one member of every Russian family, millions attended his funeral cortège and nearly a thousand of them were trampled to death by the frenzied throng that followed him to his final rest. To honor his memory, his victims mummified his body and put it on display. His Kremlin tomb became a national shrine. Legions of his benighted subjects made annual pilgrimages to pay homage to his glory. In a poll conducted fifty years after his death, Stalin was voted the third most popular Russian in his nation's history after Alexander Nevsky and Peter the Great.

As the Inquisitor observed, the human yearning for a higher authority is a collectivist passion, the desire to find "a community of worship." Dostoevsky called this "the chief misery of every man individually and of all humanity from the beginning of time." Driven by the desire to have everyone submit to one God, men have gone to war from time immemorial. Even as they seek desperately for a common object to love, so they yearn for a common enemy to hate, which is why the quest for an earthly redemption has led to the greatest crimes.

December 2010

I

I have never been a collector of objects from the past; but through all the moves I have made and the losses I have suffered, I have managed to keep in my possession a faded photograph that was taken when I was still a toddler, barely three years old. In the photo I am standing in my shorts and suspenders with my head straining upwards at the figure of an immense equine. The picture was taken by my father during a family vacation in the country, and my mother catalogued it for the family album, inscribing the words "David and the Giant" on its obverse side. Among the thoughts this image provokes is this oddity: I have come to the end of an urban life to find myself nested in a rural setting in the company of horses, and I feel as much at home here as in any place I have lived.

Ever since the time of the emperor Marcus Aurelius, a dwelling on the land among horses has been an odd circumstance for a Jew. When the Romans conquered Jerusalem, they scattered its inhabitants to the four corners of the globe. Afterwards, Jews lived among strangers and were rarely ranchers or farmers. If the right to own land was not denied them, they avoided it for practical reasons. Forced to settle among peoples who regarded them as infidels, they were perpetually on the alert for a hostile turn in the environment that would force them to move on. Over centuries of persecutions, they acquired the instincts of flight animals. Knowing that things could go very badly and quickly, they kept their assets liquid and their papers at hand.

At the turn of the last century my grandparents became part of yet another Jewish exodus, fleeing from Moravia and Ukraine to seek refuge in America, a country that offered itself as an exception to the historical rule. The American founders had separated church and state, while a Constitution devised by immigrants removed their status as intruders. Consequently, when I acquired a homestead in the Santa Rosa Valley nearly two and a half centuries later, my little odyssey had no greater significance than the breaking of a family mold.

II

A Jewish wisdom holds that when a human being dies, a whole world is lost. Having observed my dogs over many years, I am sure this is true of animals as well. Within a single breed and even the same brood, no two dogs can be said to be the same. My black- and-white spot, Jake, is perpetually on edge and shadows me like a bodyguard, afraid I might disappear. When I leave the house he sits at the front window, a lone sentry awaiting my return. When he thinks I am about to leave he grows agitated and is unable to eat. If I put a dish in front of him, he jumps back as though it might strike him. At night I can hear the ticking of his nails across the hardwood floors and then the crunch of the food I have put out for him, as he eats in the safety of the dark.

Lucy is his polar opposite. She lunges to seize the food from my hand and makes her own way about the house, perching on her favorite chair in regal isolation. When I let the dogs out in the yard, Jake is the last to venture forth and then only briefly for relief. Lucy bolts through the sliders and walks the far edges of yard, stalking animals and neighbors as they pass, until I summon her back. I have no idea why their personalities are so different, but they are; and I know I will not be able to replace them when they are gone.

Chihuahuas attend to movements around them, and strange intrusions will cause their entire bodies to shake with fear. Bewildered by our absences and elated at our returns, their anxiety over the unknown future is not unlike that of the Aztecs who took them as companions long ago. Not understanding what kind of beings we are, and unable to discern our purposes, how can these little dogs look on us as anything but gods?

The helplessness of these little creatures is a way to measure the gratuitous cruelties of which human beings are capable, and have been since the beginning of time. Not long ago the wife of a soldier away at war went on a shopping run. While she was out four young men broke into her house and ransacked it, stealing what they could, and turning her home into a rubble. As if the damage was insufficient, they lingered to play some additional pranks, urinating on the clothes in her closet. Then they took her pet Chihuahua, shaking with uncomprehending fear, and shoved him into her freezer, and slammed the door shut.

III

"People speak sometimes about the 'animal cruelty' of man," Ivan Karamazov observed to his brother Alyosha, who was studying to be a priest. "But that is terribly unjust and offensive to animals. No animal could ever be so cruel, so artfully, so artistically cruel." The conversation between them is the substance of another famous chapter of The Brothers Karamazov which Dostoevsky called "Rebellion," placing it before Ivan's fable of the Grand Inquisitor. Its subject is Ivan's argument with God, his rebellion against the idea of a redemption that requires children to suffer. "Men have a great love of torturing children, even love children in that sense," he comments with caustic irony. "It is the defenselessness of these creatures that tempts the torturers, the angelic trustfulness of the child who has nowhere to run and no one to turn to..."

The suffering of the innocent and the torments of the helpless provide Ivan with a case against the future harmony of mankind that Christians are promised. His meticulously collected examples begin with a newspaper account of Muslim soldiers in the Balkans, cutting the unborn from their mothers' wombs and tossing nursing infants onto the points of their bayonets. He then cites a newspaper report describing an eight-year-old boy who has been tortured to death by the master of his estate. The boy, whose parents are serfs, had inadvertently injured a favorite dog. Irate, the master orders the shivering child to be stripped naked in the arctic winter, then commands his hunting dogs to attack the terrified victim and tear him to pieces.

Ivan asks Alyosha to reconsider the "reconciliation of all with all" that God has promised. While the mother of the child may forgive the torturer for her own suffering, she has no right, Ivan argues, to forgive him for the suffering of her child. And if that is the case, what universal harmony, and therefore what redemption, is possible?

Ivan is referring to a redemption in the hereafter. But what does the wanton cruelty of human beings, their love for the suffering of others, say about the possibility of a redemption in this life? Human perversity is such that not merely strangers but parents will abuse and torture their children. Ivan is ready with examples. For inadvertently soiling her bed, a girl of five is beaten without mercy by her mother and father, who are educated people: "They beat her, flogged her, kicked her, not knowing why themselves, until her whole body was nothing but bruises. Finally, they attained the height of finesse: in the freezing cold, they locked her all night in the outhouse, because she wouldn't ask to get up and go in the middle of the night (as if a five-year-old child sleeping its sound angelic sleep could have learned to ask by that age). For that they smeared her face with her excrement and made her eat her excrement, and it was her mother, her mother who made her! And this mother could sleep while her poor little child was moaning all night in that vile place."

In the foul and freezing dark, the little girl had prayed. "Can you understand," Ivan cries, "that a small creature, who cannot even comprehend what is being done to her, in a vile place, in the dark and the cold, beats herself on her strained little chest with her anguished, gentle, meek tears for 'dear God' to protect her—can you understand such nonsense, my friend and my brother, my godly and humble novice, can you understand why this nonsense is needed and created?"

It is the same question that Job puts to the God of the Old Testament, and that men of religious faith have asked since the beginning of time: If there is evil, how can the creator of the world not be its author? And yet how can He permit it? How can a God of perfect love be the author of perfect hate? Ivan finds the thought unbearable. If human harmony requires the suffering of one innocent child, he berates his brother, it is "too high a price ... and so I return my entrance ticket."

Despite Ivan's rebellion, believers can still maintain their faith by appealing to the limited horizons of our mortal estate. We see through the glass darkly, ignorant of God's plan. Since His design is incomprehensible to us, the possibility exists that it may yet prove just. Through this logic, believers can hold onto their faith, which they do because otherwise they could not go on.

Atheists will scorn their choice as the consolation of the weak. But is this scorn well placed? If believers confront a dilemma that seems insoluble, consider the problem encountered by those who lack their belief. To create a world that is harmonious and just, secular redeemers must put their trust in human beings. But how can human beings create themselves anew? A glance at the human record reveals this to be a much greater leap of faith than relying on a God unseen. Divinity is by nature unknowable, but we are known and our ways familiar. Unless we are in denial, we cannot doubt what the outcome will be.

Consider that those who worship a God of perfection will want to obey His moral law. In seeking to bring about a general happiness, they will resist the sacrifice of the innocent. But what moral authority restrains the social redeemers who speak in the name of an imagined future? To what God do they answer when they are tempted to shed blood for a greater good?

Would human beings have imagined a world of bliss if the one they had created were not so heartless? What is the basis, then, for the hope that they can create a world that is different? How can creatures so consumed with hate, and so steeped in blood, fashion their own salvation?

IV

In the Oval Office of the American White House, a wheat-colored rug has been installed with this testament to the progressive faith: "The moral arc of the universe is long but it bends towards justice."

But does it? How do innocents fare today compared to the "reactionary" past? Terrible as the examples Dostoevsky provides, they do not begin to push the limits of human depravity. In this modern (and therefore enlightened?) age, John Couey kidnapped Jessica Lunsford from the safety of her bedroom. She was nine years old. Couey held the child prisoner in his own house and raped her for three days, locking her in a closet while he reported to his regular job. On the third day he bound the little girl's wrists with speaker wire and stuffed her in a garbage bag. Then he buried her alive in a shallow grave, and left her to suffocate beneath the earth.

Horrified lawmakers crafted a law in Jessica's name providing mandatory prison sentences for those who prey on children, and requiring them to be electronically monitored as long as they are alive. "Jessica's Law" is only one of several statutes to save others from such fates that have been named for those who were not saved. There is Megan's Law and there is the Amber Alert, and there is the Adam Walsh Child Protection and Safety Act.

Adam was only six years old when he was taken from the parking lot of a store near his home. Sixteen days later, police found Adam's severed head 120 miles from the scene of his abduction. A convicted serial killer confessed to the crime, and described to the police in gruesome detail the sexual torments he inflicted on Adam before beheading him. The killer then taunted Adam's grieving father, offering to sell him information about the location of his son's body parts. The offer was refused, but authorities never filed charges for the crime. They were of the opinion that the killer was merely boasting to enhance his reputation to the similarly inclined.

The law inspired by Adam's death requires criminals who commit sexual crimes to register with authorities and then to update their information at three-month intervals, with failure to register a felony. Yet the law was only passed over the widespread objections of "human-rights" advocates who were concerned that the liberties of sexual predators were being infringed. At the time of its passage, there were an estimated half a million sexual criminals in America, and the whereabouts of a hundred thousand already identified were unknown.

According to information provided by the National Crime Alert Registry, six out of every ten rape victims are under the age of eighteen, and half of those are not even eleven. The chance that a boy will become the victim of a sex offender is one in six, a girl one in three. The National Center for Victims of Crimes informs the interested that the sexual abuse of children is a family affair and more than half of rape victims are kin. This makes attempts to identify and prosecute the criminals difficult and often impossible. It also poses an obstacle that is almost insuperable to the detection of these crimes in the first place. When the bonds of love are set against the claims of justice, how can there be one or the other?

Abuse begets abuse, generation on generation; adult criminals are spawned by the cruelties of their parents, and the misery proceeds through time without end. Subtler forms of torment that families inflict also scar the innocent and prompt the victims to punish strangers in return. Can there be an end to this chain of suffering? Laws against child abuse have been enacted by governments throughout the civilized world, but the tide flows unabated. A hundred years after the Emancipation Proclamation, there are tens of millions of children sold into sexual slavery the world over.

But what practical remedy is available? How can we prevent the sins of the parents from being visited on their children? By monitoring all families, abrogating their privacy and individual rights? By the forced removal of children from their homes to raise them under the auspices of the state? And who will monitor the overseers?

The moral arc of the universe is indeed bent, but there is no one, and no way, to unbend it.

V

In the morning, when I prepare for the day ahead and shave the new-grown stubble from my cheeks, I often think of my father who has been gone these twenty-five years. The bathroom where he performed these same rituals also served as our family field hospital. I was an avid competitor in neighborhood games and often ran shoeless in the streets, which led to scrapes and cuts requiring attention. Among the comforting memories I can still retrieve are those of my father as our resident medic dressing the wounds I acquired at play. As an adult I was able to see that he was a weak man, unable to rescue himself from the deeper hurts that life inflicted. But when I was young he was my Gibraltar, and I was confident he would never fail me.

Every morning I would wake up early to watch his preparations, sitting on the closed bowl beside the sink, or standing discreetly to his rear, my head rising just above his waist. His towel would be draped around him, his small athletic frame faced to the mirror and his bowed calves visible under the towel edge. The routine that followed never varied. He would lather his cheeks and puff them out, first one and then the other, then pull on his chin with his free hand until the surface became taut and smooth. In measured strokes he would draw the razor down from his ear in the same deliberate manner with which he applied the bandages to my wounds. Then, when the foam was swept away, he would tear a tissue into little squares and place them over the spots of blood where the skin had been nicked by the errant blade.

Ever since my angina I have had to be careful about cuts. The blood thinners prescribed by my cardiologist create a moderate hazard when the skin is pierced. A slight break barely noticed before could cause blood to pour like an open faucet. Fortunately, as a result of technical advances over the intervening years, the disposable razors my father used have been greatly improved. Gone are the single-edge Gillettes whose scratch and tug led to inevitable breaks. My razor now bears the same company name but comes with a track holding five finely spaced blades that vibrate with an electric pulse regulated by a microchip. The shave this complex device provides is so smooth I can hardly feel the hairs being severed as it passes.

This is the detail that provokes the memories. For though my father was normally silent during his morning routine, he would sometimes halt his razor mid-stroke and turn to where I was standing to explain to me the sinister designs of its makers. These were the capitalists, who were in business to make profits and not to serve human needs. Consequently, Gillette would never create a perfect blade, or one that would last longer or even forever. He delivered this homily on many occasions, varying his examples to illustrate the evils of the system he hated, and to demonstrate how its profiteers blocked his hopes for a better life.

Summoned from memory, these sermons became irresistible occasions for my own second thoughts. Whenever a company came to market with a new product, I was inspired to review his long-ago claims. One razor manufacturer even produced an "Infinity Blade" to last forever. It hardly mattered whether the promise was realized. The claim reflected a market reality that nullified my father's gloomy suspicions. To succeed, capitalists had to develop products that met their customers' needs better than those of their rivals. What made profits possible was the satisfaction of human needs. My father had overlooked so obvious a truth that I realized he never understood the system he was so desperate to overthrow. Each time a product innovation made life better—and for more people than ever in the past—it caused me to think of the wasted devotions of my father's life.

One summer I had occasion to visit the Czech Republic and found myself on a tour of Prague Castle, an imposing edifice overlooking the River Moldau. The castle had housed the kings of Bohemia since the 12th Century and had been the seat of the Holy Roman Empire after that. But for me it provided a conclusive text confounding my father's faith. Its royal rooms were arched by forty-foot ceilings, and were fitted with the finest furniture and rare tapestries. But these august chambers were lit only by candles, and their cavernous interiors were heated by wood fires, and there were no bathrooms in sight. Water was brought in with buckets, and the only toilets were wooden baskets. It occurred to me that the ordinary home of the poorest worker in the capitalist societies my father hated was richer in human comforts than the most opulent palaces of the kings of old. It was a gift of the very system that continues to oppress the utopian imaginations of progressives everywhere.

VI

We seek to persuade ourselves that the past is more substantial than a dream by speaking of its actors as people who have "made history," as though an elaborate architecture was in the process of completion. We describe events as "historic," suggesting that a cornerstone has been set in place. But this is a metaphor, and there is no such architecture. One day we will forget the heroes and their stories, and history itself. Its path is not an upward slope as progressives like to think, but a cycle of rises and falls, as the Romans long ago understood. Those who triumph in the present will be conquered later, and what is built today will be gone tomorrow, and no one will be there to mourn its passing.

We live inside the historical drama in order to gain the comforts of a religious faith. Unlike the narratives of our individual lives we cannot bring history to a halt. It is a fiction we do not control, and it will roll on without us. Consequently, the illusion of a historical progress creates meanings for our individual stories, and not even the wisest among us seem able to do without them.

Despite his exceptional insight, even Dostoevsky was unable to live with the idea of a history without purpose. Sometime in his mid-fifties, at the peak of his creative powers, he persuaded himself that history was, in fact, structured like a novel with themes an artist could decipher, and he became a prophet in the process.

In January 1877 he wrote: "It is evident that the time is at hand for something eternal, something millenarian, something that has been in preparation in the world since the very beginning of its civilization." He was referring to a conflict now nearly forgotten that was brewing in the Balkans, which were then ruled by the Islamic empire of the Ottoman Turks. Four months after Dostoevsky wrote these words, the Russian Tsar declared war on the Ottomans, putting his country at the head of a coalition of Christian nations seeking to liberate themselves from four hundred years of Muslim oppression. To Dostoevsky these events appeared as the road to Armageddon since Russia's war might lead to the liberation of Constantinople, which had been the holy seat of the Orthodox Church before the Islamic conquest. In the prophet's imagination, a Russian victory would prepare the way for a theological utopia in which the world would be ruled by an authentic Christian faith.

Earlier, Dostoevsky had written in his notebooks: "I want the full kingdom of Christ." He had then crossed out the words "I want" and put in their place: "I believe in the full kingdom of Christ." And then: "I believe that this kingdom will be accomplished, and it will be with us in Russia." Other nations lived only for themselves but Russia was different, he believed, a nation that lived for Christ. "Now that the time has come," Russia would take the lead in establishing the kingdom of God, "becoming the servant of all for the sake of universal reconciliation [and] the ultimate unifying of humanity." Dostoevsky had become his own Inquisitor incarnate.

Dostoevsky knew that the secular world would look with scorn on his vision of a Christian millennium. But he had an answer: his messianic vision mirrored their view of a progressive future. "You believe (and I along with you) in a common humanity—that is, that at some time the natural barriers and prejudices that until now have prevented the free communion of nations through the egoism of national aspirations, will someday fall before the light of reason and consciousness, and that only then will peoples begin to live in a single spirit and in accord as brothers, rationally and lovingly striving for general harmony. Tell me, gentlemen, what can be higher or more sacred than this faith...?"

What indeed? Dostoevsky remained convinced that this was the faith for which Russia had been chosen. Until the current historical moment, he wrote, Western civilization had been dominated by two failed attempts to achieve the universal community of man. These were the utopian quests embodied in the Roman Church and in secular socialism, which he thought of as different versions of the same promise. Socialism was a totalitarian religion that sought "nothing other than the compulsory union of humanity." It owed its provenance to "an idea derived from ancient Rome that was subsequently completely preserved in Catholicism." But the true Christian idea of individual freedom had been preserved in the Eastern Orthodox Church—or so Dostoevsky convinced himself. Now, under Russia's aegis, "the fulfillment of the destinies of humans on earth" would be achieved voluntarily through a spiritual conversion to this Christian truth. The reconciliation of humanity's warring factions would finally be achieved through the defeat of Islam and the unification of the Slavic peoples under the Russian imperium where Christianity was a living creed.

VII

Every quest for a redemption in this life faces a necessary enemy in the opponents of its promised future. So it was with Dostoevsky's quest for a universal harmony in Christ, whose path was blocked by a people who resisted the faith and were, by nature, insular and self-centered—the Jews. "The Yid and his bank are now reigning over everything," Dostoevsky confided to his notebooks, "over Europe, education, civilization, socialism." The Jew "will use [his bank] to uproot Christianity and destroy civilization."

Like every would-be redeemer, Dostoevsky viewed the apocalypse as imminent: "The Jews' ... reign is drawing nigh! Coming soon is the complete triumph of ideas before which feelings of love for humanity, the longing for truth, Christian feelings ... must give way." He regarded Jews as a self-regarding, self-seeking tribe among the nations who refused to be assimilated to the cultures they inhabited, and thus to the common good.

On the other hand, the same characteristics contributed to the fact that Jews were a people that had outlived every other. "Even the mightiest of the world's civilizations never lasted half of forty centuries," Dostoevsky marveled, yet insularity and egoism were an insufficient explanation for this fact. "In order to lose so many times their territory, their political independence, their laws, almost even their religion—to lose these things and each time to unite once more, to be reborn once more," the Jews had to be continually reinvigorated in "their old idea."

This idea was the belief that they were chosen by God who gave them His covenant, which Dostoevsky described in these words: "Go forth from the other nations, form thine own entity and know that henceforth thou art the only one before God ... even when thou art scattered over the face of the earth and among all other peoples ... pay no heed; have faith in these things that have been promised unto thee." The promise of redemption had given the Jews the will and strength to be reborn in defeat, and to survive above all others.

There was an irony in this rebuke. Fåor the same promise was also the self-centered heart of the mission that Dostoevsky had embraced—a Russian salvation of the world. How did this irony escape the artist whose Inquisitor had identified the need of human beings to worship a God in history who would release them from insecurity and doubt? The torment of their uncertainty was so great, he warned, that "even when gods disappear from the earth, they will fall down before idols just the same..." For the sake of a god to worship, they will make war on each other and will do so "to the end of the world."

VIII

When I have vanished like those before me, my family name will soon be gone as well. Of my four grandchildren, three are females who will probably take the surnames of their husbands, should they marry; the fourth is my daughter's son, who bears the surname of his father. But this eclipse will mean little. In our family the name "Horowitz" is hardly three generations old, having been invented for my grandfather by immigration officials at Ellis Island when he came to America in 1905. Who knows who we were before that?

About our family prior to their arrival in America, I know very little, which probably reflects my father's discomfort with the past. He was incurious enough about his lineage that he never seems to have inquired about the actual name of his own father in the country of his birth. "Gurevitch or Gurevoy" was all he said to me. Because he had a particular disliking for the relatives on my mother's side, whose men were more successful, our contacts were rare, and I had little of their family history imparted to me as a child. My mother went along with this prejudice, perhaps choosing it as a path less stressful than resistance. As a result, all the knowledge I have of the lives that preceded me is a thin line of memories beginning with my mother's father, whose name was Shmuel Braunstein or Bronstein—I have no idea which.

Shmuel was a Rumanian Jew who emigrated to America before the turn of the last century and was one of eight wine-making brothers who left Rumania because they had been forbidden as Jews to own land or cultivate a vineyard. In America they became merchants, owning dry goods stores in New Haven and New York. They shed their family name, half of them deciding to call themselves "Brown" and the other half "Stone." In this American transition my grandfather Shmuel Braunstein became "Sam Brown."

I must have met my great uncles as a youngster but I have no memory of them. Like most of the details of my grandfather's life I do not know the dates of his passage to America. But sometime after his arrival, he married

Rose Abramovitz (or Abramovich), a young girl of eighteen who had been born on these shores. I know the year they were married, which was 1898, because it is stamped on some serving pieces made of blue glass, which my grandmother received as a wedding gift and handed down to my mother, who left them for me. About her family I know nothing except that they arrived with the first great immigration waves after the Civil War. Rose and Sam had two children whom they called "Blanche" and "Harold"—names, as my mother observed, that were somewhat bland and hardly Jewish.

My uncle Harold was a talented musician who studied with the composers Leonard Bernstein and Aaron Copland. He was also a man of strong and often inflexible views when it came to defending the integrity of his art. Consequently, although he lived for seventy years, his works were rarely played, and he failed to receive the recognition he deserved. In his forties he taught at the High School of Music and Art, where he created the Renaissance Chorus, which was devoted to the era that was closest to his heart. After his death, his students kept the chorus together but met at infrequent intervals. When they were themselves in their sixties and seventies, the chorus members organized a concert of his works on a weekend that would have been his 100th birthday if he had lived so long.

I went to New York to attend his centennial, which was held in the Advent Lutheran Church on the Upper East Side, and there I heard his music for the first time. The organizers provided concert notes which contained an excerpt from the diary of the composer Ned Rorem, one of his students, and which offered this observation: "If forty years later he died unknown while ever superior to many an interferer, some of us feel that in his surly urge to avoid the reeking herd—in his not playing the game which is part of the rat race—he sailed above the storm but, unlike the Eagle of the Rock, he sailed quite out of sight."

Out of sight. This could also be said of the entire family of Braunsteins and Horowitzes. One day it will be true of me as well.

IX

We can look back thousands of years through the images left by those who went before us and still see ourselves in them. Their thoughts and hopes, emotions and disappointments, are all familiar. But in one respect a gulf has opened between us that cannot be bridged. Scientific advances have progressed to a degree that has made our own lives unimaginable to our ancestors. A result of these advances is that it is now possible for a Jew to trace his lineage through a single gene sample back to the time of Aaron and Moses.

The opportunity this provides is a consequence of the inbreeding of our forebears, and also the isolation imposed by our sense of entitlement, and our persecution by those who resent us for it. On the other hand, as Jews we do not need genetic markers to determine our identity, since our history is itself a genome. Consider that two millennia after our dispersal by the Romans, the Horowitzes and Braunsteins were still on the run; they had left a hostile country for a strange new one; and they were still pursuing the Promised Land.

When I consider how my life and the life of the Jews have been shaped by these facts, I cannot help wondering about the illusions that possessed our ancestors to take on the most powerful empire the world had ever seen. As it happens, this question arose at the time of their rebellion and was recorded for posterity by Yosef ben Mattithyahu, one of the Jewish generals who defended Jerusalem against the Roman advance.

In the course of the siege, Yosef was captured by the Romans and became their historian and also their counselor. He changed his name to "Flavius Josephus" and under this Latin pseudonym wrote a seven-volume account of the conflict called The Jewish War. In his history, Josephus put the argument against the rebellion into the mouth of a Jewish leader who sought to dissuade others from their fateful campaign: "What confidence is it that elevates you to oppose the Romans? Are you richer than the Gauls, stronger than the Germans, wiser than the Greeks, more numerous than all men upon the habitable earth? . . . You are the only people who think it a disgrace to be servants to those to whom all the world has submitted. . . ."

Josephus understood the passion of his people, which was to submit to no God but their own. It was the covenant that promised their salvation. But the Romans also knew that a common worship secured a common rule, and they required subjects to bow to the gods who sustained their empire. Eventually, Rome's emperors declared themselves to be gods, and demanded a religious adoration from their subject peoples. When they attempted to place their statues inside the Temple in Jerusalem, the Jews rebelled, and responded, "No king but God," for "God is to be [our] only ruler and lord."

X

Five centuries after the Romans drove the Jews out of Judea and Samaria, the land their God had promised was conquered by Islamic armies and brought under Muslim rule. The Muslims built a mosque over the ruins of Solomon's Temple, and made Jews across their empire a subject people. Centuries later, the Muslim empire was defeated in World War I. The European victors divided up the ruins, granting the descendants of the Jews three slivers of desert land to create a Jewish state. After nearly two millennia they had finally come home.

But Islam's prophet had cursed the Jews, warning his followers the day of redemption would only come "when the Muslims fight the Jews and kill them, when the Jews hide behind the rocks and the trees, and the rocks and the trees cry out: 'O Muslim, there is a Jew hiding behind me. Come and kill him.'" As Muslim fortunes revived, the war against the Jews began again.

Atheists attribute the hostility that has followed us through the ages to theology—a hatred that emanates from rival religions. This is true of the war between Muslims and Jews, but in what god did Hitler put his trust? Jew-hatred also exists in countries without us, like Malaysia and Japan, and Poland after its Jewish population was destroyed. As one writer observed, it is a venom that is in some ways absolutely unique. "Sinhalese who don't like Tamils, or Hutu who regard Tutsi as 'cockroaches,' do not accuse their despised neighbors of harboring a plan—or of possessing the ability—to bring off a secret world government based on the occult control of finance." Belief in the conspiracy of the Jews is the heart of an atheistic as well as a theistic faith. It puts a comforting order into the world, and feeds the illusion that a salvation awaits if the culprits can be removed.

XI

At seventy-one years, I have lived longer than both Marcus Aurelius and Dostoevsky, and indeed most of the people who preceded me on this earth. The ability to extend our lives is one of the gifts of science that encourages us to believe that things are getting better, and to this extent they may be. But the same advances have enabled us to monitor each other more closely, constricting our freedoms, and to kill each other more easily and on a far greater scale than ever before. It has also brought the warring sides of humanity into closer proximity, making no place safe.

Here is a Jewish perspective: It is three millennia since Moses led us to the border of the Promised Land, which was situated on the West Bank of the Jordan where Muslims now rule. It is almost two thousand years since the Romans expelled us from this very territory, Judea and Samaria, and renamed it "Palestine." This is time enough to review our progress and weigh the balance, which is this: Wherever we have migrated in our exile to make our homes, we have built thriving and creative cultures, yet we are still among the most hated and hunted people on earth, and the only ones who have been chosen for this role the world over.

He who has seen present things has seen all, both everything that has taken place from all eternity and everything that will be for time without end....

Deep in the millennial past, Jews were the original progressives and invented the idea that we are headed towards a brighter future, which perhaps is why our history is so filled with tragedy and defeat. We have survived so long now and are spread so far and wide as to provide a measure for those who can handle it, of where we are going and where history is actually headed, which is nowhere.

XII

Several times a week now, I take a walk alone to the end of the long and leafless driveway in front of my house in the Santa Rosa Valley. I walk past the avocado grove on my neighbor's side and onto the street where I turn the corner, which is lined with hedges, and go out the community gate. Once beyond the perimeter, I follow the horse path up the hill until I can see the valley floor below me. There is an agricultural plain in the crease between the mountains that has been planted with a fresh crop, and the hillsides are green again from the recent rains.

If I push myself too hard on the upward slope my chest begins to tighten, and I am reminded of what I have come through and where I am headed. If the pain is too strong, I stop to rest before making the turn to come alongside the pastures and pipe corrals where the Warmbloods loiter with their colts in the shade. Then I make my way down the hill to complete the circle and return home.

Unlike my walks in Calabasas or the shorter outings I take within the gated community, I do not bring the dogs with me. Winnie's joints have become too sore for such strenuous exercises, and while the little dogs are still limber enough to make the walk, there is no way the big dog would understand why we had left her. So I leave them all behind.

Sometimes I stop to look down at the valley below and reflect on its ghosts. The Chumash Indians lived in these environs before the Europeans came, and probably before the times of Moses and Christ. Their stay ended when the californios crossed over from Mexico and Spain, carrying diseases for which the natives had no defenses. The Hispanics took their brief turn, and were then replaced by the English-speaking conquerors who preserved the names of their ranchos, which still mark the landscape and are occupied by people like me. And who will come when we are gone?

Despite all that I think I know, I still return to the security of my stories, and am content to live in their worlds. And what is the alternative? Without our stories our lives would be chaos and our existence unbearable. I keep moving forward, as I always have, though my steps have slowed and my passions are dimmed. My time is spent reflecting on these facts, and carrying on the work that has taken me this far, looking out for family, friends, and animals as I go. Beyond these personal obligations I have concerns for my country and for the perils of the Jews because their fates cannot be separated from mine. Most of all, I try to be a support to my wife and do what I can for my children and their children, who are quite independent of me now and have lives that go on without me. I am impelled forward by my writing, and that is the reason for doing it. Although there is always a feeling of loss at the completion of a book, I am content to be coming to the end of this one, and look forward to its publication, even though few people will read it, and then there will be none.

I do not dwell on thoughts of oblivion but refer to the advice of the Roman, using my knowledge of the future to muffle the distress of the present. Sometimes I take a sentimental turn and imagine that when it is my time to go I will be joining my daughter Sarah and, along with her, my parents, and also the members of our family known and unknown who went before me down the ages to the beginning of time.

Some days I sit on my back porch looking up through the trees and their shivering boughs to the sky above, and think about going, and find myself completely at peace with this prospect. I have felt this way for some time now, comfortable with the idea that soon I will be no one and nowhere, and comforted in a stoic way by the knowledge that it doesn't add up. Perhaps my daughter's passing helped me to arrive at this peace. In any case, the loss ahead of me is no different from any along the way, except that there will be no pain. We are wounded by losses and rage to have them reversed. But eventually we come to terms with our fate, knowing that this was all there was ever going to be.

In the year gone by, I fulfilled an obligation to my daughter by putting together a book of the writings she left behind, which occupied so much of her short time on this earth. My children built a library for her among the Abayudayah, a tribe of African Jews in Uganda, whom she served and to whom we have sent a package of her books. And that, in the end, is what my father left me, too, and what each of us leaves to our children: a bookshelf and a death.

Because of his interest in creating a new world, my father generally lacked interest in the improvements to this one that did not hasten its coming. His grandchildren have been freed from this illusion and understand that the life we have now is all we will get, and therefore is what is important. My sons and daughters have worked to bring health and pleasure to others and to aid troubled and disabled children. They understand that if the world is to be redeemed it will be one individual at a time. I take satisfaction in that.

At some point in every day I return to my writing. It is not that this work is important to anyone, though long ago I acquired an audience to whom it may seem so, and perhaps there has been some good that has come through my words. I do this work because it is important to me.

Often I play music in the background when I write, and sometimes it is the Requiem Mass that Mozart wrote in his thirty-fifth year for an anonymous stranger. It was the last piece he ever composed. While he was working on the Requiem he was stricken with an illness so severe that he told his wife he was writing it for himself. His intuition was correct, and he died some days later before he was able to finish a piece that has been played by millions through the centuries since. The only parts of the Requiem he was able to complete before taking his last breath were the Introit or "entrance" (Grant them eternal rest, Lord, and let perpetual light shine on them) and the Kyrie (Lord, have mercy on us). He left behind him sketches of the rest, and was still writing on the last day he was alive.

BOOK III
"You're Going to Be Dead One Day"
A Love Story
(2014)

1
May–June

I generally have a soft spot for family occasions and warm weather, which is an obvious reason for my contentment today. Not only is the sun shining down on a brilliant spring morning, it is also Mother's Day, and my wife April and her sisters have planned a small gathering at our house to celebrate. At this moment I am off by myself in a corner of the sitting room where the windows meet, contemplating how occasions like this inevitably bring bittersweet memories to the surface, and looking forward to them.

Since it is still early, I have settled into a luxurious leather chair that my wife bought for me recently. The new chair is also elaborate with stainless steel rails and machinery that electronically tilts the user back and raises the legs to an optimal therapeutic point. It is equipped with a glass holder and a retractable desk that allows me to write with the least discomfort. The manufacturer calls my catbird seat "The Perfect Chair," and from where I am perched I would not argue. Its price, if you were curious, has been set accordingly, and would discourage many people from even considering the option. It certainly would have discouraged me if the decision had been mine. But it was a surprise from April on my release from acute physical therapy unit in Los Robles Hospital, where I was laid up for two weeks for reasons I will divulge shortly. It is one of many gifts that bear the imprint of a wifely concern for my wellbeing, which is a healing balm in itself.

Along with the chair, she has set up a new moveable desk by my bed. These two pieces of furniture are where I spend most of my time now, since I am no longer mobile. A little over a month ago, I went into the hospital for what I thought was a routine hip replacement, but while I was under the anesthetic the surgeon slipped up and damaged my sciatic nerve, leaving me with a paralyzed left foot and a reservoir of neuropathic pain. Until this mishap, I took my limbs for granted, as most people do, and had no idea how a useless foot and damaged nerves could take a person down.

My wife is understandably upset about my condition and pressing me to sue. I have contacted an attorney but am skeptical about securing any positive result. In the litigious environment of the medical profession, doctors have availed themselves of elaborate defenses that are difficult to breach. Only time will tell whether I will ever recover the use of my limb or whether the courts will deliver me a modicum of satisfaction.

When I signed up for the operation, I had not the slightest inkling that a calamity like this might be awaiting me. I had undergone a similar procedure on my right hip ten years earlier, after which I was out of the *hospital in a day, and functioning reasonably well within a few weeks. This encouraged me to follow my normal approach to problems: just get them out of the way and go* back to work. But when I woke from this procedure in my hospital bed, I knew immediately that something was very wrong. My foot was hanging lifeless from the ankle, a syndrome known as "drop foot," and instead of my release papers the hospital had provided me with a morphine pump. I could not move my toes. I could not *feel* my toes, and barely feel the foot itself.

My doctors have told me that my present condition is not hopeless, and some sort of recovery is likely. But they remain evasive as to when this might materialize and what it might be like. Nerves apparently have their own schedule and manner of repair. Whether they will heal enough to restore what I once took for granted remains disconcertingly uncertain. Nonetheless, I have accepted the ambivalent prognoses and canceled engagements for the next several months, at not a little personal cost. Two of the speeches I was scheduled to give would have been before thousands of people and carried with them honorariums I now have plenty of use for. I have accepted this setback with as much philosophical attitude as I can muster, having found in the course of many lost battles that it is better not to fight the inevitable when it is staring you in the face.

It is also wise to try to enjoy the life you have before the gates begin to close. In the years before sixty, I led a physically robust existence and never paid much attention to matters of health. But in 2001, as the country reeled under the attacks of 9/11, I was diagnosed with a prostate cancer and underwent a radical prostatectomy to remove it. I seem to have been battling significant ailments ever since. I don't wish to exaggerate these trials because, until my present unfortunate case, I have managed each of the problems without too much disruption of my activities and accepted the new limits my body has laid on me.

Entering this new world inevitably prompts thoughts about "last things." I have written three philosophical memoirs about aging and death and the lessons to be drawn from our brief journeys on this earth, and this is undoubtedly the beginning of a fourth. I began this series with a book called *The End of Time,* a title with dual meanings. The "end of time" can refer to the purpose that we give to our lives, or the purpose that our limited allotment of time gives to them. In this book I also included observations on the utopian quest for a perfect world, which is a secular religion for many, and has been the focus of most of my thinking life. This quest is really an attempt to deny the permanence of injustice, of which death is the exemplary case.

The second memoir, *A Cracking of the Heart,* was about the admirable life and untimely death of my daughter Sarah. You do not really know death until you have lost someone you love, and lost her forever. Writing about my child was a way of salving my grief, and the book has been helpful to others dealing with irreparable loss. The third volume, *A Point in Time,* while slim like the others, is actually a summa of my life's work. Its focus is again the social redeemers who want to escape the meaninglessness of life by pursuing the fantasy of a heaven on earth, while sewing the seeds of catastrophes along the way.

While I am awaiting the family's arrival, I can enjoy an interlude of undisturbed solitude in which to ponder these matters. Of course I could fill my head with happier reflections, but I won't. Thinking about our mortal condition, and the way it affects how we live in the here and now, remains as seductive to me as ever. It provides my old age with the frisson of youthful discovery and has been the inspiration for some of my most satisfying compositions. Others may suppose that so morbid a preoccupation on a bright spring morning could only be inspired by the fact that next week I have a long-standing appointment to see my oncologist. But I can assure you this is not the case. After all, I have lived with the same cancer for thirteen of the most productive years of my life. And who isn't facing a death sentence?

Nonetheless, my reflections on mortality are disturbing to those like my wife who are immersed in the life around them and instinctively understand the utility of fresh air and sunshine to the human spirit. I appreciate and respect this attitude, which is why I choose to conduct my ruminations in a corner by myself.

Family Matters

Mother's Day has not always been a tradition in the Horowitz family. As a reflex of his communist politics my father dismissed the occasion as a "greeting-card holiday" invented to make profits for Hallmark. I was long influenced by this presumption until a Mother's Day came along when April said we should buy a helium-filled party balloon shaped like a heart and send it to my mother Blanche with our prayers. The idea was pretty alien to me. My mother had been dead for twenty years, and the idea that we could communicate with her through a plastic balloon sent skyward seemed ridiculous. But the little ceremony April contrived and put her heart into brought tears to my eyes because her thoughts for my mother were so sincere, and put me in reverent mind of the woman who was once such a towering presence in my life.

It is April's family who will be joining us this morning. Her younger sister Kim is already with us, and has been staying in the house since April's accident (which I will come to shortly), taking only a few days off now and then to attend to her own household in Huntington Beach. This has been a great help in our family crisis as Kim does the cleaning and cooking, and, equally important since April and I are both on medications, drives us to our respective doctor's visits.

April and Kim were the youngest in a brood of ten but were separated twenty years ago when Kim and her husband, Jim, were forced to move to Indiana because of a work-related problem. When they returned to California, they settled two hours down the coast and kept to themselves. It was only when April's mishap occurred that she and her sister were reunited and began to resurrect the tomfoolery of the happier times they spent together when they were young.

Now their laughter rings about the house, triggered more often than not by April's manic impersonations and pranks. The two women are on the back porch now, attending to seven yelping canines who inhabit the environs when Kim is here with her three. When the dogs are done with their breakfast, they will exit the kitchen door to romp about the sprawling lawn at the back of our house. There are four Chihuahuas and three Boxers. Two of them, named Max and Ollie, belong to Kim. A third, named Merry, is ours. April bought Merry and Ollie as puppies almost a year ago, just before the car accident, and we gave the male to Kim out of gratitude for her help.

We will not be a large group this Mother's Day, but sufficiently entwined to make the occasion work. April's older sister Cheri will be driving up from West Covina with her husband Wendell, a Vietnam vet. Kim's husband, to whom I owe a debt for lending us his wife, is coming up from the beach, while their son Ryan will arrive separately to complete the family cohort.

Unanswered Questions

My solitude has begun at the far end of the house from April's and Kim's laughter and the dogs' happy cries, and I am deep into my head and the dark thoughts that preoccupy me. A stream of light pouring through the living room windows has brightened this pleasant interval of not-so-pleasant concerns, making them even more incongruous. But press on I will.

All questions about death begin with observations for which only a religious faith can provide solace. I have no such faith, and therefore my posing of these questions is unfiltered by the religious hope that a life eternal awaits us where a Divinity will sort things out and make everything clear. Those of us without such faith must grapple with these stark facts: there is no one to tell us when we will be gone from this life; there is no one to tell us why we are here and waiting to be gone in the first place; and there is no one to tell us what happens then—whether we will enter a life eternal or soon be nothing at all, with every memory of us vanished.

These unanswered questions at the heart of our existence are formidable loose ends of our earthly stay, which threaten to undermine it at every turn. It is remarkable to consider that even though they are central to our lives, we are no closer to answering them now than when Pythagoras discovered that musical notes could be translated into mathematical equations.

The gloomy dialogue that goes on in my head in response to our dilemma is the product of a lifelong conviction that we should strive to understand the existence into which we have been cast, and not merely endure it as we would a case of drop foot or a dose of bad weather. Is there something strange about this? Or is the subject merely averted because it might ruin our day?

A Hidden God

At seventy-five I have reached what would once have seemed to me a formidable age, but hardly feels that way now that I am here. Having begun to understand how the game is played, I would welcome a second round. However, for reasons unexplained, the game was not set up that way. One and done. After years of reflection on this fate, I have grown used to it, and to a surprising degree accepted it. Yet the finality of a cosmic emptiness still rankles, like a puzzle missing its central piece. There is just no satisfying way to comprehend the possibility that everything one has lived and worked for and loved will be erased and gone.

The 17th-century scientist and religious thinker Blaise Pascal, whose poignant life ended when he was only thirty-nine, devised his own approach to these questions. He attributed the darkness at the heart of our existence to the paradox of a Hidden God. Only God could fill the emptiness for us, but chooses not to. He will not even reveal to us that He is there.

In this season of medical ordeals, I have encountered my own paradox, which is fortuitously temporal and happy. It fills the only life I have and thus trumps Pascal's lonely despair. April and I have been together for twenty years and age has overtaken us, but in the midst of our medical woes I find myself possessed by a passion that I would have thought reserved only for the young and innocent. And these feelings marvelously are shared. I ask myself, how can adults schooled by time and aware of each other's inoperable flaws fall again so deeply in love? As with so many other important things I cannot explain this, but it has brought a happiness to my physical suffering that has made me perversely apprehensive of its ending.

Two Sensibilities

Over the years, April has made many concessions to my intellectual distractions but has never reconciled herself to the morbid reflections of my late memoirs. Perhaps this intolerance derives from the age gap between us, which prompts her to visualize the emptiness I will leave when I am gone. She, the optimist, is a pessimist about this, which might account for her near-panic when she hears me utter phrases like "the end of time."

Our different sensibilities do not end there. April is instinctively apprehensive that the future may turn dark, while I, the pessimist, am upbeat about my own future and rarely see disasters coming. How do I reconcile these contradictions? I don't. Like Walt Whitman I could answer by saying I contain multitudes, but probably my heart is simply incapable of following my head. When I look for the cause of my optimism, all I can come up with is this: I was brought up in a quasi-religious environment where my parents and their friends were on a mission to "change the world" and enter a promised land. As a result, from a very young age I was convinced that despite the improbabilities, despite the fact that our community of communist believers was tiny and hunted, the brave new world we were seeking was just beyond the horizon. My expectation, regardless of the obstacles, was therefore always of a positive outcome. Tragic experience has taught me the destructive folly of this attitude, but habit and instinct continue to say otherwise.

Asking how a pessimist about human beings and their prospects can still be optimistic about his own is like asking how an atheist can still be moral. Obviously this is possible, unless you believe all atheists are criminals. There is a dimension to our lives, finite as they are, which contains possibilities that are not. So there is nothing strange in agnostics like me embracing them.

Our different outlooks also affect the way April and I view my current benighted state. April agonizes over the details of my new life—the pitiful sight of me hobbling across the floor with my walker and therapeutic boot, the agonies I suffer when the pain is severe, my return to a childlike dependence requiring her assistance with such simple tasks as putting on my clothes, bathing, adjusting my bedding, or getting in and out of the wheelchair we take on outings. How utterly transformed my life has become! How it has shrunk under the knife of an incompetent hand. Such thoughts roll into a rage inside her, which can be assuaged only by thoughts of retribution.

I, on the other hand, have few of these feelings. Of course, I can see her point and am touched by the way she assumes the role of my defender. But unlike her I do not dwell on these circumstances or rail against the forces that have brought me low. My opening bout with prostate cancer was also my first stoic lesson, and my daughter Sarah's untimely death seven years later provided a brutal completion of the course. What they said to me was this: life is unfair and you are not an exception. This is my code. It is not something I think about; it is the way I think.

For this reason, I haven't spent any time agonizing over the injustice of a botched operation or imagining scenarios in which it never happened. Unfairness is embedded in the genome of our existence. Therefore, accept it and move on. My focus during these days of post-operative doldrums is on getting through them, and doing what needs to be done so that a recovery of whatever sort might take place. When the stabs of pain threaten to lift me out of my chair, I tell myself these are the nerves re-firing, and that augurs well. I have no idea if this is the truth, but I am encouraged by others to think it is, and thinking so certainly helps me to get by. I have disciplined myself in patience, having learned the hard way that improvement is not going to proceed according to any schedule of mine.

In the meantime, I focus on the daily satisfactions that are within my reach. These lie in what I can accomplish with my brain, and the perfect chair April has provided for me. I am currently preparing the text and publicity plan for a book called Take No Prisoners, which will be published two months from now, on July 28. I also have a larger literary project in the editing and completion of a nine-volume edition of my collected writings called *The Black Book of the American Left*. Yet another preoccupation is an organization I created nearly three decades ago, now called the David Horowitz Freedom Center. Communicating with my staff and board by email, I have been able to see to fruition several projects that bring a special satisfaction to me because they are the brainchildren of the young team I have hired, which will one day replace me.

Finally, there is the task that I do for the sheer pleasure, posting photos of beautiful equines on the Facebook page "Heart of a Horse." I receive help in this from my grandson Jules, whom I hired several years ago to assist me. With Jules' help I was able to post to the page every day I was in the hospital and have continued since returning home. The page is the public face of the Heart of a Horse Foundation, which April created to rescue horses six years ago, and which has proved a more trying challenge than we imagined when she began. It was created to promote love for horses, and in the course of time has attracted six hundred thousand viewers from Iceland to

Australia and Poland to Argentina. I derive a deep pleasure from posting the images on this page, which are provided by world-class equine photographers and artists. Whenever I sit down to it, which is usually in the early morning hours, I am drawn into a zone of calm and emerge refreshed for the more combative tasks ahead.

Complicating my optimism, which seems stubbornly innate, is the law of unintended consequences. The outlook that has seen me through predicaments that might daunt others can also be a kind of denial, leading to disasters like my hip surgery. Why was I so sure this operation would be as easy as the last one? Why did I pick this doctor off the Internet? Why didn't I conduct a diligent search for a surgeon who had consistently good results? The answer is I was too busy to be bothered with the details, too eager to get the procedure out of the way so I could get on with what I thought, mistakenly, were more important tasks; too confident that there was no danger in rushing ahead.

The hard knocks I have received throughout my life have never fully overridden my instincts and taught me the lessons they probably should have. Though chastened and somewhat more patient, I still catch myself attempting to barrel my way through the ordeal of this recovery as though the paralysis of my foot were something to endure and then be done with, like mumps.

I would not be candid if I did not admit that sometimes my optimism fails, and every now and then I run into a wall that nearly flattens me. The day April surprised me with what she called a "get-along scooter," one of those electrical go-carts you see the disabled go about on, I was forced to confront the dark side of the equation. Settling into the small vehicle and riding it up to the mailbox at the end of our driveway, I was suddenly overwhelmed by a vision of the emptiness that might lie before me—a state in which I was permanently crippled. Suddenly I was seeing a hypothetical future the way April did, black as a moonless night. Its futility overwhelmed me, and though I was able to hide them from others I could not hold back the tears.

Yet, in an ironic twist, the get-along scooter quickly proved a great convenience and even a pleasure. It allowed me to move around the house with ease, especially on days when the pain was so great I could not bear to put my foot on the floor. The very next time I took the cart outside for a spin, the boyish thrill of wheeling around the driveway at what felt like reckless speeds was exhilarating. April, who had a great time riding on it herself, said it was the first time in weeks she had seen me smile.

Faith

I try to honor April's wish not to thrust the darkest of my philosophical thoughts in her direction and to keep a lid on them when company is around. I do this not only because I love her but because her own vibrant conviction—that there is indeed a God, and a place beyond death which will unite us—provides our home with a comforting, inspirational light. Nor do I dismiss her faith out of hand. I am continually impressed by the unsolved mysteries of our existence and by our inability to understand them; how the inexplicable persists despite the advance of knowledge, and how it is all around us; how science, as advanced as it has become, has no clue as to how the universe was created and cannot explain how life began.

And there is, too, the undeniable fact that I am not without faith myself. I have lived my life as though my actions meant something and everything would add up in the end. Without thinking about it, I have had a conviction so deep it might have been encoded in my genes—that while there may not be providence in the fall of a sparrow, as Hamlet supposed, there is nonetheless a purpose to our ends. Though I cannot articulate it, this purpose causes me to conduct myself as though my wife, not I, were right.

A Near-Fatal Incident

Nine months ago, April was in a terrifying car accident that almost took her life. In an instant of dizziness at the wheel of her Ford truck, she slid onto the soft shoulder at a turn in the road, went through a flimsy fence and plunged down a steep incline. Within seconds she had glided off the rim of an agricultural drainage pipe and gone airborne before crashing into the steel of its inner wall. The impact at the end of her thirty-foot drop was so powerful that it demolished her truck, which was only a month old. The vehicle landed on its side, leaving her suspended by her seat belt, while the airbag failed to open, and her chest was slammed against the door. Only the steel of the cab, which remained intact, saved her.

She hung in midair for what seemed an interminable interval, passing in and out of consciousness. Fortunately it was rush hour, and commuters stopped their cars to descend the hillside to locate her and call the para-medics. When the rescue workers arrived, they pried her from the wreck and rushed her to the emergency room at Los Robles Hospital, and then to the Intensive Care Unit. There she was diagnosed with a contused heart, a collapsed lung, a broken clavicle, and six broken ribs.

I was alerted to what had happened by a call from Los Robles saying that my wife had been in an accident but was all right, by which they meant she was alive. I rushed to the hospital to see her hooked up to monitors and IV's with a drain in her side. She was in a semi-drugged state and kept repeating "I was airborne" and then "I was hanging almost upside down and screaming your name." I held her hand, told her I loved her and assured her she would be better soon, and tried to listen to the fragments of her tale. I was so glad to see her alive that I never quite took in the fact that I had nearly lost her, or that she was not out of danger yet.

Because of the contusion and collapsed lung, the hospital held her in the intensive care unit for over a week, while doctors kept coming in to monitor her condition and to worry about her heart. Her doctor told her, "You're lucky. If that contusion had filled your heart with blood, you would be dead. As it is, you can be thankful to be here." Every day I came to reas-sure her about her recovery and refused to consider the possibility of life without her. From its beginning, I dealt with this as I did bad news generally. She was going to be all right and nothing in our lives would change.

But, of course, they already had. I cannot adequately describe the phys-ical agonies she went through over the next nine months, or the after-effects of the injuries she is still dealing with even as she tries to nurse me back to health. The psychological impact of the accident was almost equal to the physical—the acute sense of being brushed by death, the exaggerated fears that ordinary incidents now provoked, the anxiety that she would never be able to raise her arm again and never ride the horses she loved.

This was all crystallized for her one day in her tack room at the upper end of our ranch when she picked her lunge whip off its hook and swung it weakly. There was no way she was going to be able to crack it, no way she could work her horses. She thought: "My body is broken and my life is changed forever." Feelings like this undermined her sense of normalcy and security. They haunted her for seven months, until the day came when the pain partially receded, her frozen shoulder began to thaw and, seemingly at that moment, my own trauma reversed our roles.

Mother's Day

When everyone finally arrived at the house, the sun was overhead. April and I had been hosting brunches almost every other Sunday for these same family members, so it was going to be hard to make Mother's Day seem special. But with three mothers present, we were ready to give it a try. April and Kim had made up a quiz for everybody's amusement. The first question was, "How did Mother's Day begin?" Cheri drew the question and surprised us by saying confidently that it began as a holiday to celebrate military mothers who had lost their sons in the First World War. Everyone agreed it was the right answer and complimented her. But in fact we were all wrong. According to Wikipedia, an antiwar activist named Anna Jarvis invented Mother's Day in 1905 to commemorate the death of her mother that same year. It had nothing to do with the military.

With everybody talking at once, the conversation quickly shifted to anecdotes of the sisters' childhood, as it usually did in this group, focusing on rivalries and jealousies they tried to carry into the present. Kim was claiming—and not for the first time—that Cheri had stabbed her brother Joe with a cooking fork when she was twelve and he was thirteen. Kim was only three at the time. Such a bone of contention was not implausible in a household that had been run by siblings whose parents were frequently absent, and often for long stretches. Although it had happened nearly fifty years ago, this particular quarrel was a regular feature of family gatherings thanks to Kim's obstinacy.

As it happened, about two weeks later on Memorial Day, Kim and April and I made a visit to brother Joe's house and then to the Queen of Heaven cemetery to lay flowers on the grave of their mother, Mary Pauline. Before departing for the cemetery, we asked Joe if Cheri had actually stabbed him. He smiled and then explained that she had been slapping him in a fight while he was cooking. He had been holding one of those large forks used to lift a roast, and one of her slaps had poked one of its prongs into her own forearm. Then he smiled again at the way the canard had had a life almost as long as theirs.

After the games and jibes at our house, we drove over to Sabor, a Mexican restaurant that was serving an elaborate buffet for the holiday. They also served gigantic Margaritas, one of which was sufficient to medicate my pain. Before it took its full effect, I hobbled over to the buffet with the aid of my cane, and with only one hand free to put the food on my plate was once again confronted with how helpless I was. Seeing my fluster, April came over and began gathering dishes for me. When I returned to our booth I found the conversation unchanged, as it would always be. After we had eaten as much as we could and said our goodbyes in the parking lot, we all were able to agree that this had been a good time, and we would do it again.

The Heart Has Reasons

It is odd that April can have such dark worries about my life expectancy but refuses to hear my reflections about the cosmic emptiness toward which we all are headed. It is all the more puzzling because I have no intention of letting these views of darkness influence my actions. If one were indeed to act on the opinion that we are nothing and nothing matters, one would end up a nihilist or sociopath. But I don't live by what I *think* the future may hold. My stoicism tells me to cherish what I have and hope to make the worlds within my reach a little better. I accept the contradiction— that my head should tell me one thing and my heart another—and listen to my heart.

I am not ashamed to admit that I don't know the answers to life's most important questions. I believe there is even an advantage to having a perspective that accepts the mysteries at the center of our being. An open mind can open new worlds.

I am going to relate two stories that will illustrate and perhaps even illuminate this observation. One story is about two people and a dog, and the other about an incident that happened to April and me, which science cannot explain. To forestall any unwarranted assumptions about my gullibility, let me begin by saying that I have never had experiences of the kind that lead others to claim with confidence that they have touched unseen worlds. When I am told of such experiences, I am inclined not to believe them, though I have seen enough acts of improbable intuition not to dismiss them entirely either.

The first story concerns my late daughter, Sarah. Or perhaps it does not concern her at all. That is one of the questions I cannot resolve, and it typifies the enigmas that surround the meanings of our lives.

I will not try to capture in a paragraph or two the amazing life of my daughter, which ended at the age of forty-three from the effects of a birth condition known as Turner Syndrome. My book about her life and death is called *A Cracking of the Heart,* which refers to the humbling one must go through to let knowledge in, but also to the effect of her passing on me. The first chapter of the book is titled "You Resurrect the Dead," which is a line from the Jewish funeral prayer to promote the ascension of the souls of the departed. Sarah believed in a resurrection of the spirit, and had found such a concept, called "a rolling of the souls," in Judaism. She was not afraid of death and was in this, as in all she did, a model for the rest of us.

Two days before the incident I am about to relate, April was rummaging among the shelves in my office, searching for a copy of *A Cracking of the Heart* to give to her sister. When she found it, she handed it to her, and as she did so two black-and-white photographs fell from between the pages. One was a picture of Sarah, still an infant, sitting on the grass in our backyard in England, where she was born. The other was a picture of me as a young father. When the two women saw the photos fall from the book, they gasped, perhaps not realizing that it was I who had put them there.

Two days later April awoke in the early morning hours and went to the adjacent bedroom so that she could retrieve some of the sleep she had lost because of the snoring of our three Chihuahuas and me. When she was settled in the other room, she fell into a deep dream state in which she suddenly saw Sarah's face, and was then bathed in such a warm light that she felt utterly at peace. When she awoke, she came to me and told me about her dream. By then it was six in the morning, and I was sitting up staring at my computer where a photo of Sarah had suddenly come up on the screen. When April looked at it and saw how sad I was, she said, "Let's get out into the morning air, and while we're at let's find a place to eat."

Without much thinking about it, we agreed to have breakfast at a Jewish deli in a local strip mall where we had eaten before. We sat down on their wooden chairs and ordered matzo ball soup and potato latkes. While we were waiting for our orders, we took some plastic plates and metal utensils from a general counter and put them on our table. April's soup came first and I availed myself of one of her bagel crusts and began opening a small package of marmalade with the idea of applying it to the bread. But at that moment, in the swiftest motion and without any warning, my plastic plate lifted off the table and struck me in the lower chest.

We both saw and were taken aback by this impossible movement. "What just happened?" April said, and then asked me if I thought it was

Sarah trying to contact me. Later when we were in the car, she asked me again. She remembers me assenting but I can't imagine I did. On the other hand, I did toy with the idea of seeing Sarah again and an immense wave of pleasure swept over me when I did. But it didn't alter my view that my daughter was gone.

There was no way I could explain what had happened. No door was open to allow a sudden gust of wind to blow the plate into my chest. The table was anchored by a heavy metal base. What we both saw was inexplicable. April would not let go of the incident. Several times she brought up the episodes that had put Sarah's energy into our lives: the book and photos, her dream, the fact that I had been thinking about Sarah too. But although I was at a loss to explain what had happened, and even though I wanted the cause to be Sarah and continued to mentally explore the happy possibilities if it were, I could not make myself believe.

If someone else told me this story, I would reject it out of hand, probably with a roll of the eyes. Plates do not just fly off tables. But it happened to me. Therefore, I am forced to file it as one of those mysteries that I cannot explain. And, of course, each of us has encountered the inexplicable at some point, and probably dismissed it as something that science could explain if called upon to do so. But there are probably an equally large number of people like April who don't dismiss these experiences, who resurrect the dead. I am grateful to her because her belief brought my daughter close to me and set me to thinking about her and wondering if I would ever see her again.

I do not pretend to understand how the chemistry between April and me works, but it has. Just as I have brought her into my worlds, she has taken me on journeys I would never have embarked on if we hadn't met. I would never have owned a dog, for example, if she had not dropped one on my doorstep, and then another and another. People whose hearts are not open to animals could never understand how these acquisitions came to affect me. One of my friends is a retired attorney named Carl, a smart man but overly cerebral. When the dikes broke during Hurricane Katrina and thousands of people were threatened with drowning, Carl said to me, "Can you believe that there are people in the middle of this flood who won't get out because they don't want to leave their pets behind?" Carl said this with a smile big enough to let me know he thought such behavior absurd. But to a dog person it is Carl's attitude that is absurd. Someone like Carl could never understand what these relationships bring to us, or the feelings that would make it difficult if not impossible to leave our companions behind.

The short life-span of canines is one of the reasons they affect our thoughts and feelings so deeply. They make us aware of the cycle of time that frames our own stay. We love them, they are integral to our lives, and then they are gone. And this brings me to my second story.

At Christmastime two and a half years ago, April and I were out for a drive. We had gone to Calabasas to have lunch and were heading north again back home. April was at the wheel and began taking roads that steered us somewhat out of our way and then to the Agoura Hills animal shelter. This was a partially hidden complex of buildings, constructed unceremoniously with large blocks of concrete painted grey. Later she observed that she had passed this complex many times before and never gone in. The only way she could describe what had come over her on this trip was that she felt as though someone was waiting for her.

As you would expect, the pound was an indescribably sad place. There were maybe seventy dogs, some young and spirited, some old and passive, all waiting for someone to pick them up, and all destined to be put down if no one showed up to do so. The woman who greeted us was friendly and solicitous. As she led us through the holding pens, she explained that this was the final stop for the dogs that animal control had captured. They had all come from other facilities, where no one had adopted them. If they weren't taken this time, within a few weeks they would be put down.

April asked the lady to show us the ones who were running out of time. In the very first stall she took us to, there was a coffee-brown Chihuahua with very short legs, a white bib at her throat and white accents over her eyes. The plate on the stall said her name was "Coco," and the lady told us they thought she was thirteen years old. Coco was standing on her hind legs and pressing her little body against the cage netting, and wagging her tail as though she and April knew each other. The tip of her tongue, hung from the side of her mouth where some teeth were missing, giving her a goofy look. April commented later that her little black eyes called out in a way that said, "Please take me. I may be old but I'm a very good girl." To this imagined appeal, April replied, "Hello, Coco, you have a silly little tongue," and got the goofy look back.

When April reached into the cage and picked the dog up she detected a putrid odor coming from Coco's mouth indicating it was infected, a

common and serious issue for Chihuahuas. The woman told her that Coco
had been found along with a pack of other dogs in a house in Belmont,
which they suspected was a breeding kennel. The owner had died and the
dogs were removed to another shelter where they were held for several
months. No one had taken Coco, so she was shipped to Agoura.

It was obvious why Coco would be used for breeding Chihuahua puppies. Her markings were beautiful, her coat sable-like and her expression
precious. She had a spirit that soared over her circumstances. Instead of
cowering in a corner of her cage at the shelter, she had rushed to the front,
stood on her hind legs, and tried to catch our attention. It was also clear
from the decaying state of her teeth that no one had looked after her health
for years, probably forever. Her beautiful coat had been marred by two large
tooth-marks on her rump, probably the result of an attack by a bigger dog.
The fur that had overgrown them was gray rather than brown and looked
like splotches on her otherwise perfect coat. Perhaps it was also her goofy
tongue-drag that spoiled the image for some prospective adopters, causing
them to leave her behind.

For us, it was Coco's flair sealed the deal. As April described it to me
later, when she saw Coco run to the front of her cage it was as if she was
saying, "Hey *me*, adopt *me*. I have lots of love for you, and if you look at me
with kinder eyes you'll see how cute I am." Of course dogs don't talk. But
neither do we know how they think or what they are trying to communicate. Whatever the cause, a bond was struck between April and Coco that
was to be the little dog's salvation.

We asked the woman to open the cage, and Coco came right over. April
picked her up, gave her a kiss and said, "Boy, Coco, your mouth smells really
bad." She put her fingers on either side of Coco's jaw and opened it and said,
"Oh my God, your teeth are discolored and infected. That must really hurt.
I am going to take you to the vet right away." After paying our fifty-dollar
pound fee, that is just what we did. As soon as we left the building, April
dialed her friend who was a large-animal vet. He told her an infection such
as she was describing could easily be fatal and advised her to take Coco
directly to a dog vet he knew in Ventura.

The vet's name was Lori, and after inspecting Coco, she said it was the
worst mouth infection she had ever seen. There was a hole in Coco's nasal
cavity, her jawbone was eaten away and her teeth were so far gone that if
she didn't have immediate surgery to remove them the infection would

most certainly kill her. "I can't imagine the pain this dog has been in," Lori said. "Do anything it takes to save her," April replied.

The operation took four hours and cost a thousand dollars, which gave me a little jolt. But since Coco was ours, I could hardly deny her the attention that would keep her alive. Coco's teeth were so rotten that they crumbled when Lori began to remove them. Eventually, she had to take out all but two and sew up the hole in Coco's nasal cavity. When it was over, Lori told April that if she had brought her in a little later it would have been too late. As it was, she was going to be fine. April picked Coco up and kissed her all over, and said, "Coco, I'm your new mommy, and now I'm going to take you home."

Coco proved to be an exceptional addition to our household. Despite her age, she was full of curiosity and energy, warbling and making other amusing sounds as she explored her new home. At night, she immediately took a place in our bed near our heads, and nestled up close to me so I could stroke her fur until one of us fell asleep. Coco also had a melodramatic growl, which was hilarious to us but intimidated all the other animals, including Winnie, the large Bernese mountain dog. We wondered whether the drama queen was an inborn personality or had developed out of the hard life she had lived in the breeding mill and the battles she had been forced to fight in order to survive. We worried about her age and what we had been told was her enlarged heart. We didn't know if she had only months to live.

In the event, she fooled us all. She ran with the pack, sometimes tumbling over herself when she tried with her little legs to keep up with the larger dogs. She was relentless about getting the most out of life, setting an example for everyone else. Her antics amused all who encountered her, and it could be said that with all the love that was showered on her these last years were truly golden. Recalling them afterwards gave April and me a tremendous lift every time we thought of how a fortuitous stop along the way had given Coco a new life, and us a new companion.

When we took her in, we hoped that Coco would go on at least for a year, and when she passed that milestone we came to wish that she would live forever. But as she neared the end of the second year she was struck by an illness the vet never quite identified. It put her in intense pain that did not respond to the drugs the vet provided. When the pain continued for weeks, so that she no longer ran in the yard but crawled under the furniture, hiding as animals do when they are ready to die, we visited the vet again to take her out of her misery. The vet had a place for the euthanasia, which she called the Rainbow Room. I have a vivid image of Coco cradled in the vet's arms, looking at me with almost a wink of peace as the drug took her out of her pain and she slipped away from us for good.

We buried her in a little graveyard along the outer fence near the upper yard where our horse arena and stables are located. The lone occupant of the gravesite until then was our loveable Winnie, who was with us for nine years and whom we had put to sleep in the same Rainbow Room a few months earlier. She had lost the use of her legs and any quality of life. It was as terrible to see this sweet and loving dog in such pain as it was to lose her. April laid hearts and flowers at the graves and set two kneeling angels to watch over them.

You can call these feelings sentimental, or the intuitions and compassion that bonded Coco to us delusional. Dogs don't talk, and Coco's "thoughts" were likely what April projected onto her. But what of it? Whatever the source of the feelings that had created the bond, they had led to great pleasure for us and a new life for Coco. How would a stark "realism" affect the passion to rescue little creatures like Coco and share the unforgettable lives they give us? In the end, all that really matters is the presence of a passion, born of whatever faith will foster it, that inspires one creature to step forward to save the little life of another, and to give and receive the pleasure and happiness that come from such a bond.

The Paradoxes of Youth

I conceived this memoir as a meditation on age and, as a result, am in danger of obscuring the work of younger years when I was nurturing a generation that would one day replace me. As we all grow older there is a bittersweet quality to parenthood and to the reflections on days that are past. In a perverse way our children's lives become a measure of our own decline as their exciting steps lead to a future without us.

On Mother's Day my thoughts turned to April's twenty-eight-year-old son, Jon Jason (or Jon J, as we call him), who could not be present, and to what his upbringing reflected about his mother. From the year of Jon's birth, April found herself on her own, a single mother working a full-time job to support them both. Her mother, who had been absent for long stretches of

April's childhood, was home for Jon's, and took care of him daily from the end of school until his mother returned from her job doing skin care in a plastic surgeon's office. Although April had never gone to college herself, she recognized the intelligence of her son and encouraged high ambitions for him. She put him in a Montessori school and supplied him with the books he wanted, and encouraged his interests, which from an early age were scientific. And she took care to give him the stability and security in his young life that she had lacked in her own.

One of the first things that made me realize that April was someone I could trust in marriage was, paradoxically, the way she hid Jon's existence from me for months after we began seeing each other. I was so impressed by this that I wrote about it when I told the story of our romance in *The End of Time*, pointing out that her concern to protect her child's love told me how careful she would be with mine.

Jon was eight when I met him, a sensitive, shy boy and, as time proved, an exceptionally good son. I don't remember a day in the twenty years we have known each other that I had cause to raise my voice or speak a word in anger to him. His biological father, "Big Jon," is a craftsman who builds custom cars and trucks for journeymen and municipal governments. I quickly saw that he had imparted to his son a respect for work and a sense of integrity. Over time Big Jon showed his son the love he had found so hard to give to their infant family at the beginning.

However, it was five years before Big Jon agreed to meet or even talk to me. This was because April's brother Patrick had planted poisonous thoughts in his head. *He's going to make your son a Jew and a Black Panther and get him killed.* These canards kept Big Jon away until the thirteenth birthday party April and I held for his son at a local eatery. The atmosphere between us was cool at first, but then I made a point of letting him know that I admired the good work ethic and the honesty he had instilled in his son. I would always respect, I said, the fact that Jon was *his* son, and would always welcome him in our home. From that moment the tension between us disappeared, and over the next fourteen years we became better and better friends, until at Jon's wedding on our back lawn in 2012, Big Jon and I hugged each other with tears in our eyes.

Although April and I were passionate about each other within months of our meeting, it took two years of wooing to get her to move in with me, and another two before we were married. This caution on her part was the perfect antidote to my reckless disregard, which had caused me such trouble, including two absurd marriages whose embarrassing details I have noted in *Radical Son*. The first was actually agreed to within six weeks of my meeting the prospective bride. Not surprisingly it was over within three months of the wedding vows. April put restraints on this rashness, which I had confused with adventurousness. She has provided a welcome discipline to such impulses ever since.

I had never said a political word to Jon J, whom I had only recently met, when April showed me a "Letter to Santa" he had written as an exercise in his Montessori school. This was during the Clinton administration and its sexual scandals.

Dear Santa,
I wish I had these things. I wish I had a new president. I wish that people would help themselves. I wish that people would respect America. I wish that people would think twice before having baby's [sic] that they cannot love and care for. I wish that all Americans, black, white and brown would be proud to be Americans together as one. I wish that I could have a bike. And new stuff for my computer.
Love,
Jon J

I sent the letter to Rush Limbaugh who read it on air, causing a little stir of pride in the family.

In 1996, the three of us moved into a fixer-upper in the Pacific Palisades. At first Jon J didn't want to move in because he was scared of the big hole that our renovations had temporarily left in the living room floor. We tried to address his insecurity by having an artist paint a mural of an astronaut and spaceship on his bedroom wall. It proved to be the initial step in winning him over. For the first two weeks in our new home he insisted that April sleep in his bed until one night, as he became more comfortable with his new life, he said to her, "You don't have to sleep with me anymore. You should be sleeping with David."

Jon was now in the fifth grade and facing life in a new school. Although it was a charter elementary school in an upscale neighborhood, it had the same problems as schools everywhere. The schoolyard was terrorized by a bully who systematically singled out kids in the yard for torment. Finally, Jon's turn came. For days the bully taunted and jabbed at Jon, who was still very shy but physically much bigger. When the day came that this troubled youngster decided to attack, instead of pummeling him and paying him back for the blows he had inflicted, Jon just held him down until the adults came over and pulled them apart. Later he explained to his mother that he didn't want to hurt him. Jon was just that kind of kid.

April was a force for stability and promise in her son's life. She never allowed him to get down on himself or set his sights low, and she shone a constant light of love on him. My own mother had stood behind me much as April stood behind Jon but could not handle the intensity of feeling contained in the word "love." As a result it was mostly absent from the Horowitz household. Not so from April's. The son was constantly washed in his mother's affection. I had never witnessed so much frank exchange between a mother and her child before. I am sure that this played a role in inspiring his compassion for others and in encouraging him to have dreams and pursue them. I am sure that it planted in him the most important confidence of all—that he had the power to make his dreams become real.

But this confidence did not flower overnight. There was a daunting shyness in him that I took it upon myself to help him overcome by including kids from the local playground in basketball games I played with him. The most peculiar manifestations of the anxieties that festered inside him were severe stomach pains, which caused him to throw up nearly every day he had to go to school or when he had an exam. It was particularly hard to fathom because he was such a good student. Nonetheless, for as long as these symptoms persisted, which was until he entered college, he was only a good student, not the extraordinary one he became.

As he grew older, Jon became a somewhat spiritual person, like his mother. But in his case it had an institutional dimension as well. We had pulled him from a disastrous public middle school and put him in a Lutheran one. When he was ready for high school we enrolled him in Saint Monica's, a Catholic school where the religious instruction was Jesuitical and also Marxist. At Saint Monica's John came under the influence of a benevolent priest who recognized his talents and converted him to Catholicism. He went on to Loyola Marymount University, another Jesuit school, where he majored in biology and the level of his studies became too erudite for me to follow.

During these years, it was one of my great pleasures to engage Jon in intellectual conversation and try to offer guidance drawn from what had suddenly become a considerable accumulation of life experience. The most important advice I ever gave him, I think, was that he had to look after himself, because no one else would, which sounds a lot colder than it is. No matter how dearly we loved him, we could not live his life for him. We could never keep abreast of all the details of what was going on in his world and affecting him. In the end he was going to have to make the crucial assessments and decisions for himself. I have no idea whether this advice ever made an impression, but I was gratified that as he grew older and was faced with difficult decisions about what graduate school to apply to and what career to pursue—decisions about which I was in no position to make informed judgments—he took hold of them like a man and made them himself.

During these years, I was writing my philosophical memoirs about mortality and faith with which Jon was familiar. Consequently, we had occasion to explore some of these questions together, which gave me a chance to find out what he thought. I knew that he had a sober attitude toward the church and its fallibility, and a healthy concern about the corruption to which even "men of God" were prone. It was the time of the molestation revelations in the Catholic Church, where priests who preyed on young boys were protected at the highest ecclesiastical levels, revealing the moral rot that is endemic to human institutions and reminding us that, in the end, *we* are the problem (which is a prominent theme of my writings). For Jon, faith was a personal matter rather than an institutional one. He attended church regularly and participated in its social activities. But in the matter of belief he was and would always be his own man.

In June 2009, Jon graduated from Loyola Marymount. That Father's Day he gave me a card that provided me all the satisfaction for the years we spent together that I could ever wish for. It was one of those corny greeting cards with a cover that said "Dad, You Rock." But it was the words inside that got to me: "From the beginning of our relationship some sixteen years ago, you instilled values in me that I am forever grateful for. You helped show me how to be a great husband with the support and unfailing love you gave my mother throughout your marriage. You exposed me to the beauties of classical music, opera and literature, as well as encouraged me in my intellectual pursuits. Most importantly, you did all of this happily and with warmth and love. I may not be your son by blood, but you have loved me like one of your own."

Jon was admitted into the master's program at UCLA with a research appointment that helped finance his education; and in 2012 was awarded a Master of Science degree in microbiology, immunology and molecular genetics, with a thesis titled "Polarization of the endothelium governs monocyte differentiation and function." There was no way I could have helped him along this path, which was beyond my intellectual reach. I had the same experience with my biological sons, Jonathan and Ben, and my daughter Anne. There was a time when I had a sense of where they were going and could maybe give them advice along the way. Then, with such swiftness that I didn't see it coming, there came a moment when their knowledge and careers accelerated at light speed and left me in another building with my nose pressed against the glass.

It was the crossing of a Rubicon in our relationships. I was no longer their mentor, no longer drawing them out of their shyness, worrying about the directions they were taking. No longer a parent in the sense I had once been. A whole world that had been mine was gone. Now they were independent, and my relationship with them was as an equal, in their areas of expertise a pupil at best. Being a parent is an awesome power and responsibility, but my tide had run out. I was now a helpmate with experience to share. There was satisfaction in that, but it was also a diminishment, as great as, or even greater than the one apparent in the weakening sinews of my aging frame.

While he was still at Loyola Marymount, Jon met a young Filipina woman named Kathleen Alejandro and fell in love with her. Their engagement lasted through all of Jon's years in graduate school until September 2012, when they finally tied the knot. April and I offered them our house for the wedding, but by the time April finished re-landscaping the half-acre that was our back lawn, filling it with rose bushes, and building a gazebo to serve as a chapel, it was more accurate to say that we offered them a new addition to our house. When the day came and the guests arrived two hundred strong, it proved to be a memorable event. Jon had strung lights through our trees, giving the evening celebration a magical air. All the families and guests danced on a floor that was laid out on the lawn. If I live to be a hundred (as April insists I must) I don't think I will ever see its like again.

Jon had won a competition to be among twenty students who would attend the University of Colorado as both an M.D. and Ph.D. candidate

("MudPhuds" as they were called), with the National Institutes of Health funding his education and support for the six years it would take. It was a long way from the broken home he had come from.

In his first year in the program he was told to come up with a research project that could be submitted to the NIH or some other funding agency. This was merely an exercise for new students and not for actual submission. Jon had done most of his graduate work in immunology and was aware of the link between psoriasis and cardiovascular disease. His proposal was a research project to identify the gene that linked the two diseases and open the door to a way to diminish the cardiovascular consequences for psoriasis sufferers.

Jon looked at his detailed research project and thought that it could and should be funded. So he sent his paper to a husband-and-wife team on the Colorado faculty who were heading a large research program on the link between psoriasis and heart disease. They agreed with him, submitted the proposal to a funding agency, and offered to make him the head of the research project he had designed.

Jon told us this in a phone call a week before our Mother's Day gathering. I was immediately interested in his project because five years earlier I had had an angina. My "widow-maker's artery" was almost completely clogged, yet I had no history of heart disease in my family and for years had been on Lipitor, the drug that controls cholesterol. But I did have psoriasis, and this link seemed now to explain it.

Jon's call from a distant location underscored the irony of families. Your children are dependent on you and inseparable, and then one day they are grown and largely gone. April shed many tears when Jon went off with his bride to explore their new horizons. She felt she was losing a big part of her life and her identity as a mother. But at the same time there were also tears of joy at what a remarkable young man her baby had become.

Adventures With the Foot

While I was still in the hospital after the botched operation, a man came to my bedside and took a mold of my calf and foot. Days later an AFO boot was delivered to me. AFO stands for "ankle foot orthosis," and the idea is that this hard plastic boot will brace the ankle and also raise the foot the paralysis has dropped. When I tried it out in the hospital, it worked pretty well. But then a day came when it caused me such unbearable pain that I had to hop around and pull it off. After this experience, I switched to the clunky therapeutic boot that April had brought home when she broke her navicular bone. You see skiers with these boots all the time. The clunky boot was serviceable for a while, but then I began to get medical advice that I needed to wear the AFO because it is designed for patients with drop foot. The advice came first from a nurse who didn't have much experience with the problem. But then I went to a podiatrist who insisted that I wear it. If your AFO hurts, he said, it needs an adjustment. You must go to the manufacturer and they will do it.

So I called the hospital and found the manufacturer and made an appointment with a seemingly knowledgeable man who took my AFO and adjusted it. He put a pad in the arch and reshaped it a bit, and put it back on my foot. Again, the pain was excruciating and I had to take it off immediately. He said, "You are suffering from neuropathic pain. It's not the boot. It's you." When someone with expertise is so decisive you don't want to challenge him, and I didn't, even though I had my doubts. I returned home and put on the therapeutic boot, and my doubts were confirmed. I experienced nothing like the pain from the AFO. I could walk with the clunky boot, so I did.

It seemed at the time as though I had a medical appointment every day. Shortly after my unsuccessful visit to the AFO maker, I had an appointment with Dr. Vimal Lala who had an Advanced Pain Medical Group. On my way to see Dr. Lala, I began to visualize a sandal that would keep my foot close to the ground, and unlike the boot would be flexible. At this point, I wanted to feel the ground because I sensed that my foot was actually coming back. It had been two months since my operation, and I had been trying to move my toes for weeks. Then one day they did move, if only a few millimeters. I kept on trying to flex them, until a day came when I could move my whole foot, and move it up and down, and the toes as well. I no longer had drop foot, or if I did my case was much improved.

I showed Dr. Lala my foot and the movement I had achieved and explained my problem with the boot pain. Dr. Lala practically pounced on the reference to the AFO. I shouldn't be wearing any therapeutic boot, he said, and certainly not an AFO. These boots were braces for people with broken bones. What I needed was to restore the muscles and nerves that were not working. Ideally, I should be walking around barefoot.

On hearing these words, my desire for a flexible footwear became irresistible, and with April as my escort and the get-along scooter as my transportation, I went to the mall and bought a pair of leather sandals that were just about perfect. When I put them on I felt I was walking on air. Hobbling on air would be more precise. My foot was still weak and also swollen, which caused enough pain, especially in the morning when I woke up, to keep me on an opioid—as it happens, Percocets—for the early part of the day.

At this juncture April began oiling and massaging the damaged limb. It was an idea suggested by the podiatrist, who had his assistant do just that. Despite the odd nerve reactions in my foot, which felt uncomfortably electric, these manipulations felt good enough that I asked April if she would do it regularly for me. We figured that the lymph was causing the painful swelling. April had had a case of lymphedema, so she knew what she had to do to bring the swelling down. The results were dramatic. The swelling came down, and for the first time in months I could see veins on the top of my foot, which had begun to look like an actual foot again. The movement I could achieve with it was now even greater than before.

Just How Much She Loved Me

Just as this partial recovery was taking place, I was faced with a dilemma that put me in conflict with my wife. We both found this situation particularly difficult because during our convalescences our passion for each other had risen to such a high pitch. I had become so dependent on her, and she worked so tirelessly and lovingly on my behalf as both nurse and caregiver, that friction between us was even more painful than normally.

An event was coming up on the calendar—a dinner and discussion in a hotel suite followed by an all-day meeting to which I had been invited. It would be my first venture into the outside world in the two months since my operation. I wanted very much to go to this meeting, but April was against it. She felt I was not physically ready, and under her pressure I canceled it. But then I received a call from Dr. Bob Shillman, the sponsor of the meeting and a member of the executive committee of my board, urging me to go. I was deeply committed to the purposes of the meeting and didn't want to let Bob down. I also felt that it would be psychologically important for my recovery if I went. So I raised the issue with April again, but she was still opposed. She was unmoved in her conviction that I was not ready for such exertions and would suffer a setback if I went. She was also concerned about how I would look to the others attending, given the amount of medication I was taking, and worried that it would damage me if I didn't do well. And she was concerned that under the stress I might fall and injure myself, not an unreasonable concern given how wobbly I became when tired.

The event was a private meeting of five leaders of organizations who were dedicated to combating the anti-Semitic campaign that had been launched on college campuses by front groups for terrorist organizations. The goal of these organizations was the destruction of the Jewish state and the extermination of its Jews, and they were making disturbing progress. It was, in fact, remarkable how these groups had received the tacit support of college administrators and become a prominent and intimidating force on American campuses through the efforts of the Muslim Students Association, an arm of the Muslim Brotherhood, and Students for Justice in Palestine, an offshoot of the terrorist organization Hamas.

These Islamist groups had teamed up with the anti-Semitic left and were conducting anti-Israel demonstrations across the country, spreading two genocidal lies that the uninformed found persuasive. The first was that the Jews had stolen Arab land to create the state of Israel. The second was that Israel was not a democracy but an "apartheid" state. In fact, Israel, along with Syria, Lebanon, Jordan, and Iraq, were all created from land that had belonged to the Turks—who were not Arabs—for four hundred years previously. In other words, the Arabs had a weaker claim on the land around the Jordan than the Indians had on the United States. Equally malicious was the lie that Israel was an "apartheid state." Israel is actually the only state in the Middle East that is tolerant toward its minorities. Although the claim was laughable, its effect on the ignorant was to delegitimize Israel and make it easier for the terrorist armies of Fatah, Hamas, and Iran to destroy the Jewish state.

I was not a Zionist and had never been to Israel, but I believed Israel's tiny democracy was the frontline state in the war that Islamic-Nazis had declared against the West. Their special message for the Jews: In the name of Allah, we will exterminate you. Each year for several years my Freedom Center had conducted campaigns on more than a hundred campuses to combat these malignant forces, which had the protection not only of college administrators but also the Jewish groups on campus—in particular Hillel, which was afraid to offend Muslims and was extending them an ecumenical olive branch by attacking their critics.

April was familiar with my efforts but was not swayed from her view that I should not attend the meeting. I had been engaged in political battles forever, and one meeting was not going to change the world. She continued to fear for my health and for my public persona. She also feared for my safety and hers. The left had put itself in the service of the Islamist holy war and was personally vicious toward me. Because I opposed them, they had identified me as "the godfather of the anti-Muslim movement." Calling opponents of Jew-haters and terrorists "anti-Muslim" is a typical leftist tactic. The Southern Poverty Law Center, which was responsible for this libel, couldn't (and didn't) point to a single statement among the millions of words I had written and uttered (and which were also captured on videos) that could remotely be described as "anti-Muslim."

Another factor in April's thinking, which went unmentioned, was that the Islamists I opposed were terrorists, supported by the left, and no one could dismiss the possibility they would seek retribution for my stands. We had always lived with this possibility, first from the Black Panthers and now from the Islamists. But in the end, despite her fears and despite her concerns about my health, she saw how much I wanted to go, and she agreed to take me to the Century Plaza Hotel, an hour's drive from our home, and stay with me for the times I needed her. Not for the first time in our embattled life together, I was grateful for her support.

Then, as luck would have it, on the day of the meeting I had a serious mishap. I was in the bathroom shaving and my feet were bare. As I was exiting the room I stubbed the big toe of my good foot on the doorsill and lost my balance. As I was falling, I grabbed for something to stabilize me, but it turned out to be the handle of an upright vacuum cleaner, which immediately folded under my weight, and I went tumbling down. During the fall, I managed to flip myself over to my right side, protecting my injured foot and the new hip, as I went down with a thud. Our cleaning lady, who was close by, called out in horror to April just as I uttered the words "Don't tell my wife." Soon everybody was standing over me, while I tried to explain that my left leg was okay, even as I felt a pain in the calf, and I could see no one believed me.

I was able to rest for a few hours until the pain subsided, although my big toe continued to throb and I had a tender bruise on my right buttock. I told April as firmly as I could manage that I still wanted to go, and disturbed as she was by what had happened, she consented. We put the get-along scooter in the bed of the black Ford F-150 I had bought her after her accident and got into the cab. But as soon as we started driving I could see that she was disturbed, although the apparent focus of her distress was the vehicle rather than me. We had hardly left the driveway when she noticed a message on her dashboard that said "Off Road," indicating that the truck was in four-wheel-drive mode. She couldn't stop fretting about this as we drove down the Santa Rosa Road. Would the car break down if we drove it on the freeway? Would the engine be ruined? Would it explode?

As she turned the truck onto Moorpark Road, the very stretch of highway where she had had her accident, she became so panicked that she began to ask if we should go back and get my car. I told her to stop the truck and call the Ford dealership and ask them about the message. The service manager told her to look for a toggle switch and move it back to the two-wheel mode, but she couldn't locate the switch. He then assured her that she could use the four-wheel drive for the freeway and it would just mean greater wear on the tires and poorer gas mileage. When she had a chance, she could take the truck to any Ford dealer and they would fix the problem. And so she decided to push on.

But as she drove and we talked I could see that she was still agitated and it was getting worse. Finally it poured out of her. "You are reckless and you are not aware of how reckless you are. When you drive the get-along you bump into things. The other day you almost ran over a child in the mall. Even when you are walking you don't notice how wobbly you are, and how you bump into people." As she unloaded on me, it was not her words that I focused on so much as her expression, the anguish in her voice and the fear in her eyes. "I'm so frightened for you," she said. She was shaking and in tears. "You don't realize what you do." She didn't have to articulate the next words because I knew what was coming: "You are thinking only of yourself. You don't consider what you put me through."

I may be dense and in denial sometimes, but I am a feeling person, and I love this woman with a fierce passion. It didn't take a heartbeat to see what I had done. It was not just the bravado, which had made me want to ignore my drugged and crippled state, drive a little recklessly on the scooter, and take on more than I should. It was my life that was pressing down on her. This was a person who had not been brought up to do battle in the world of political savagery that she had inadvertently entered when she fell in love with me. As a result of her injuries she was in physical pain herself and psychologically raw. I could not dismiss what she had said. I did bump into walls and people. Because of the drugs I was taking I was not myself, but pretended I was. I did have enemies who hated me enough to want to see me dead. And I had not taken her anxieties or her warnings seriously enough. She knew how much my political causes meant to me, and because she loved me, she had been ready to put herself through hell to support me. She was driving me to the meeting to which she did not want me to go, and to which I could not have driven myself. She was fighting through her fears because she wanted me to be who I was. She loved me that much. It did not matter if her fears were fully justified. It mattered how she felt. It was about how at this moment what I was doing was torturing her, and I had to man up to it.

I was silent as these thoughts ran through my head, reflecting on how this moment had been repeated many times in the twenty years our destinies had been tied together. I thought of how she had stood by me through crises and trials when others might not. How she helped me to live a life she would never have chosen for herself. As we reached the hotel room, I let the dam break. I told her how deeply sorry I was for putting her through this, how much I appreciated what she had done, and that I would try to be more attentive to her concerns. The tears were running down my cheeks as I thanked her for what she was doing for me, and how appreciative I was at her understanding that while I could try to change some things, I could not change who I was, and how grateful I was that she loved and supported me anyway.

We lay in each other's arms in the hotel room for a while. My words had calmed her, and her concern was now for me and for how I would pull myself together for the meeting. She didn't want me in tears, didn't want me feeling guilty. She just wanted us to be one and at peace. And then it was time for me to go upstairs, where the meeting was about to begin. We had planned that she would spend the night with me at the hotel and help me to get ready in the morning. Then she would go back home to take care of the animals and maybe oversee some of the construction projects she had undertaken around the house. She would return in the evening to pick me up.

I mounted the get-along scooter, which saved me from having to hobble down the long halls with my cane. When I arrived at the meeting everyone was solicitous, as people usually are with someone in my condition, and we began our talks. I felt my powers returning as I spoke, mindful about slurring my words (as April had cautioned me) and trying to appear less injured than I was. The next day I made it through the all-day meeting, gratified by the influence I was able to exert and surprised by the stamina my body had shown.

When the meeting concluded I returned to the room, and April and I ordered room service and a salmon dinner, with capers for her. The time we had spent together had been good for us both. She was pleased that things had gone well at the meeting and that I had come through it better than she feared I would. We were both somewhat chastened and happy to be on track again. I knew I could never eliminate her concerns about me or the pressures my life brought to bear on her. But I was certainly going to try harder to do just that.

A Harrowing Call

On Mother's Day, when we were all gathered, I received a phone call from Elissa, the mother of my children. Elissa and I were married for nineteen years and have been divorced for thirty-six, but we have remained connected—first through our children and grandchildren and then as two people who have cared deeply for each other through life's trials, particularly the untimely death of our daughter Sarah.

When I answered the call, Elissa told me that our oldest son Jonathan, who was only fifty-three, had just had a heart attack and was in intensive care. It was hard for me to hear her say, "I feel like I've been a bad mother. I'm not supposed to outlive my children." Then she corrected herself—"But Jon's not dying." Yet she, more than anyone else in the family, understood that we all are.

Fortunately Jonathan's episode was not as serious as we feared, and he was able to leave the hospital within a day or two. As soon as I learned of his condition, I attempted to phone him to see how he was doing, but I couldn't find the hospital he was in and had to wait a day to reach him. I left a message for Renee, the woman he had lived with and loved for twenty-five years, and soon heard back that he was doing all right. Even before I received this news I called my other son, Ben, who was in Israel on business. Jon and he were very close. Ben had become a man of considerable influence, and my shortsightedness in choosing an orthopedic surgeon was weighing on me. I didn't want Jon taking any chances, so I asked Ben to see if he could get him a good cardiologist. I knew he would have contacts at Columbia University Medical Center because he had recently been made a trustee of the school and his mentor and friend Bill Campbell was chairman of the board. In a few days, Ben was able to get the head of the Columbia Medical Center to call Jon and fix him up with excellent care.

When I finally spoke to my son, I was much relieved. The doctors had performed an angiogram and inserted a stent, just as they had in my case. I told him of my own experience and not to worry, he was going to be all right. There was a little anxiety in his voice, but over the next few days, the cheerful take-it-in-stride character I knew so well was back. And I also learned that he had put himself on a dietary regimen that would help his condition, and that he had already lost weight, and that relieved me too.

My Musical Son

Years before this episode, my labors in the vineyard of parenthood had been upended by the crime that exploded my political faith. Perhaps there were other forces that would have ended my marriage, but the depression that then overtook me and lingered for seven long years sealed its fate. My divorce from Elissa in 1978 was a continental divide in my life and, to a lesser extent, in my relations with my children. Jonathan was seventeen when the marriage unraveled and well on his independent way. But the other three were still at home. I stayed close by and tried to maintain the family whose bonds I had broken, but a significant part of my authority was gone, and there were many times in the years that followed when I feared I might lose my children. They never turned their backs on me, but an internal space opened up where we would meet as strangers. It would be a space that without their permission I could not cross.

Elissa and I always knew that our first child had a musical aptitude. When Jonathan was ten months old he would stand in his diapers at the front of one of my speakers, which was as big as he was, hold on with one hand, and bounce his knee to the beat of the music. Before he was two he could identify every instrument in the orchestra by its sound, something he learned from listening intently to Benjamin Britten's *Young Person's Guide to the Orchestra*. When he was an adolescent I asked him what instrument

he liked and bought him a saxophone. When he was seventeen and just out
of high school, he moved to Los Angeles and formed a band. Although he
had played the sax in his high school bands, he was now playing the bass.
He was always a quick study like that. Better yet, he also wrote the songs,
both lyrics and music. I went to Los Angeles to see him play at a club called
the Lingerie and was warmed all over by what I saw and heard. It brought
out the youngster still in me, and the lyrical quality of his music was almost
as old-fashioned as I was. As his dad, of course, it did occur to me to ask
him how he managed to do the band and also his classes at UCLA. "Oh, I
only go to class when there's a test," he replied. I might have reprimanded
him, but he was an honor student on the Dean's list, so how could I argue?

I will always remember his graduation from UCLA, even though I couldn't
make him out among the ten thousand students who were packed into a sports
stadium for the ceremony. When we did meet in the parking lot, he was easily
identified by his dyed-black, bouffant, rock-and-roll hair and the pink and
turquoise high-heeled boots poking out from under his academic gown.

He was a remarkably talented songwriter. Granted, I am his father, but
in my opinion he is up there with the best professional lyricists. On the
other hand, he is so much a limelight avoider that it's hard to find a trace of
him or his songs on the Internet, even if you know where to look. He has
long been something of a cult figure among the music crowd, and that's the
way he prefers it, mysterious and hidden. When I asked him if he had copies
of his lyrics he emailed back, "I don't; they may be online somewhere. That
record was a long time ago—pre me having a computer." I'm not sure I
understand this casual attitude toward his work. He doesn't seem bitter that
he is not better known as a songwriter, or that the albums he produced were
not the hits they deserved to be. Far from it. He will give you a dozen good
reasons why celebrity is a prison and a curse. Shortly after he sent the email,
on the other hand, he was able to locate some of his lyrics.

Quoting a couple of them can't justify the claim I made, but it can provide a taste of how intelligent and clever and musical they are. He started
out with a band called Candy, and this was one of his refrains:

> *What if every time was like the first time*
> *Then all those things I told you would come true*
> *Because if every time were like the first time*
> *Girl I'd never walk away from you.*

In his third album, which featured a band called The Loveless, the lyrics grew melancholy and bitter:

> *Staring at the holes in the wall,*
> *Where your pictures used to hang.*
> *Reading your old letters*
> *Listening to the rhythm of the rain.*
>
> *And I'm wondering if I'm on board your train of thought.*
> *And I'm laughing 'cause I can't remember why we ever fought.*
> *And it's times like these I almost miss you.*
> *And it's times like these I almost wish you were here.*
> *And it's times like these I almost miss you.*
> *Wish that your ghost would disappear.*

I always wondered what wound had caused him to produce such lyrics, and was even concerned about it for a while. But then he had such a cheerful demeanor generally and was so creative that I stopped worrying.

Unfortunately, Jonathan had chosen to enter an industry that was on its deathbed. I already knew from his first album, which he had written when he was in his early twenties, that the music world was a bad-news business. In those days, there were MTV shows that featured "countdowns" of the hits. Candy's first video debuted at number eleven in the Los Angeles market. But there were no Candy albums in the stores. The reason? Just before release, the record company that made the album was bought by Polygram, and the Polygram executives didn't want the A&R representative who had been responsible for Jon's album to have a success and gain a leg up on them. So they killed the record.

This turned out to be the norm in the business. You step over the bodies of the weaker to get to the top. There was even an incident where the megahit band KISS stole one of Jon's lyrics. One of the KISS band members used to hang around Jon's gigs at Madam Wong's and other L.A. clubs. Jon had written a song with a clever refrain: "You put the X in Sex." Without so much as a word of explanation or request, KISS changed the lyric to "She puts the X in Sex" and made it a hit. Although they were multi-millionaires themselves, they didn't even throw a bone to the youngsters whose work they had pilfered. I was furious, but my son just took it in stride, as he did many other adversities, and went on to the next challenge.

Because of my concerns about the effect of the divorce on my children, it came as a surprise and a grace to me in 1984 when Jonathan asked me if I would like to move to Los Angeles and share an apartment with him. The four members of his band had been living in a flat together but had broken up the household when some of them decided to move in with their girlfriends. I was still in Berkeley, living in a cottage-like house that I bought after the divorce but I didn't hesitate to say yes. I sold the house, packed up my things and joined my son in a one-bedroom apartment I rented in West Hollywood.

My internal disorder was not over, however, and the joint domicile with Jonathan lasted only a few months as I was busy making one of the many mistakes it would take before I found my balance again. Within six weeks of moving to Los Angeles I was engaged to a woman I barely knew and who barely knew me, with the result that I was soon single again. None of this turmoil interrupted the post-divorce connection I had with my son. It was part of Jon's easygoing nature that he was able to take in stride events that might feel like earthquakes to others.

In anticipation of my misconceived marriage, I had bought a house in Griffith Park. Jonathan's band played from the roof of my garage at the ill-fated wedding. After the breakup, I offered him a small room with a private entrance in my new home. Excited by the prospect of having him live with me, I began building him a beautiful apartment on the garage roof with a wood-beamed cathedral ceiling. But when it was completed, he didn't move in. Instead he left Los Angeles to pursue new musical horizons in New York. I was disappointed by the move. But I wanted him to succeed in the musical career he had chosen, and he thought he could do this better in the "Big Apple," as he liked to refer to it.

In New York he formed a new band and put out his second and third albums but soon came up against the brute facts of an industry that was on life support. A company called Napster had effectively destroyed the record business by creating an Internet swap site where recordings could be obtained for free, effectively killing the ability of the artists to make money off record sales, and facing Jon with his biggest challenge. In retrospect, Jon described the challenge this way: "For me Napster was a new punk rock. Punk rock was why I got into the music business in the first place. It had a do-it-yourself spirit and an anything-is-possible/no rules attitude. Napster had the same charge for me."

To succeed in the music world now became a test of ingenuity and industry savvy which, it so happened, Jon had in abundance. So much so that he was sought after by the record companies over the next years as he used his fertile brain to find ways to succeed in a mortally wounded business and eventually to make his way to the top. To make ends meet he had gone to work for the Sony Corporation as an accountant and was so good at what he did they offered him a job running the department, which he turned down. It was no mystery to me why after I visited him in the Sony headquarters, which reminded me of the nightmare corporate future portrayed in the film Rollerball. As I've already noted, one of the things I've always loved in my son was the way he enjoyed life, and always seemed to be nursing a silent chuckle. But when I visited him at Sony I was shocked to see how depressed he was. His shoulders were slumped and there was no sparkle in his eyes. I was happy when he quit Sony and went to work for a music publishing company called Fiction.

It was the end of the 1990s, and the money stream of the record companies with their giant overheads had dried up. In his typically casual way, Jonathan summarized how the new environment affected him: "the Internet happened and I got interested in music online." What he meant was that he saw in the Internet a way to promote bands without the record companies. His insights were so keen and the strategies he devised so effective that one day in the not too distant future, a major record company would ask him to come and run it. He turned that offer down too.

In 2001 Jonathan formed Crush Management, a company that would publish music, manage bands, and most importantly figure out a way to make them popular and profitable. He likes to describe Crush as "a futuristic music company." Since Jonathan was a cult figure, people came to him with ideas and bands looking for management. One of the early bands he picked up was called Fall Out Boy. He explained to me why he liked them: "The lyrics to a song they had, called 'Dead on Arrival,' stood out to me: 'This is side one / flip me over / I know I'm not your favorite record.' It seemed like they came from someone with a great mind." Great mind or no, they were certainly original, which is a scarce commodity in any corner of the popular culture. The problem, however, was how to make a name for Fall Out Boy so they could sell records, attract crowds on tour, and make money. When I asked my son how he did it, he said, "The wizard never steps from behind the curtain." So I can't tell you more about his secrets than he has been willing to share with the public, which is not much.

He and his partner Bob McLynn, who joined him in 2002, worked for three years to make a name for Fall Out Boy. In 2005 they succeeded. Fall Out Boy's album From Under the Cork Tree sold three million copies, unheard of for a new band in the desert that Napster had created. Crush had also signed another band, Panic! at the Disco, which was selling two million albums. Both bands were featured on the cover of Rolling Stone, and Jonathan's charges were so popular they were able to sell out venues like Dodger Stadium.

When I had just finished setting down these words, I turned on the Today show, and there was Fall Out Boy, promoting its latest album Save Rock and Roll. This was ten years after Jonathan had helped them launch their careers, and as the host Matt Lauer explained to the television audience, their new album was already number one on iTunes in twenty-seven countries.

My son had created a musical miracle that would not stop. By Father's Day 2014, the twenty-one groups and artists he signed had sold seventy-seven million albums, had collected $165 million in touring receipts, and had 730 million YouTube views. His clients include the hottest songwriter in the business, Sia, who has written hits for Beyoncé, Rihanna, Eminem, Katy Perry, Jennifer Lopez, and herself. On accepting the Songwriter of Year award in 2014 Sia thanked my son, the "best manager in the world," and her new album, A Thousand Forms of Fear, went to number one on the charts and number one worldwide. Jon and his partner also resurrected the band Train, which in 2012 had the number-one single of the year and the biggest single in Billboard's history. That same year, a song by his group Gym Class Heroes was chosen to be the official song of the Olympics, and another of the group's works became the official song of the New York Giants.

I am proud of my son's achievements, and particularly pleased with the way he continues to be such a happy and thoughtful person, despite the pressures that go with his success. He wears all this lightly, as he should. One thing that intrigues me is that although I remember him as a voluble youngster, he has grown into a pretty reticent adult, no doubt part of his business strategy. Although I don't want to exaggerate his diffidence, you sometimes have to pry his thoughts from him, and even then he likes to remain, as he puts it, behind the curtain. Perhaps this is a reaction to his preachy old man. I don't know if it is, and it wouldn't bother me if it were.

Because of his reticence there are a number of things we don't bother to discuss. Among these is politics, except obliquely. I've already mentioned how the divorce made me cautious around my children for many years, although that's now no longer an issue. Another factor affecting our communication has been the public attacks on me from my opponents. From the moment I broke with the left, my enemies regularly took positions of mine and turned them upside down or inside out until they had no relation to anything I had ever believed or said. They would claim, for example, that I supported slavery, or was a Torquemada intent on suppressing ideas I disagreed with, which were both the opposite of the truth. In an uglier vein they said I was a racist and a bigot, and wanted the poor to suffer. It was all so ludicrous, but that didn't stop them from spreading their malice across the Internet and other public media.

When I was approached by people, even friends, who were not familiar with what I had said or done recently, I never knew what opinion they might have of me. The attacks had a similar effect on my relations with my family, who were dispersed across the country and out of touch with my current thinking and public actions. How did they view me? What did they think of me? For several years I could not make facile assumptions about the answers, although over time, through many conversations and books written by me, that changed.

Jonathan is not a political person. I enjoy this feature of his personality. He is in touch with what I would call the normal world that looks askance at politics and politicians and is busy taking advantage of the amazing opportunities that America affords. My talks with Jonathan have the effect of bringing me back to earth. He probably voted for Obama, but I don't really know or care. I've avoided this area in our conversations because I don't want my conflicts to burden him. His bands have played the White House and Kennedy birthday parties. The entertainment community doesn't spend a lot of time thinking about political issues but reflexively embraces leftwing opinions because it finds them "cool." My son does not share this shallowness, but there is no need for him to confront it either. When I thought about it, I didn't want to create a situation where he might feel put on the spot, caught between his father and the world he moves in. I wanted him to enjoy his success. Even more important, I didn't want my enemies to become his. So I just bypassed the political in our conversations. If he wasn't interested in discussing politics, neither was I. In the conversations we did have, however, we were quite close in our outlooks and our assessments of people, and that was a comfort I could live with.

Jonathan's observations are always interesting to me. He is a shrewd judge of character, as you would expect a man of his achievements to be. I enjoy the times I am able to spend with him and always feel sad when they are over and he has to leave. This is a problem that stems from our geographical separation and his success. I have to be content feeling close to him in my heart and enjoying our phone conversations and the times when we are able to sit down together in Los Angeles or New York.

Like my other children, Jonathan has his own life and his own world now. They are a mirror that shows me my own limitations and makes me wonder about the different paths I might have taken, and whether they would have turned out better for me, or worse—who knows? Parenthood, it turns out, teaches you about yourself, and not always in a reassuring way. You see your failings starkly, and hardest of all you have to accept the distances that the dance of life creates. My connection with my son is different from what it was when he was in the bosom of the family that Elissa and I created. The loss is painful to me, but it is the course of life and I accept it. I also left my parents behind when I ventured out into the world. Now I understand their case.

Father's Day

While I have been writing this, another holiday has crept up on me. The second Sunday in June is Father's Day, and while there is no family gathering scheduled, the occasion is nonetheless affecting me emotionally, not least because of the vulnerability I am feeling as a result of my slow recovery and continuing pain. It has been two and a half months since the operation, and I still feel weak and dependent and unsteady when upright. This is unsettling, especially in the way it makes me feel older and feebler than I am.

My first present is from Jonathan and Renee—a bottle of Silver Oak cabernet with a note that says, "Hey pops. Happy Father's Day." They send me a present of fruit or cheese or wine on every calendar occasion. Perhaps I am overly sentimental, but it invariably puts me in mind of how Jonathan opened his door to me after the divorce now more than thirty years past. The cabernet came in a leather case, and April and I gathered it up and set off for a local Italian restaurant. I hobbled in, uncorked the cab and ordered a dinner of filet mignon with a mushroom risotto. April's preference was salmon and a white chardonnay. Then we topped off the evening with a latte and Tiramisu. When I reported the menu to Jonathan, he said I should have been the one to have the salmon. I explained to him that the surgeon who crippled me had also caused me to lose a third of my blood and I was on a diet of red meat to harvest iron and restore my red-cell count. Besides, steak goes better with a cab.

Jon Jason and Kathleen have sent me two jars of marmalade, a favorite of mine going back to when my grandmother Rose used to read me the poems of A. A. Milne, especially the one in which the king wanted butter for his bread but the queen and all his servants offered him marmalade instead. As a marmalade man, I found the Wilkins & Sons "orange with malt whiskey" a particularly savory treat.

Ben and Felicia have sent orchids, as they always do on occasions like this. But it is the note in Felicia's hand that justifies the good feelings I have despite the trials of my seventh-fifth year: "Happy Father's Day! Although we are far away across the Atlantic, we are thinking of you on this special day. And we want to let you know that we love and treasure you in our lives."

My Onetime Friend Florence

Two weeks earlier, unbeknownst to me, Elissa took another blow in a life that seemed too filled with them. Her best and oldest friend, Florence, expired at home in New York after a three-year battle with leukemia. Florence had been one of four particularly important women in Elissa's life, including my daughter, Anne, who is thankfully still with us. The others— Elissa's sister Barbara and our daughter Sarah—were also taken from her in untimely fashion, Barbara by a cerebral hemorrhage, Sarah by causes undisclosed but probably connected to her birth condition.

Elissa and Florence were inseparable girlhood friends. In fact, it was through their friendship that Elissa and I met, when she was only sixteen and I but two years older. At the time, Florence was seeing a friend of mine who asked me if I would like to double up with him on a blind date. I said yes, and Elissa and I immediately became a couple. Florence was not too happy with her date, so we introduced her to one of my college classmates with whom I was also close and had encouraged to become politically radical. When I graduated college, Elissa and I married and moved to Berkeley, where I was admitted to graduate school. Florence and my friend soon followed so that he could pursue his own studies at the university, and then they too married, beginning an odyssey in which our families grew together.

It was politics that eventually separated us. In 1974 the Black Panthers murdered an innocent woman named Betty van Patter, whom I had recruited to help them, and whose death changed the course of my life. When I confided to my friend what had happened, he shocked me by defending the murderers because they shared our progressive views. Like the rest of our leftist friends, he blamed the "power structure" for the crime—not because the "power structure" had anything actually to do with Betty's murder but because, in the radical playbook, blacks were oppressed and therefore innocent, while whites were oppressors and therefore guilty. Shortly after the murder my marriage began to unravel, and Florence and her husband aligned themselves against me.

It is strange how life works this way; you begin it with great gambles you are completely unprepared to make, and then you must painfully undo the messes you create for yourself and others along the way. I have no regrets about marrying Elissa, who has been a wonderful mother to our children. I cannot speak for her, but despite the pain of the divorce, it finally worked out for me. One could say I have had two lives; I went through rivers of pain to change my understanding of myself and others, and become what I am today.

As the years progressed, and we grew older, I made some attempts to see if the relationship with Florence and her husband that politics had torn apart could be repaired. This was quixotic no doubt, since I had dedicated the second half of my life to combatting the malignant delusions of the left, while they had marched along the same communist lines they had grown up in. Still, I did not want to turn my back on the non-political dimensions of our lives or the bonds we once shared. But events proved otherwise; the weight of our political commitments was too great.

I have never considered all or even a majority of leftists to be bad people despite their political views. After all, I was one of them once. But the historical saga has a diabolical twist in which destructive illusions about the future can seduce good people into the arms of evil. Consequently, when

leftists are able relate to me in a decent way—however rare that may be—
I am ready despite all differences to reciprocate. An Irishman named Ernie
Tate was a friend of mine in the days I worked for Bertrand Russell in London. Ernie had little formal education and was schooled instead by his comrades in the Fourth International, a Trotskyist sect. I was a leftist not of his
persuasion, and I noticed that he never got angry when I challenged a view
he held but just smiled at me as though I were a child unable to grasp the
arcane wisdom of his Trotskyist faith. After I left England, fifty years went
by during which we did not see or communicate with each other. Then I
was contacted by someone writing a book about the events we both participated in who told me Ernie had written a memoir called *Revolutionary
Activism* in which he treated me kindly. When I read the book, I was no
more surprised by the fact that his political views had not changed at all
than I was to see that he did treat generously a one-time friend whom his
fellow leftists now regarded as a monster. He was that kind of person. I
wrote and thanked him and he replied. But as we exchanged pleasantries
about the past, I came to realize that there could be no future in the relationship we had resumed because our conflicts now were in the present and
he could not forgive me for that.

I think Florence had some of Ernie's openness. She was naturally curious
and could see more sides to an issue than perhaps she allowed herself to concede. Some fifteen years ago, when I spoke at New York University, she came
to hear me, even though my subject was the malignant effects of the left to
which she was so wedded. Afterwards she came up to me and, if she was
hostile, concealed it well. I was happy to see her, remembering the days of
our friendship. But when I sent her a copy of *Radical Son* and inscribed it
"For the good times," she told Elissa, "There were no good times." She had
that kind of capacity for vindictive anger, which in my experience is generally
shared by people convinced that they can make a better world.

When a person dies, you get to look over the life and assess it as a whole.
I tried to do that with Florence. Her work had been as an attorney practicing
family law. While her political activities involved a constant war against the
enemies of the left, in her daily routines she had dedicated herself to helping
the poor and the outcast. I would be remiss if I were to overlook these
admirable efforts.

When she died two Sundays before Father's Day, an obituary appeared
in the *New York Law Journal*. My sister Ruth sent me an email from Nova

Scotia with the link. The obituary said that Florence had headed up two family units for the Legal Services Corporation in Brooklyn and Queens and had "spent much of her career ... serving low-income families, incarcerated women and victims of domestic violence." Even in retirement Florence was active, volunteering with the Incarcerated Mothers Law Project, "often visiting women in prison to advise them on their parental rights. She also served on the advisory board of the New York Asian Women's Center, which helps women and children escape domestic abuse."

This was worthy work. In the larger scale of things, this counts. Florence was a good wife and mother and raised two fine children, and that counts too. And she was a best friend to Elissa for more than sixty years, right to the unhappy end. And for me that counts a lot. I'm sorry that her political engagement—and no doubt mine too—created a wall between us that was insurmountable. It was a loss for both of us.

My Wilderness Sister Ruth

I have mentioned my younger sister Ruth without introducing her, so let me repair the oversight. Like offspring, siblings are with you always and measure the distances you have come, and therefore all that you have left behind.

Ruth made a decision forty years ago that causes family occasions with us to be so rare they are practically nonexistent. In the early 1970's she moved to the remote northeastern tip of Nova Scotia, a thousand miles east of Maine. The weather there is so raw and unpredictable that her house is equipped with a barometer to warn of incoming storms. The only time I was able to visit—more than twenty years ago—it took me longer to get from Toronto to her home in Nova Scotia than it did to get from Los Angeles to Toronto. When I was ready to return to California, she had to drive me to the airport in Sydney, a hundred miles away, through a snowstorm so intense there were complete whiteouts along the way. The only occasion when she has been able to visit us was our wedding, and I was grateful that she did.

When she moved to Nova Scotia, Ruth met and married a Vietnam War resister named Ian Sherman. He is a visual artist who works in wood and marble, and in his day job has built and maintained coastal hiking trails around Inverness. Now retired, he volunteers time to the trail organization he founded and also to a local human-rights group. In 2007, Ruth also retired from her job as the librarian at the local high school, where she had worked for twenty years. Recently they became grandparents for the first time.

Ruth has made a quiet and satisfying life in Nova Scotia, a place of imposing natural beauty. It doesn't snow there all the time, and in the months when it doesn't she is a devoted gardener. Her move to this remote setting has a philosophical underpinning which she summarized in a letter to me: "Our life here is about tending the land, being more or less self-sufficient and living in harmony with the natural world. We are back-to-the-landers." As a political person, she incorporates this modest ambition into a comprehensive world-view: "We take a real, deep, and complete interest in global issues, our local community issues and our day-to-day life in our valley, which we see as entirely interconnected."

My sister is a private person, which is one reason she moved to the wilderness. She did not like even the small mention I made of her in *Radical Son,* so I am trying to be respectful of her privacy now. When *Radical Son* was published there was a political gulf between us, as she remained on the left even as I gravitated right. I don't hold her politics against her but I can't say the same about her attitude towards me. This saddens me but there is nothing I can really do about it.

I have written a book about my second child Sarah, and will leave it at that. I was fortunate to have been able to compose a portrait of her life. She was a beautiful person and is gone.

My Business Son

My third child, Ben, began life as a shy, neurasthenic child, physically small and thin, almost afraid of his own shadow. I remember watching him have a meltdown during an egg-and-spoon race at a local camp as I looked skyward and silently pleaded, "How is my son going to survive in this rough-and-tumble world?" Those days are long gone. I am certain that the transformation took place around his fifteenth year, after my departure from the household, when he joined the Berkeley High football team to play as its center. My reaction to this—he was the first Horowitz ever to put on a football uniform—was to worry that he might be crippled by an injury. But there was no way I was going to stand between him and his desire. Fortunately my fears proved overwrought as he bulked himself up and became a man.

When he came of age to go to college, I urged him to apply to Columbia University rather than UCLA like his brother. I didn't like the size of UCLA and, for reasons that don't seem so compelling to me now, I wanted him to be exposed to Columbia's core curriculum, which introduced students to the great texts of Western Civilization and had a big impact on my romantic self, forty years before. Columbia was an expensive school and I was by no means rich, but I put together every extra dollar I had to pay for his tuition. There was an irony in this. Both my sons are shrewd with money, and both are somewhat bemused and not a little critical of the way I manage my accounts. For whatever reason, I have always spent what I had. I wanted the best for him and didn't think twice about my decision, even though it would drain my account. I know Ben shakes his head at what he regards as my prodigal ways but, as it happened, paying for his Columbia education was one of the best investments I ever made.

The core curriculum in Western Civilization proved to be a minor aspect of Ben's study. He was drawn instead to the school's computer science program and on graduation took a master's in the subject at UCLA. Then he went out for job interviews, and I was able to help him get an appointment at Silicon Graphics, the cutting-edge company in the field, through my Berkeley friend who had married its CEO. I couldn't get him the job, only the interview, but that was enough. He was immediately hired, and that became the first step in what was to become a remarkable career.

I was also able to be of service to him in another way. That apartment I had built over my garage for Jonathan, which he never occupied, came in handy for Ben. While still at UCLA, he married a USC grad named Felicia Wiley, the youngest child of a family of African Americans whose parents had migrated to Los Angeles from Shreveport, Louisiana. Felicia was the first member of her family to go to college, and when Ben met her was a supervisor in the complaint department at Toyota. I offered the couple my house for their wedding reception and the freshly built apartment over my garage to live in.

A year later, when Ben was hired at Silicon Graphics, he and Felicia and their first-born child, Jules, moved north. The next years were stressful for their family as Ben transitioned through jobs at NetLabs, Lotus, and Netscape. I gave him some fatherly advice, advising him to be aware that the demands of his career were stressful for his wife and family and therefore to pay attention to what was going on in his household. Years later he wrote a number-one bestselling business book called *The Hard Thing About Hard Things*, which gained such an impressive reputation that Rupert Murdoch bought a thousand copies to distribute to his managers. In telling the story of the company he created, Ben included some autobiographical details among which was the advice I had given him. At the time, he was not making that much money and was reluctant to invest in an air-conditioning system despite a heat wave that was distressing his wife. As he related it, the anecdote sounded a little bizarre but was probably accurate. "Son, do you know what's cheap?" I apparently asked him. "Flowers. Flowers are really cheap. But do you know what's expensive? ... Divorce." Or so he recorded it. He got the message and the air conditioning, and he and his gracious wife Felicia have been inseparable now for twenty-five years.

This was the last useful advice I was able to give Ben for many years, as he was moving in a world that was not only foreign to me but involved such complex decisions that I wouldn't have had a clue what to tell him had he asked me. At Netscape he met and became friends with Marc Andreessen, co-inventor of the browser. When Netscape was bought by AOL, the two of them put in their required year and then launched a company they called LoudCloud, with Ben as its CEO. In an incredibly adverse economic environment, which came close to bankrupting the company, he changed the name to Opsware and the company mission to software, and in the course of a dramatic white-knuckle saga made it an amazing corporate triumph. Less than seven years after he created the company he sold it to Hewlett-Packard for $1.6 billion, forty times its value only a few years before.

Ben's story has become a Silicon Valley legend. He has told it in gripping prose in his book, and told it so well that I would be foolish to try to duplicate any part of it here. Reading about his travails as he battled market crashes, dealt with corporate rivalries, and coped with the unexpected to prevail in the end, I was taken by a thought that I wanted to shout from the rooftops. The thought was this: If leftists were to read this book with half-open minds and see what the life of a real CEO is like—the judgments he has to make, the risks he has to take, the personnel issues he has to handle, the corporate puzzles he has to solve, the adversities he has to soldier through—they would instantly see the folly of their beliefs and abandon their delusions about "surplus value" and corporate exploitation and capitalist enemies. They would throw their socialist texts in the trash where they belong, and be awed at what it takes to create an enterprise and steer it to success through the "gale of creative destruction," as Schumpeter once described the turbulent weather of the economic marketplace. But this will never happen. Even if leftists were to read Ben's book, they would not believe what they read because it would shake the foundations of their beings. This is why ignorance rules the political world, and always will.

Ben's account of the challenges he faced and met filled me with a paternal glow and also with wonder at where all that brilliance and sharp-eyed character assessment came from. When I put this question to him, he said that it came the hard way—by learning from his mistakes as he went along and by not making the same mistakes again.

Reading his book made me marvel at the differences between him and his old man. For I was driven—one might say obsessively—by a mission that blinded me to many things at the periphery of my sight. The mission was to "change the world" and, when that came to grief, to confront those who continued the misguided quest. I was so absorbed in pursuing these wars that I didn't pay proper attention to many things I should have. As a result, I didn't have the breadth of vision of either of my sons, or their sharp judgment of character, and consequently, unlike them, did repeat my mistakes and paid the consequent price.

A parallel difference was my confrontational attitude, a product of my upbringing in a family of communists who saw themselves as revolutionary soldiers facing a determined enemy. Ben was not unaware of this and made his own observations about it in his book. He recalled how he started out in the corporate world following my example, but quickly found that it led to dead ends. And so he changed. Both he and Jonathan were able to locate grooves in the system they could run along, outwitting their opponents and finding ways to succeed. I have the greatest admiration for both of them, for this ingenuity in working their way out of the family mold. Thinking about their successes has contributed to my speculations as to what my own life would have been like if I had not been brought up in a household whose goal was to sharpen the conflicts and confront the enemy.

Reading Ben's description of the crises he faced, I experienced shivers of regret over the fact that I was unaware of his trials at the time and had failed to provide him a shoulder to lean on. Where was I indeed? And then I remembered: I was facing my own crisis with a prostate cancer and the efforts to get on my feet again. But there was more to it than that. A point comes, sooner than we think, when our children set out on their independent courses, and the possibility of influencing them or giving them the shoulder they once had is all but gone. Still, I can't help wishing that circumstances had allowed me to give my son help in those dark years.

Today Ben is riding the crest of his success. After selling Opsware, as part of the corporate deal he had made, he was required to spend a year of what he regarded as indentured servitude running Hewlett-Packard's two-billion-dollar global software division. The day he was liberated, he began implementing his next career step: the creation of a venture capital company called Andreessen Horowitz, which in less than five years has grown to be a $4.3 billion company at the top of the Silicon Valley food chain. His appearance on the cover of Fortune in March 2014 confirmed that he had taken his place with the titans of the digital world.

Ben has instincts very much like those of his brother Jon, with whom he is close. They are generous souls and often join in efforts like building a library for Uganda's Abayudayah tribe in the name of their sister Sarah, who spent a summer teaching the tribal children. Ben has a son, Jules, and two daughters, Mariah and Sophia. Mariah was born with a severe autism which requires round-the-clock care, and autistic charities are naturally an important Horowitz family philanthropy. Although Sarah and Mariah were the inspirations for these efforts, the real force behind them is Ben's wife, Felicia, who has grown from the anxious and pressured young mother I first got to know into an alluring hostess, social organizer, fund-raiser, and active philanthropist. She is also an extraordinarily talented quilter whose works are auctioned for tens of thousands of dollars to help her worthy causes. Ben and Felicia have provided scholarship funds for African-American students at Columbia and equally munificent sums to American Jewish World Service, which is the organization through which Sarah worked and which focuses on helping abused women of all religions and races all over the world.

The cause of oppressed women is a passion for Ben, as he explained on the Internet in an article called, "Why I Will Donate 100 Percent of My Book Earnings to Women in the Struggle." You can find that at bhorowitz.com, his business blog with ten million followers. He begins every column of business advice with an illustrative quotation from some rap artist. As a result, Ben has become fairly famous as an enthusiast of the genre—not to mention a rebel in the world of business journalism—and has become friends with Kanye West, Nas, and other hip-hop figures. Nas's iconic album Illmatic draws on his growing up in the Queensbridge projects where, ironically, as a twelve-year-old I once distributed communist literature. Ben's advocacy of hip-hop led to an invitation from Henry Louis Gates to give a seminar on the subject at Harvard. When I queried him about all this he said, "Dad, you have to understand that rock and roll is communism, hip-hop is capitalism." I said, "Are you going to tell them that at Harvard?" He said, "Yes I will." And he did.

As you can see, there is a bit of a chip-off-the-old-block here, which is immensely gratifying to me. I am struck by how different Ben's career (like Jonathan's) is from mine, yet how close we are in outlook and understanding. April and I feel very much at home when we are with Ben and Felicia and enjoy the large extended family that Felicia's parents, sisters, aunts, and uncles have brought into our lives. I gave a eulogy for Felicia's father John at his funeral, which was inspired by my son's great love for him. John Wiley was a good man, with little formal education but with a shrewd mind and gentle instincts. As a young father he worked on oil pipelines and followed them to California. Before he died, Ben gave him a present of a ride around the track in a Formula One car with Mario Andretti at the wheel. His widow Loretta is a ray of sunshine, always looking to the bright side even though her life has had its share of heartbreaking tragedies. "My attitude," she says, "is it's one time here. Be grateful for what you get. That's all there is." And so it is.

It's an odd experience watching your children take over and render you fairly useless and old hat. It accelerates the sense of diminishing horizons at the same time it ignites fires of love, and feelings that despite your shortcomings you did things well, and you can look back on the life that is vanishing, and feel good.

Healing

While savoring these family passages I still have to cope with my daily condition, which continues to weigh on me. When I wake in the mornings my leg feels like lead, and there is pain shooting through my foot, and I'm wondering how I will be able to walk or make it through the next hours. When I finally roll out of bed, the first thing I reach for is my cane, which will help to take the pressure off. But even with this support, shuffling along I feel a hundred years old, and can't see how I will ever be whole again. On the TV the talking heads are droning on, reminding me that I will not be part of that dialogue again soon if at all, nor will I be traveling cross country to deliver the speeches that have been an important part of my work. During this convalescence, I practically dropped out of a debate in which I have been engaged for half a century. The younger bodies and livelier brains of my children's generation are taking over and leaving me behind. I am not unaware that these thoughts of oblivion are premature and somewhat overwrought. When my foot is better and the pain subsides, I will probably come back in some semblance of myself and get in a few more rounds. (And so it transpired. Two years later, I wrote a book about President Trump that became a *New York Times* best-seller, and was touring the country making three or four speaking appearances a month.) But then I will be gone with John Wiley and all the rest.

My Rebel Daughter

Of all my children, my youngest, Anne, appears to be the one who picked up the confrontational gene that shaped so much of my life. Anne and I share fundamental traits, and yet despite our similarities, so obvious to others, there is a distance between us which I cannot fully explain. I long attributed it to the divorce, since Anne was only nine at the time. When she and Sarah came to my foredoomed second wedding in Los Angeles, she insisted that they both wear black and be rude to my bride. Sarah refused to go along with the rudeness side of the plan. I don't know how to assess what goes on inside the heads and hearts of others, but Anne's rebel streak was there from the outset and has not been directed only at me. She is the one child in the family to have dyed her hair purple when that was a teenage fad, and the only one to elope and get married in Tahoe with no family member present. Both episodes were far more disturbing to her mother than to me. She made amends after the elopement by having a reception many months later in Berkeley.

Shortly after our divorce, Elissa and I went to a parents' night at Martin Luther King Junior High, where Anne was a student. We gathered in one of the classrooms with a group of other parents and children, and listened to Anne's teacher talk about the class and his students. Toward the end of his remarks, he complained to the parents that our children weren't always attentive, and it bothered him that they talked among themselves while he was trying to teach them. No sooner had these words left his lips than a voice that I immediately recognized as my daughter's shouted, "If you weren't so boring, maybe we would want to listen to you."

I was appalled by this embarrassing outburst and show of disrespect. When we left the room I scolded my daughter, much to the disapproval of my now ex-wife, who was understandably angry with me for other reasons. In retrospect I can see how a distraught father would react the way I did, worrying that a thirteen-year-old should show more deference to her elders. But I also see how bold my daughter was in speaking up for herself and her classmates against a form of abuse from tedious instructors that is not uncommon in classrooms. On another occasion, I had to go into her school to confront a teacher who should never have been in a classroom and who failed her on an exam because she wrote her answers in orange ink. Another incident that got my dander up was her school adviser telling her she "-wasn't college material." She obviously was.

Anne was accepted by the University of California, Riverside and after two years there by UCLA, where she received her RN degree, and went immediately to work in an abortion clinic. Anne has never been a political person, but she soaked up many Berkeley attitudes and felt both that women should have the choice whether to abort their babies, and also quality health care if the choice was to do that. But she soon found she didn't like nursing because, once she had mastered the routines, the job was "boring." She went back to school, this time to the University of California San Francisco Medical Center where she earned a Nurse Practitioner's degree, which gave her more authority and flexibility than her previous credential.

Her first job was in a community clinic, where she was left on her own since there were no other pediatric specialists. After a year she took a job at another community clinic, where 95 percent of the patients were Spanish-speaking. She already had some facility in the language and quickly brought herself up to speed. At the clinic she worked with foster children who had a level of sophistication that she felt other children didn't. She decided she wanted to develop an assessment tool that could be used to evaluate the maturity of a foster child who desired emancipation. It was the rebel at work. She went back to school and entered a Ph.D. program, but as school started she got pregnant and left. She hated the program in any case because of its extreme academic focus. "No one really was interested in my wanting to create something practical," she said later.

In the millennium year she gave birth to a son named Elvis, and sent out a notification to the family that proclaimed, "The King has arrived." When Elvis was about a year and a half old she took a job at La Clínica de la Raza in Oakland, where she worked for seven years, ministering to Hispanic families and providing quality care for their children. In 2007 she took a new job in the pediatric clinic at the Juvenile Justice Hall in Alameda County. While she was there, she still maintained a position at La Clinica as an after-hours triage clinician, and also as a laser clinician in a program to remove gang tattoos from youngsters who wanted to start a new life.

I have to confess that her work with criminals, even though they were youngsters, bothered me. It took me back to my experience with the Black Panthers and made me nervous for her safety. I discussed this with Anne more than once, but if I have conveyed here anything of the spirit of my daughter, you will understand why I could never rest assured she had listened to me or, if she had listened, heeded my advice. I was afraid that in befriending these criminal youngsters she would cross invisible lines that might make them mistake her kindnesses and come after her for more than she was prepared to give. I was also fearful for my grandson Elvis, a precocious and good-natured child who might become a target if Anne wasn't careful.

As it has turned out, my fears have been unfounded, and so perhaps my bad example did have an impact. Meanwhile my daughter has been a Good Samaritan to many troubled youngsters. I will confine myself to two examples. E., a Juvenile Hall inmate, started getting arrested when he was eleven. He had sickle cell anemia, but all he knew about sickle cell was that sometimes he had priapism—a painful erection that lasts for more than six hours at a time. He had other pain and was supposed to take antibiotics daily, which he refused. Anne asked him point-blank if he knew what sickle cell anemia was. He said he didn't really know, but that he knew he would die by the age of twenty-five from it. He was fifteen at the time.

So Anne talked about it to him. To explain the importance of hydration she used the example of Cheerios in milk. She made a plan for keeping him hydrated so he wouldn't get priapism. Eventually he got to a point where he wanted to try daily medication to avoid crises. This required frequent blood work and adjustments to the dose, but he agreed and stuck with it. E. told Anne that he wanted to be an astronaut. "Ninety percent of my kids tell me they want to play pro football or basketball, and I am pretty sure that they won't, but an astronaut I had never heard before." She didn't tell him that he would never qualify because of the sickle cell, since even a normal plane ride requires oxygen for so-called "sicklers." So she told him, if he completed his next program she would send him to space camp at Stanford. With that as an inspiration, he finished the program. But while she was trying to raise the money for him to go to space camp, he got arrested again. He was placed back in the same program, and they made the same deal. Anne was having trouble raising the money, so she decided she would just pay for the space camp herself. Unfortunately she never got to make the payment. E. ran away from the program and was murdered shortly after his eighteenth birthday.

Anne is philosophical about her work. "I don't think I can save anyone. I don't think I can really change anything," she told me. I was struck by how she had come to the same conclusions it took me so long and cost me so dearly to arrive at; how different her attitude was than mine had been for the first half of my life. Then she told me about one of her successes:

"B. was a very shady character, full of stories that I think he himself believes. He had been in and out of the Hall for a few years on different types of theft charges. Then he came in and we got a call from a doctor at his school health center. He had a positive HIV test but had not returned for follow-up. In trying to locate him, we found out he was in Juvenile Hall. One of the most awkward conversations I have ever had was trying to tell this fifteen-year-old boy that I knew he was HIV-positive, and I knew he knew, and I knew he didn't want me to know. He was in some of the most amazing denial I had ever seen. He got released and disappeared, no meds, no follow-up.

"Then he got picked up again. We got to know each other well over many discussions regarding whether or not he would be compliant with treatment, where he would go for treatment, where he was going to live, etc. I remember one day he looked at me, almost startled, and said, 'I really have this, don't I?' When he got released again, a lot of disasters followed. During his final detention, we requested the judge keep him past his eighteenth birthday so we could stabilize him and complete therapy for a secondary condition. During this time we created a team of outside and inside people who would continue to support him in the community. While this is not unusual, most kids don't get to sit with their entire team and help dictate the plan of care.

"B. is about twenty now, and even though I cannot continue to provide him health care, I provide him the support of a knowledgeable friend whom he trusts. So he will call the clinic when he knows I am there to ask what to do about a rash, or that his meds are running out, or that someone asked him to get a TB test and do I know what he needs to tell them. I get great satisfaction out of being B.'s friend, and there to help."

My daughter helps a lot of people. She also has the ability to anger people, including members of her family. I love my daughter and am proud of the good she does, but I wish the rebel in her would mellow and settle down, even though its progenitor is probably me.

Max

The dogs in our household are its life. They are the children one can actually handle after reaching middle age, which is one reason we miss them so fiercely when they are gone. About midway between Mother's Day and Father's Day, Kim's brindle boxer, Max, died. This was accompanied by days of mourning in our household. Boxers are prone to cancers, and Max, who was almost ten, had a tumor as big as his stomach pressing down on his spleen. Max had large black eyes and a fearsome look, which scared strangers. But to those of us who knew him he was a sweetheart.

There is another reason the passing of our pets affects us, and that has to do with what I call the happiness of dogs. They are happy to see us, whenever that is, and happy when we acknowledge them, if only by a look or a scratch behind the ears. In the morning, all I have to do is stir from my slumbers and my Chihuahuas will set up a yowling and a cackling, a yipping and a yapping, as though Gabriel had sounded the trumpet summoning us to Judgment and a life of eternal bliss. It is no great mystery why we miss them when they leave.

Max was Kim's shadow in the same way Jake, my white Chihuahua with black cow patches and bubble eyes, is mine. Jake has been with me thirteen years and has kept watch over me all that time—through the prostatectomy, the first hip replacement, and now in my present hobbled state. When I get up, he will follow me from room to room as if spotting my position and checking to see that I am all right. He shadows me so closely that sometimes I will look around for him only to discover he is underfoot.

It is Lucy, however, our auburn with the Flying Nun ears, who April is sure will be next. Age has slackened the flesh around her mouth and turned many of her hairs white. She is twelve and overweight and has a heart murmur and a wheeze, and is prone to laze around the house. But she has been doing this for some time. I take my hope from that.

The short lives of dogs offer lessons to us. They teach us the evanescence of life and get us used to the fact that everything we love will be lost. Not that this recognition will make the next passing any easier than the previous one. But these exits raise our awareness of life's true progress, and teach us to embrace what we have before it is gone.

The vet put Max to sleep in the same Rainbow Room where we said goodbye to our little Coco. The rainbow idea seems to have originated among horse people. In a legend of loss and reunion, horses, when they die, are said to pause at the foot of a "Rainbow Bridge" to wait for their owners to follow them. An unknown author has written a poem about the bridge that every horse person knows.

> By the edge of a woods, at the foot of a hill,
> Is a lush, green meadow where time stands still.
>
> Where the friends of man and woman do run,
> When their time on earth is over and done.
>
> For here, between this world and the next,
> Is a place where beloved creatures find rest....
>
> Their limbs are restored, their health renewed,
> Their bodies have healed, with strength imbued....
>
> Then all of a sudden, one breaks from the herd.
>
> For just at that second, there's no room for remorse,
> As they see each other ... one person ... one horse.

So they run to each other, these friends from long past.
The time of their parting is over at last.

The sadness they felt while they were apart
Has turned to joy once more in each heart.

They nuzzle with a love that will last forever.
And then, side by side, they cross over ... together.

This is the statement of what I call a creative faith. The secular and skeptical will dismiss it as merely a saccharine fantasy to salve the wounds of a bruised heart. But that is precisely its utility for those who believe. Does it matter if there is such a bridge or not? This is a question no different from whether there is life after death. Or whether there is a God. No one knows the answers to these questions and no one can know. Therefore, both answers—yes and no—are expressions of faith. The only real question then is how these faiths affect the lives we have.

My wife is a believer. When I asked her about the Rainbow Bridge, she said, "To me the Rainbow Bridge means peace. I thank God for the Rainbow Bridge because it will guide my loved one to the other side, and one day to a reunion. I hope so, because I want to see Coco, and I hope to see the ones I failed so I can make it up to them." As she said this her voice cracked and there were tears in her eyes, which is the way it is whenever she thinks of losing Coco. But it is this same passion that caused her to save Coco in the first place.

Two Types of Faith

When we are confronted by final questions, there is only faith to guide us. Atheism is no less a faith than theism because we cannot know the answers to the questions it addresses. But not all redemptive faiths are the same. What I call "creative faiths" are those that look to a divine reality to resolve the contradictions of this mortal one, and provide a consolation for irreparable loss. What I call destructive faiths are faiths whose consolation is a mission to transform the world we inhabit into one that the faithful desire. Consolation comes from the illusion of contributing to the creation of a world redeemed from the miseries of this one.

Such faiths are destructive because the goal is impossible, and requires its prophets to be endowed with God-like powers. People who resist the goal—unbelievers—are seen as enemies of humanity's salvation, and therefore worthy of damnation. The primary passion of a destructive faith, therefore, is hatred of those who don't share it. Jihadist Islam is such a faith as are Marxism and progressivism, and all quests for a perfect world.

For the first half of my life, I was guided and inspired by such a quest until events overtook it and broke my heart. I came by this faith innocently, having been raised in a progressive household whose desire was "social justice" enforced by the powers of a like-minded state. But the only way to accomplish this ideal would be to transform human beings and make them different from what they have been since the beginning of time. The only way to accomplish this would be to suppress human freedom, and thus destroy the very world they sought to achieve. The religion I was born to was communism. Its adherents desired a "kingdom of freedom" but their practice was the totalitarian state.

In my family and throughout our community, the progressive illusion was an unspoken condition of parental love. This may sound brutal, but as a child of loving parents I wasn't conscious of the coercion. Instead I was lifted by my parents' passion to heights of self-righteousness and self-regard. What could be more intoxicating than to be called on to save the world, and to have family and friends applaud every step taken along the path to that goal?

Secular faiths are even more difficult to relinquish than religious ones, since they offer similar consolations but lack the warnings against a pride that flows from serving a noble cause. Consequently, millions of intelligent and caring people remain wedded to the destructive idea no matter how many victims it accumulates. Crimes in the name of the revolution are routinely denied, or dismissed as unfortunate "mistakes." But they are not mistakes. They are the predictable consequence of ascribing God-like powers to self-centered, needy human beings, prone to treachery, self-aggrandisement, and deceit.

In mid-life, my commitment to social justice involved me in a crime that opened my eyes and changed the course of my life forever. A woman I had recruited to the cause was murdered by my political comrades. This confronted me with the way revolutionary vanguards acted as though they were sanctified by a law higher than the ones that governed everyone else.

No one in the crusade for social justice stepped forward to hold them accountable. The faithful closed their eyes to protect the beautiful dream. For the first time in my life I no longer felt righteous. For the first time, I was able to listen to the voices of others who did not share my faith. For the first time I felt an irreparable guilt, which I could not rationalize or dismiss.

Now I had a debt to pay and justice to seek. It was no longer the justice of progressives, which denies the rights of individuals in the name of an imagined good. The justice I sought was for this world — for individuals like this innocent woman, who were victims of the progressive faith.

Divergent Paths

It probably hasn't escaped your attention that none of my children have pursued political careers like their father's. Even my daughter Sarah, who took up many political causes, did so within the framework of a deeply felt Judaism. Her religious philosophy guided her politics, not the other way around. When the writer Walter Isaacson read an earlier version of this manuscript he raised the following questions: Why were my children not political? Why, on the other hand, was I so passionately political, and why did I continue to be political throughout my life, even when I moved to the other side? How do my children's choices and mine reflect on the general human desire to extract meaning from this life? Here are my answers:

Taking up Isaacson's first question, I asked my son Jonathan about his choice of a musical career. His response was this: "Children normally run away from their parents. Only dummies go into the family business." It was a characteristically wry reflection but a bit facile as a general observation. The desire to establish an individual identity is indeed strong but so is the dynastic pull, and many worthy offspring follow in their parents' footsteps. Philip was the king of Macedonia, but his son Alexander conquered the world. Leopold Mozart was an accomplished composer; his son Wolfgang was a voice for the ages. The reason Jonathan chose music as his own career was because that was his first love. He never gave politics or any other profession a second thought. This was true of each of my children: they loved what they pursued and found in their pursuits a meaningful direction for their lives.

I was one of the dummies Jonathan referred to, entering the family business. It was actually more a religious calling than a business, a passion that informed the moral life of everyone who was part of it. My decision was dictated not only by my parents' devotion to the progressive cause but also by the fact that the members of our entire community were committed followers of that cause. It was not only a worldview that enveloped me but a world, so that I don't remember ever thinking I was free to pursue a different course. If I had done so, it would have been seen not as an alternative but a betrayal.

The lesson I eventually took from this was to avoid raising my own children as I had been raised; that is, to enter the family faith. I didn't want to narrow their choices by making their approval of my work or my political opinions seem to be conditions of my affection for them. If Jonathan had been raised in my father's household — to make the point — he would have faced daunting opposition to his rock-and-roll career, while the opposition to the religious and business courses that Sarah and Ben pursued would have been even stiffer.

The decision to set my children free was made easier by the fact that as they were entering adolescence I was increasingly plagued by doubts about the wisdom of the path I had chosen—or that had chosen me. But when those doubts finally became overwhelming—when I was able to see that the political movement to which I had dedicated myself produced sinister results—why did I not just quit the political life? The lessons I had learned from my experience were set forth in my autobiography, Radical Son, which was my declaration of independence from the cause I had been born to. Why not end it there and find a less combative world to enter?

Would that matters had been so simple. A light did not suddenly go on for me to illuminate everything wrong about the past that had engulfed me. From the time of Betty's murder, it took twenty years before I was able to reach the point where I could write a book like Radical Son. Before I could understand a movement so deeply inscribed in the psyches of its followers and formulate a response to it, I had to free myself from its confines, and in particular from an outlook that was inseparable (or so I thought) from my core identity and being. Those two decades were years of gut-wrenching self-interrogation and inquiry. The process was ongoing, and made it impossible for me to complete the odyssey I had begun as a very young man and terminate it with the book I had written.

Having been inside one perspective and now looking at things through very different eyes, I was able to understand—to see—how the best intentions led to troubling and even evil results. I even managed to capture this new insight when I created a motto for the online magazine I came to publish: "Inside every liberal is a totalitarian screaming to get out." Of course I meant by this that every progressive who imagines that a beautiful future is written into history's code will be tempted by its very beauty to go along with the means necessary to achieve it. Out of good intentions, therefore, dreadful results. To confront the siren-song of the left and warn others about its consequences was a calling I could not refuse.

As for Walter's final question—what meaning do my present efforts impart to a life?—they don't. They provide the satisfaction of opposing bad causes and perhaps contributing to good ones. In that sense, they could be said to make a life seem meaningful. But I don't believe, as progressives do, that the moral arc of the universe is bent toward justice. Therefore, in the long run, the battles I have fought and the many volumes written have as good a chance of adding up to nothing as they do of contributing to happier endings. In the long run, history does not move in a positive direction. Or any direction. If I entertain a hope of historical progress, it is limited to this: that my children and theirs will live in a freer, less threatened, and more humane environment than I did. I cannot engage the future any further or more widely than that.

Yet we all seek a larger purpose to our lives, and this quest for meaning is inescapable; it is part of our genome. How should we deal with the desire to make the world whole, and to make it make sense? My advice is this: Keep a wary eye on such urges, which cannot be satisfied. Be careful about what you seek. Where large matters are involved, a modest ambition is usually the prudent one. Tend your garden. Cherish friends and family. Our lives are enlarged and our sense of who we are is enhanced when our children turn out well, and when we can be of help to others. Find satisfaction in these modest goals, in completing the tasks you undertake and in fulfilling the responsibilities that are yours. Bear always in mind that only a religious faith can impart meaning to our existence. It does so through the vision of a life hereafter that repairs the irreparable in ours and makes us whole. Now we see through a glass darkly, only then face to face. This is the only faith that has a chance—and it is only a chance—to succeed without destructive consequences.

By contrast, the bad faiths—the faiths that seek to change this world and purge it of evil—lead inexorably to passions that are themselves evil:

the desire to take away freedom and to suppress opponents. That is why missions to redeem the world by making it just are responsible for the great calamities of our times.

This is what I have concluded through bitter experience and what I feel called on to testify to others, and will continue to do so until my final breath.

July-August

Karma

April and I began living together in 1996, and once we were nestled under the same roof, animals began appearing. I use this grammatical construction advisedly because I was surprised by their appearances and not involved in their coming. First, a dog named Barney; then a Maltese named Buddy, whom we called "Fat Man;" and a Shih Tzu named Molly, who rode in my lap to and from my radiation treatments in the winter of 2001 for the prostate cancer that had leaked into my system. Then came Jake and Lucy and Lucky, who are with us still; and Winnie and Coco, who have only recently passed.

In the eighth year of our marriage we were living in Calabasas. April had begun riding a gorgeous paint named Alvin, who was boarded at a ranch about twenty minutes away. Soon she was buying the horse, and then we were buying an acre-and-a-half ranch in the Santa Rosa Valley so that Alvin could be with us all the time. As soon as we had acquired the ranch, April bought another horse named Diddy to be Alvin's companion. No sooner had we settled into our new home than April began rescuing horses that people had abandoned. To help her, I set up a foundation which she named Heart of a Horse, to raise money to fund her rescues.

As soon as we were set up on our new ranch with Alvin and Diddy in the stalls, April began rescuing abandoned and neglected horses. One day the Ventura County humane officer called to tell her about a horse that had been left in a stall near Lake Casitas. The horse had not had anything to eat for a long while and was in very poor condition, and was going to be removed from the property. The humane officer asked April, who was becoming known in the area as the "Heart of a Horse Lady," if she would take the horse, rehabilitate him, and then find him a home. April agreed to meet her at the site in Ojai.

The abandoned horse, an Arabian, had been owned by an illegal immigrant who had been arrested on a criminal charge and sent back to Mexico. Several other horses were stabled in the same location, but none of the owners had bothered to feed the Arab who had been left behind. April drove her truck to the site. It was a dry field, parched and dusty, and there were only a few trees to break the harsh rays of the sun overhead.

Across from the entrance, April saw a cluster of semi-open shacks that served as stalls. There was no water in the stalls. April glanced at her dashboard and saw that it was 108 degrees outside. She got out of her truck and walked over to the edge of the stall where the abandoned horse had been left. "I saw a bay-colored skeleton that appeared to be an Arab," she told me later, "although he was so emaciated and his body so distorted that I had to look twice to make sure. His flesh was shrunken from lack of food and seemed to hang from his spine, making his head, which was down, seem exceptionally large. His flanks were sunken and instead of being rounded his rump was all angles where the flesh had receded, bringing his bones to the surface. He had a tattered black mane and a ragged tail, and, most heartbreaking of all, he was on his knees in the manure, as though he had given up hope and was simply waiting for his misery to end. I thought to myself, 'this poor fellow is ready to die.' But the moment I stepped into the muck inside the stall, he lifted his head and looked up at me."

When he did, April began talking to him. She said, "I don't know your name, or who you are, and you don't know me. But I'm going to help you. Just hold on, sweetheart. I will rescue you and find you a home." Outside the stall there was a bucket filled with empty beer cans. The humane officer and April dumped the cans out, rinsed the bucket clean, filled it with water, and brought it into the stall for the Arab to drink. Then April went over to her truck and pulled out a twenty-five-pound bag of alfalfa pellets. She poured the pellets into a container and put it near the Arab, and he immediately began to eat. He chewed very slowly and with great effort. "He was so weak it was pitiful," she remembers, "and the air was so hot. My heart went out to him."

Once they had provided the Arab with water and food, there was nothing more they could do for him at the moment. They needed to get a vet out to look at him and then remove him from the site to a place where he could be rehabilitated. Before April could call the vet, she needed to leave the place. She did not want to be there by the stables alone. Men with hardened faces and hostile looks were standing around. They were day laborers who owned the horses in the stalls next to the starving Arab, but had not fed or watered him. They had been warned that the law was looking into the case, and they were standing around sullenly, as though making up their minds as to what kind of trouble they might be in and what they were going to do about it. April mounted the cab of her truck and drove off.

When she got back on the freeway she dialed Dr. Smith, her vet, and filled him in on what she had seen. They agreed to meet later in the day and drive together in his vet truck to the field in Ojai. When she returned, even though it was only about four or five hours since she had been there, she could already see a change in the emaciated little Arab who still had no name. He had drunk more of the water and devoured more of the feed, and the nourishment had begun to revive him. When she looked over the wall of his stall, he was standing and holding his head up and looking back at her. His eyes had begun to have a flicker of life in them, and she imagined him saying, "Hey you're back, the lady that gave me something to eat. I didn't think I'd see you again."

They entered the filthy stall, and April helped Dr. Smith place a halter over the Arab's head. This gave them enough control so that he could administer the medication he had brought to ease the Arab's discomfort. When this was done, they attempted to walk him out; but he had been confined to the stall for so many months that he was hardly able to walk. April was a little worried that he might pass out. The two of them rubbed his body all over, then they walked him over to the wash rack across from the stalls and hosed him down and tried to flush off the dirt, which was caked on his back and flanks and legs. His head was now up and his eyes alert, but he also extended his neck towards them and seemed to want them next to him. As they put him back in his stall, April kissed him goodbye and said, "I promise I will be back tomorrow."

As Dr. Smith and April headed for the vet truck, two men came toward them and began talking in broken English about the owner who had been sent back to Mexico. One of the men asked April, "Are we going to get in trouble for this horse?" Her first concern was to avoid any possible scene that might compromise the Arab's removal, so she said, "No. There is not going to be any trouble, because the horse is leaving with me on Monday." Then she asked him as unthreateningly as she could, "Why has this horse had no food and water for so long?"

He looked at April and said, "I don't want no trouble." Holding up two fingers he pointed at the starving Arab and lied, "I give this horse two flakes of hay every day." A flake is a normal meal for a horse, and two meals is a normal portion for a day. If the Arab had been fed that much hay, there was no way he would have been in the skeletal condition he was in.

"You gave this horse two flakes of hay a day?" said Dr. Smith. "Si." Dr. Smith did not bother to conceal his anger: "You gave this horse two flakes of a hay a day and he's three hundred pounds underweight? That's a miracle. I've never seen anything like it in my practice. This horse is skin and bones and getting ready to die. How is that possible?"

"Maybe he got cancer," the man said.

The next day April could not stop thinking about the Arab with no name. She had some business to take care of before she could see him, but when her tasks were done, she drove back to the scorched field off the freeway in Ojai. She pulled up, jumped out of her truck and ran to his stall. There he was, and he was standing up straight. He looked right in her direction and his body language said, "Wow, you came back for me."

"Yes, I came back," she said out loud. "I've brought you some treats and some fly spray to get those nasty things off you." She fed him some horse cookies and began to apply the spray. Some horses shy at the sound of the aerosol, and the Arab turned out to be one of them. He probably had never encountered fly spray before or heard the aerosol whoosh. So April sprayed her hand instead and rubbed it over him. As she worked her way down from his face, and over his withers to his flanks, she could feel every bone sticking out. It made her sad to be touching his skeleton like that, but she also saw he was loving the touch. As she rubbed and soothed him, he turned his head and his big brown eyes looked at her as if to say thank you. "You are going to be coming with me Monday to start a new life," she said. Then she realized his new life had already begun.

Before driving away, she asked the men who were still hanging around what the horse's name was, but no one would tell her. On the way home, she decided she would call him Lazarus. "God put a conscience into the person who phoned the Humane Society and alerted the officer who then called me," she said. "If that person had just passed the Arab the way everyone else had, he would soon have been dead. The name Lazarus means, 'God is my help.' That phone call was the first link in the chain that brought Lazarus back from the dead." When Monday came, she returned with a hauler to transport him to the ranch where she had rented a stall to start him on the path to rehabilitation.

In the months that followed, April hired a trainer to work Lazarus, and a sports therapist to massage his muscles and stretch his joints. Dr. Smith provided him with vaccines and other medications, and a farrier shoed him properly. April organized a group of young girls to give him baths and ride him and shower him with affection. When the rehabilitation was complete, this horse that had looked like a concentration camp survivor could easily be mistaken for a show animal; he was that beautiful.

And talented too. One day the Mexicans at the ranch were playing their mariachi music, and Lazarus suddenly began to dance. It turned out that he was a charro horse, used in the Mexican rodeos which are held all over California, although the general public is hardly aware they exist. Lazarus was so full of energy and life. He would take off on a run and fly across the arena as Arabs do, making leaps in which all four of his hooves left the ground. It was a display of joy at his new life, and it lit up April's heart to watch him. She knew, however, that she would have to part with him soon. In the end, the goal of rescue is to find the abandoned animal a "forever home."

Sure enough, after several months a man from a nearby horse canyon came to adopt Lazarus. April was cautious because she did not want Lazarus to be abused again. But her concerns were allayed by the kind character of the man. He already had a white Arabian and wanted to make Lazarus his companion. When Lazarus finally left, April's emotions were a mixture of joy at his rejuvenation and sadness that he would be leaving her. She cried for a long time. She had come to love him so much, as she did all her horses.

I am in awe of my wife for the devotion she has shown to these abandoned creatures. A spiritual heart breeds compassion for the vulnerable, as the story of Lazarus illustrates. But why have I told this story in detail and at length? It says something about the cruelty of men toward any creature they consider weaker or unable to retaliate. As a critic of messianic illusions, I see it as a lesson in the irredeemable aspect of the human condition. The casual cruelty and normal deceitfulness of human beings will always frustrate hopes for a better world.

It is also a lesson in the possibility of redemption for an individual life. Each time you bring someone back from the doors of death, each time you restore them to health, you are confronted by how fragile life is and how glorious it can be. My heart is warmed every time I think of the skeletal figure April came upon and the magnificent creature that emerged through the love and care that she and her volunteers showered on him.

The story of Lazarus is also the story of a creative faith. Do horses have thoughts and emotions similar to ours? If you talk to a horse, does he understand you? Can you inspire his will to live? Does God watch over his creatures and arrange phone calls leading to rescues like this? Does it matter? What matters is a heart that is open, that can connect you to the voiceless and helpless. What is important is a faith that inspires you to see to their care and revival. Without these, none of what April did—and not only for Lazarus—would be possible.

In my view, the good deeds that are done in this world are performed by people of faith who love and are not daunted by the ordinary cruelty of others. They are performed by people who act on the belief that our lives are connected and that we are placed here for a reason, whether by a divinity or not. My wife's belief is the source of immense good to those who might never have received it. And I am its chief, if not always deserving, beneficiary.

Is it necessary to believe in a God to have this faith? I do not think so, although it is certain that belief in God, and a hidden order, can be a powerful inspiration to good deeds. There are many sources of creative faiths, but what they have in common is this: They are born of humility and love, and their adherents do not presume to act like gods and try to re-create the world.

Bury the Bad and Embrace the Good

During the days of my glacial convalescence, one thing on my mind was a book-signing party I had set in motion for July 26, which would be four months after my mishap. It was going to be held at our home, and its ostensible purpose was to celebrate the publication of *Take No Prisoners,* a book I had written about how to fight a bad faith. We were expecting two hundred people and had prepared entertainments to make the occasion memorable, with a band, a disk jockey, pony and horse rides, and a barbecue.

The theme was western and we were hoping everyone would come decked out in ten-gallon hats and cowboy boots, ready to have fun.

The real energy behind the event was April's, who had a very different view of what this party would mean. "This is a celebration for us of our return to the world, to life," she said to me. "We've been buried for so long now with our medical problems, this is a chance to see our friends and your supporters all at once. We're going to get a great lift out of this, and maybe, even, it will put you back on your feet."

While immersed in preparations for the party, we were visited by a branch of April's large family that had been missing from our Mother's Day gathering. Jim and Kim were there along with Cheri and Wendell. But the guests of the day were her sister Ramona's children, Race and Jackie O, and their families, which included five children. For this festivity, April had bought the children a store full of toys, including a stable and horse for one of Race's little girls. Afterward I asked April if these weren't the kind of toys she would have liked to have when she was a little girl, though I knew the answer before she gave it.

In the evening, when the younger generation had departed, a little gathering formed around the table under our jacaranda trees. It included Kim and Jim and April and their former sister-in-law Cindy. The conversation turned to their childhood and to stories out of school about April's parents. When Kim and Jim began talking about sexual improprieties by April's father and mother, they triggered an angry reaction. April was a fierce defender of the good she remembered in her parents, and would not tolerate the disrespect Kim in particular was showing for their memories.

Nothing struck me more forcefully than April's defense of her father, who had psychologically abused her, disowning her to her face and taunting her verbally on many occasions throughout her childhood. It was only as a young adult that she acquired the psychological fortitude to fight back. Yet at the end she had gone to his sickbed and wiped the sweat from his brow and bathed him and let him know that she forgave him. She wanted to keep only the memories of the kindnesses he had done to her and her siblings and to bury the bad memories with him. She had the same attitude toward her mother. "It is best," she said, "to remember the good. It is best for one's own heart to be at peace."

When I thought about this attitude of hers, so different from her sisters', even though I thought she was being far too generous — to her abusive father in particular—I realized that that very attitude had played a central role in our marriage. Every marriage faces formidable obstacles in the fact that two people with different sensibilities must learn to live together under one roof. Consequently, in every marriage there are conflicts which generate strong emotions. Sometimes when they rise to the surface they may even seem to preclude a life together. These conflicts are somehow resolved in marriages that work, and not in those that don't. In mine, it has more often been the readiness of my wife to embrace the good and bury the bad that has released us from these moments and reunited us on the other side.

A Partial Remission

While all the party preparations were going on, our home continued to have the feel of an *hôpital des invalides*. An x-ray had shown that April's clavicle had still not healed, and that broken bones were pressing down on her axillary nerve, causing the pain to run down her arm to her fingertips. As if that were not enough, she had also developed a case of chondromalacia, an inflammation of the underside of the knee, which was also quite painful and required physical therapy, in her case possibly an operation, to correct. At the same time, I was going through a phase of recovery (to put the best face on it) where there were hours in the day, and especially at night, when I was besieged by waves of eye-rolling pain. These episodes prevented me from concentrating on my work and had to be medicated. From where I sat, the recovery was going so slowly I was beginning to give up hope that I would be back to a semblance of normal by the time of the party.

Then, quite suddenly, I had a remission. The foot massages April was giving me were having an effect; as were, no doubt, the exercises I was doing and the passage of time. Where I was sometimes taking two or three pills a night to deal with the pain, I was now going days without needing even one. It was an amazing pleasure to walk without pain and not to feel the soreness that I had become used to along the sciatic ridge of my foot. I was still hobbling because of the frozen ankle and would tire easily as the foot swelled under the pressure of my exertions. But there was no denying the trend was positive. Twice a week I was attending rigorous physical therapy sessions, which focused on the muscles that were weak and the sinews that were still locked. It was now the middle of July, and the party was only a week away.

The therapy had given me increased flexibility, and I was beginning to think I would attend as a semi-recovered case. I was looking forward to that.

A Romance of Age

When the day finally arrived, the party proved to be just the celebration of life and return that April had predicted. Our friends and neighbors came, and my co-workers at the Center, and my supporters. It was the largest gathering of April's family outside of funerals that anyone could remember. Her sisters Kim and Cheri and Ramona were there, her brother Joe, and members of her extended family including Big Jon, who thanked her for putting the reunion together. There were about two hundred in all, and they seemed to be having an exceptionally good time.

The festive atmosphere was encouraged by the talent we assembled. My friend Joel Gilbert brought his Dylan tribute band, "Highway 61 Revisited," to play a forty-five-minute program. Another friend, screen actor Steven Bauer, brought his guitar and performed a solo set of songs by Paul McCartney, Elton John, and others. But for me the high point of the afternoon and evening came when the DJ announced he was playing "April and David's wedding song" and April and I stepped onto the temporary floor that had been laid over the grass, and began to dance.

April was in a blue and white flower-print dress, and stunning, as her blonde hair caught highlights from the sun. The misters we had put in place because the day was hot elevated the dreamlike effect, enveloping us in a gauzy vapor. Like newlyweds, we drew each other closer and kissed.

Our friend Arrik Weathers had indeed sung this song at our wedding sixteen years before, but I had first given it to April as "our song" when I had not yet proposed but knew I was about to. I knew, too, that she would have worries about what she might be getting into, since I was coming from a world so different from hers. The song was called "I Swear," and was sentimental and over the top in the way that pop tunes often are ("I swear by the moon and the stars in the sky"). But it fit the occasion and what I wanted her to hear:

> *I see the questions in your eyes*
> *I know what's weighing on your mind..*
> *I'll stand beside you through the years..*

And though I'll make mistakes
I'll never break your heart

I'll give you everything I can
I'll build your dreams with these two hands
We'll hang some memories on the walls
And when just the two of us are there
You won't have to ask if I still care
'Cause as time turns the page
My love won't age at all

The moments we danced to this song were enchanted—not with the romance of youth, which is a romance of promises, but the harder romance of age—of achievement. For twenty years I had kept these promises and would keep them to the grave. I could not say that about my whole life, but I could say it about the life I shared with April.

We were among friends, and our dance struck a chord with many, moving several to tears. The day after the party we received a note from one: "I know you have a houseful of guests and face cleanup today, but I want to thank you for including me in your party yesterday. Of all the enjoyable conversations I had and food I ate, what touched me most was watching you two dance your anniversary dance. I am truly grateful for the angel that came to you, April, in your moment of death and brought you back for David and the rest of us."

Amen.

Inspiration

I have already observed how the short lives of canines impart an important discipline to the mortals who own and love them. Their stoicism in the face of life's adversities set benchmarks for us all. April and I have adopted two rescue dogs who are missing legs—a condition that didn't have the same relevance for me when we rescued them as it does now. Lucky was the first to become part of our household. At five pounds, he is a little snip of a dog with a white coat and brilliant black eyes. We call him "knuckle-head" because the abuse he experienced sometimes triggers emotional squalls when he feels threatened. His right front leg was already shriveled when April came upon him in a Petco adoption center and was drawn to his bereft look. When she inquired about him, she was told that Lucky had been there a year. "Nobody wants him." When April heard these words, of course, she picked him up and said, "Lucky, you're coming home with me," and we have had him ever since.

The vet thought Lucky's withered leg posed a hazard and advised us to remove it, which we did. The absence of the front limb has given him a sort of hippity-hop gait, like a rabbit's. "My little jumping jelly bean" is the affectionate way April refers to him. One of my pleasures is to watch him follow the other dogs as they scamper across the lawn. Because of his handicap he occasionally stumbles, rolls over, and picks himself up to bound after them again. This all reminds me of Coco, who used to fall into a roll when she pursued the chase faster than her little legs could handle.

Abby is a deer Chihuahua with a silken black patch on her back and a brown underbelly and markings to frame it. She was found by some students hiding under a pile of wood in downtown Los Angeles. Her hind leg was broken and dangled at her side and she barked hysterically, darting away when anyone approached. The students left her scraps to feed on until they finally had the idea to bring her to us. When she arrived at our house she was screaming in pain and fear, which continued without stopping for three days.

As soon as she arrived we took her to the vet, who worked hours to save her leg but finally had to give up. There was just too much scar tissue to make the limb workable, so she removed it entirely. I can identify with Abby for the nights of pain she went through. She is still frightened of car lights and still screams every now and then, but she is a sweet and loving dog, and because it is her hind leg that is missing she can outrun any of the four-legged Chihuahuas in the house.

What impresses me is how both these dogs have picked themselves up out of tragedy and created new lives. For them, three legs, however cumbersome at times, is who they are, and they accept it. This is worth the effort we made to save them and puts a smile on my face whenever I think about it.

September 3

Testosterone

I n the idle time that an extended convalescence offers, I have had occasion to think about the fact that this is the first book I have written without any testosterone in my system. This odd fact is a consequence of the hormone therapy I began last January under the guidance of my oncologist. My PSA levels had spiked to nine, which is a lot for someone without a prostate. Fortunately, scans revealed there was no metastasis into my bones or lymph system. Nonetheless, to be safe my doctor put me on a program of Luprin shots, which reduced my testosterone levels to about zero.

I have to admit that I've been a bit watery of late, and sometimes the slightest setback in my general condition, or even something as innocuous as watching a YouTube video of Train receiving the Group of the Year Grammy and thanking their manager, my son Jon, for "saving their careers," can set off crying jags as uncontrollable as that of any female on her period.

Admittedly I am on a cocktail of other drugs, like Neurontin, which may account for these mood swings. But I don't think the medications are behind all the reactions. After all, why should tears be inappropriate when you think about how your children have gone into the world, and you realize that all those days you shared are gone with them?

As a result of this hormone-induced testosterone deficiency, I was even experiencing the kinds of hot flashes that are familiar to women during menopause. At first I resisted when my wife urged me to take a drug to eliminate them. This was a bit of male bravado, and pretty quickly I had to concede that I had overreached. The hot flashes proved to be bothersome enough that I wanted to be rid of them. "At last," my wife exclaimed, "you know what it's like to be a woman!"

Maybe—but not so much a woman that my passion for her has dimmed. Though I have known April for twenty years and despite the fact that my loins are lifeless (temporarily as I hope), there are moments every day when I see her face, or her flesh, or her form relaxed or at some task, and my chest flushes and I want to go over and kiss her just as when we were younger and my loins were alive.

In September I had another appointment with my oncologist. My PSA had dropped to 0.1, close enough to zero, and I was told that I could discontinue the Luprin treatments, at least until we could assess the result. This meant that my body would now be creating testosterone again and the missing sexual feelings would return. I look at the whole experience of their absence as a useful way of measuring the passions of the heart, which are strong enough without them.

Setback

For more than a month my bad leg had felt unusually swollen and painful, bad enough that I made appointments with my primary care doctor and my neurologist. The first appointment was on a Monday, but my primary care doctor was so busy I had to see one of his associates. She introduced herself by saying she was not actually a doctor but a "physician's assistant," which immediately undermined my confidence in the advice she was about to give. On examining my leg she said I probably had a blood clot (not unusual after operations like mine) and should go directly to a hospital emergency room and get an ultrasound to see if I actually did. But this was not something I wanted to do, having spent many hours in emergency rooms waiting for attention. Moreover, I had an appointment with my primary care doctor the next day, and my neurologist the day after that.

When my primary care doctor examined my leg he said with authority, "You do not have a blood clot," and sent me home. My neurologist was not so sure, and made an appointment for me with a vascular surgeon for the following day. After examining me the vascular surgeon ordered an ultrasound, which showed that I had an "acute" blood clot extending from my ankle up through my groin. I was immediately put on a gurney and taken upstairs to a bed in the hospital where they ran an IV and put me on anti-coagulants.

I remained in the hospital for five days, during which I had time to think about all the physical therapies I had been through, the massages of my swollen leg, which put me in a lot of pain, and the exercises I had done with similar results. I was lucky the clot had not broken into my lungs—or worse, my heart, where it could have been fatal.

Four days after I returned home, April and I took a walk up the driveway with our dogs. When we reached the top I was out of breath and had a pain in my left shoulder and part of my chest area. "It's nothing," I said, not wanting to entertain even the possibility that I would have to go back. To which April replied, "Either you are coming with me to the emergency room, or I am calling 911." On the spur of that moment I decided it would be less embarrassing to go to the emergency room if the pain proved to be nothing, so I said okay. When we arrived at Los Robles, they triaged me and put me at the head of the line. Shortly afterwards they wheeled me in for a CT scan, which showed that a piece of the clot had broken off and moved to my lung. If the clot were to pass from there to my heart or my brain, it would be all over. So I stayed in the hospital for another five days until I was stabilized. When I was released, the vascular surgeon put me on the table again and inserted a filter in my vena cava to prevent any more clots from gravitating to my upper body.

For many days I felt terribly weak, having spent so much time immobile in hospital beds. My legs, both of them, ached when I tried to walk. I was anxious in a way I hadn't been since the angina six years previously, when I had a stent inserted. For months after that, every poke of anxiety or heartburn seemed it might be the harbinger of a new assault. The experience taught me not to panic over incidents like this. Following consultations with a hematologist and pulmonary specialist, I was reassured that this too would pass, and when it did I would be all right. Gradually I returned to my routines. My bad leg was even feeling better without the full pressure of the clot, and I began looking up and outward again. It was another lesson in the ongoing tutorial of the year: you never know what the next day will bring.

At the Edge

"Once the truck was airborne," April recalled after the accident, "I thought my life was over. And I accepted it. When I hit the bottom of the drainage pipe it was a very hard hit. The airbag didn't open, and I felt this horrible blow to my chest and passed out. I was out for a few minutes but as soon as I woke up I was screaming for help and wanting to live. I was frightened. I was in such pain, and so helpless; so alone. I could feel something was terribly wrong with my body. I saw car fumes and was seized by a panic that I might burn to death. I began to scream even louder. Then I saw two migrant workers talking just outside the cab of the truck. I screamed at them, please help me. I knew I couldn't get out of the cab by myself. I was hanging from the seat belt. The truck had fallen to its side during the crash and I was suspended by the belt. One of the men climbed into the cab and got to the back of my seat and held me. He started talking in Spanish. I never saw what he looked like. As I passed in and out of consciousness, he continued to hold me. He reached out and took a knife from the other man and cut me loose. My body shifted and the pain caused me to black out again. When I regained consciousness, I saw his leg was shaking. I begged him, 'Please don't leave me.' I didn't want to die alone.

"A man was peering through the sunroof and I dreamed that he pulled me out. I felt total relief and happiness. He was smiling and his eyes were sparkling and he had such a sweet face. I started floating towards him and felt I was going to be all right. Later the rescue crew assured me I had hallucinated the man because I was pulled out of the side of the cab. When I woke up again as the paramedics were cutting my clothes off, I screamed, 'My husband is David Horowitz, please call him.' I did this over and over, and then I gave them the number of your cell. Then I passed out again. When I woke, I was on a gurney being run through the emergency room. I must have screamed because one of the nurses kept repeating, 'I didn't touch you, I didn't touch you.'"

Two weeks later an officer phoned April in the intensive care unit. She asked him about the Hispanic man who had climbed into the cab of the truck and held her. The officer said there were actually nine people who gathered at the site, but only this man was willing to take the risk of getting in. The officer said he was shaking and crying. April asked if she could contact him now, but the officer told her that the man was probably here illegally and would not want to be found.

Her brush with death caused a change in April in the months that followed. She had always wanted to fix up the house we lived in, and over the years we had done some work on it, putting in walnut floors and upgrading other features. However, the alterations we could make were limited by financial constraints, in particular by the desire not to dig too prodigally into my pension fund, which would be her only financial security when I was gone.

But now she began an ambitious construction project. It started with a gutting of our master bathroom, which hadn't been touched in thirty years. She tiled the walls in white with a crackle finish and installed a vintage bathtub with brushed nickel legs. She also showed new concern for what I ate, how much exercise I did in my crippled state, and above all my attitude—that I should never give up but fight my way to live to a hundred. The climax of all this pressure was the sweetest, most satisfying words ever to grace my ears: "Don't die, don't leave me. I love my life with you, and I don't know what I would do without you."

I had the same feelings for her. And of course, when one of us did die, the other would go on because we have children and grandchildren and that would keep us going, along with our friends and life's normal distractions. But it would not be the same. If I lost her, it would be like waking up to a world where there is only night and no day, and I know she feels the same.

I Would Have Saved Her If I Could

Before the accident whose wounds made working with horses out of the question, April had been continuously involved in rescues. But not all rescues succeed, and how could they? One day each of us will face a crisis where there will be no one to save us. Since that is life's endgame, it is wise to prepare oneself by keeping an eye on the rescues that fail. In medieval times it was common practice to keep a human skull close by as *memento mori* to encourage contemplation of our common fate. Working in horse rescue is pretty close.

One of April's rescue attempts involved a paint mare. The plight of the mare came to her attention through a phone call from a Hispanic man whom I will refer to as "Hector" to protect him. Hector said he had a horse that was ill, and he wanted April to save her. In all the time April dealt with him, Hector never mentioned the name of the horse, and no one at the impoverished facility where the horse was kept would volunteer the name over the weeks that followed. So April called her Pinto, because she was a paint.

After receiving Hector's call, April phoned her vet, Dr. Smith, and they went over to have a look. The address Hector provided took them to a collection of ramshackle stalls in a dirt yard behind a railroad track. As they entered the compound, they saw Hector waiting for them. He was young and neatly dressed, and he was soon joined by his two children, who had been dropped off from school. Hector told them that Pinto was the family horse. She had belonged to his father, and he had ridden her as a child. He had seen her give birth to five foals over the course of time. He said that Pinto had been pregnant the week before but he had to pull her baby out of her because it was already dead. He also told them that the situation had gotten so bad because he had been out of town for two months; he was shocked by what he saw when he came back. April didn't trust the explanation he gave her, but she was reluctant to challenge him. She learned too late how far from the truth his story was.

When Hector took them over to Pinto's stall, the horse was standing in a pit of manure which covered the entire floor. Every stall on the property was filthy and every animal in poor condition, but none as poor as Pinto. There was a bad odor about the horse, and every part of her skeleton, like Lazarus's, was visible through her emaciated flesh. Her hair was matted, and malnutrition was causing it to fall out. There were flies all over her. It was August, and a heat wave sent temperatures outside the stall to over one hundred degrees. Inside, it felt like an oven. April thought, "God, I hate this. How can people let this happen?"

Dr. Smith went over to the ailing mare and, after completing his examination, gave her a shot to relieve her discomfort. April said to Hector, "I can take this horse and rehabilitate her and find her a new home." But Hector did not want a new home for Pinto. He said, "No, I love this horse. I want her to stay here." Then he looked at the two of them a little nervously and said, "I don't want to get into trouble."

Sometimes people tell you things without telling you. And often you are unable to hear them. This was such an occasion. What Hector was not telling April, as she would learn later, was that he owed room and board to the owner of the property, who was also Mexican and had threatened him, warning him he had better not give the horse away. The owner wanted Hector to keep Pinto because he knew Hector loved the horse, and he was going to teach him a lesson he would never forget. He was going to starve Hector's horse to death. April never found out what the owner was holding over

Hector that prevented him from seeking help. Perhaps he was an illegal immigrant, which would have been sufficient. Perhaps it was something else. It didn't really matter.

April accepted Hector's word that he wanted to help Pinto. She could see that he was a decent man and a good father. And he obviously had a deep affection for a horse that had been with his family since he could remember. He seemed like someone she could trust to help Pinto get well. She focused on Pinto's suffering and what she and Dr. Smith had to do. She had no idea what was actually going on. She thought Hector was saying to her that he was afraid of being fined or prosecuted for Pinto's abuse, although that didn't really make sense. If she had thought about it, nothing did. April tried to reassure Hector to earn his confidence. "What you are doing now is the right thing to do. You were away and had no idea what was going on for two months." But Hector did.

April told Hector she would be providing hay and supplements, so that he could bring Pinto back to health. Dr. Smith then went over the medical program he would have to follow as part of Pinto's rehabilitation. April was having a hard time concentrating. The day was hot and the manure so deep in Pinto's stall that her boots just sank into it. When Dr. Smith had finished giving Hector instructions, April whispered, "Please tell him he has to clean up this place."

Dr. Smith was already seething over the conditions they had walked into. He told Hector bluntly that he had to shovel the manure out of Pinto's stall and attend to her hooves, which were in terrible shape. They were already so overgrown they made it difficult for Pinto to move. April told Hector she would pay for a farrier. But he said, "That's great but it won't be necessary. The owner of this property is a farrier, and he will take care of it." She was shocked to hear this. If the owner was a farrier, why hadn't he taken care of Pinto before she reached this state? The whole scene disgusted her. She said, "I can come back tomorrow and help you shovel the manure. I will help you give Pinto a bath." But Hector said, "Don't worry about it. I'll get it done. You've done so much already."

April's heart was so full at what she had seen that she didn't want to leave until she had done something to alleviate Pinto's suffering. But Dr. Smith called her over and said, "April, look around you. You are the only female here. This place can be pretty dangerous. Haven't you noticed all the beer cans and alcohol bottles lying around? I don't think it's a good idea." So they left together.

Over the next weeks, April and Dr. Smith called Hector several times. Each time he assured them that Pinto was doing great and her health was improving. "She's putting on weight. No worries." He even sent April a thank-you card. When she asked him, "Did you get Pinto's food?" He assured her, "Everything is going really well. Don't worry."

Soon after the call, April and her assistant were in the neighborhood picking up pellets and feed at the local tack store for her rescue horses. While tending to her business, she had a sinking feeling which at first she couldn't put her finger on. Then she realized what it was. She looked at her assistant and said, "We have to turn around. I have to look in on a horse named Pinto."

The heat wave had continued, and it was sweltering outside. She was hoping Hector had seen to Pinto's hooves and that she was outside in the air, where she could breathe. But she had an intuition that something was terribly wrong. When they arrived at the dilapidated stalls, her assistant was a little frightened. She had never been in such a place. April reassured her, "Don't worry, I've done things like this before. I know it looks bad, but I have to see that Pinto's okay." In her heart she just knew she wasn't.

As they approached the buildings the first thing that struck April was that the stalls were in the same filthy condition as when she had left them. Then she saw a Hispanic man standing in the yard between them and the stalls. It was the owner. He looked disturbed as their truck approached. April leaned out of the window of the cab and said to him, as firmly as she could, "Where is Hector's horse?" He didn't answer and averted his eyes. He put his head down and in a vigorous motion waved her to leave. But she was not about to go without seeing Pinto. She jumped out of the truck and walked right past the owner and over to Pinto's stall.

When she opened the door, her heart sank. It was like opening a blast furnace. The heat just came over her in waves. There was poor Pinto lying in piles of her own manure. Flies swarmed around the filth and coated her face and body. April had never seen anything like it. Pinto's tongue was hanging out and her eye that was not buried in the manure was open. Her lips were moving and April realized the horse was trying to get some kind of moisture. She realized, too, that she had come too late.

Pinto was lost. She knew now that Hector had lied to her, and none of the many people who were around the barns had bothered to call for help. Now Pinto was beyond help. All that was left was to phone Dr. Smith and ask him to come over to ease Pinto out of this life that had been so cruel to her. All April could do was to sit with Pinto, and hose the flies off her body and brush away those that had gathered around her eyes. She got some grains and carrots and tried to feed her, and whatever she could to comfort her.

She began talking to Pinto. She told her that she had been a good horse, which she had; she had served her family well. She didn't deserve this abuse. April told her that where she was going now it would be comfortable and clean. Where she was going the heat would be gone and the manure too. And there would be no more flies to bother her.

After a while Dr. Smith arrived and gave Pinto the shot that took her out of this world and the hell that men's cruelty had created for her. Through her tears April saw that Pinto was at peace at last.

All of us should have someone like this to help us pass over the bridge from this life and its injustices into whatever lies beyond. All of us should have someone to love us at the end.

Don't Cry for the Horses

After Pinto was put down, April tried to get the authorities to step in and do something about the hell-hole that had swallowed her. But the law moves slowly and, as she discovered, in cases of abused horses often not at all. In the days and weeks that followed she learned how hard it was to get justice for a gentle creature like Pinto. Her abusers had won.

Almost a year later, April stopped by the place. The filthy stalls behind the railroad tracks had been shut down by the authorities for other violations. When she drove over the tracks, she saw two big signs in Spanish that read, "Do Not Enter." Ignoring them, she parked her truck and walked around to the back of the property. The place was still filthy and brought back horrible memories, as she knew it would. The cars that used to be parked around the stalls were all gone. The stalls themselves were open and empty. She breathed a sigh of relief on seeing them. No more horses would be tortured here.

She went over to where she had found Pinto. The stall door was shut. The manure was still there but it had dried and looked like the detritus of a distant past. Pinto was gone and finally safe. The site of her torment was vacant and the grounds were overgrown with weeds. It was a scene of broken-down, empty barns that should never have been. April looked skyward and said, "Thank you, God." She felt it was payback, however small, for the torture of Pinto and her little foal. She felt a little bit of peace come into her heart

But she would never really be free of the memories of what had happened to Pinto. Each time she pictured that place, her heart was flooded with emotions from her own childhood as a little girl lost and alone. She thought of the children and horses whom no one would come to save. She could not get it out of her head that she had failed Pinto. She thought of how Pinto had lain in that foul-smelling, blistering stall, swarmed by flies, helpless and alone, waiting for someone to pick her up. And how, when she had come, it was too late.

She could no longer do anything for Pinto, but she could try to prevent a similar fate for others. She put together a campaign to tell the people who lived on those ramshackle lots, and on as many ranches as she was able to reach, that when they see horses suffering they can make a call for help and not get in trouble. My grandson Jules was working for Heart of a Horse, and April asked him to compose a brochure to inform people of the law. It was called *Keeping Horses Safe: A Guide to Identifying Horse Abuse and What to Do When You See It.* The brochure described the signs of abuse, quoted the California Cruelty to Animals Law, and urged people to phone animal control authorities and humane officers whenever they saw an animal being abused. Jules found a poem by an anonymous poet to put on the back of the brochure. It has a basic life wisdom that moves me whenever I read it.

> *Look up into the heaven*
> *You'll see them above.*
> *The horses we lost,*
> *The horses we loved.*
> *Manes and tails flowing.*
> *As they gallop through time.*
> *They were never yours.*
> *They were never mine.*
> *Don't cry for the horses,*
> *They'll be back some day.*
> *When our time is gone,*
> *They will show us the way.*
> *Do you hear that soft nicker?*
> *Close to your ear?*
> *Don't cry for the horses,*
> *Love the ones that are here.*

A Charmed Life

In my autobiography *Radical Son*, I described my painful discovery that the Black Panthers, who had been idolized by the left and whom I considered my comrades, were a murderous gang. They had killed not only my friend, Betty van Patter, but many others, including those who had no one to speak up for them, no one to save them. I described the effect of this on me in a brief sentence: "I had come to the end of everything I had ever worked for in my life." Over the next few years, the inner turmoil triggered by this event led to the breakdown of my marriage and presented me with a daunting task: how to put a life back together without the moral compass that had guided me until then.

In the crisis that followed the divorce, it was my mother who came to my support, providing the down payment on a modest but attractive one-bedroom home in the same neighborhood where my children resided. I could not possibly have afforded this myself. I was approaching forty, had no savings, no job, and no prospect of one. I didn't know how I was going to move forward. Still, I was proud that these calamities had not crushed me and that I was even thinking of moving forward.

At this point my parents came out to the West Coast. I described their visit in *Radical Son:* "My parents came out in the summer, as they usually did, and I showed them my new house. It was filled with a morning light, and summarized my sense that I had turned a corner. I had survived my trials and was beginning to pick myself off the floor and come back. I didn't know what I was going to do, but I knew I had to take the bad that had happened to me and make it work for good—first for myself, and then for others in danger of falling into the same black hole. When my parents and I had completed the little tour of the house, I asked my father what he thought. He paused for a moment and said: 'You lead a charmed life.'"

At the time, this struck me as a statement of my father's usual disconnect from my reality, with not a little resentment thrown in over my mother's gift. But now that many years have gone by, his words have taken on a different meaning. Did I lead a charmed life? I could have been killed by the Panthers, since killing people who got in their way was what they did. After Betty's murder and my divorce, I could have fallen into a chasm from which I might never have emerged because of the betrayals of those I had considered my friends and the collapse of my guiding faith. I could have been killed by the gangbangers I hung out with in Compton, where I was doing magazine stories in the early 80s. I could have died from the blood clot following my botched operation. But I didn't.

You can look at your life and rack up the losses, or you can count your blessings. I am missing a daughter who was a beautiful soul, and I can never get her back. At age seventy-five, I have been felled by an incompetent scalpel and condemned to months of neuropathic pain and uncertainty as to when if ever I will feel whole again. My wife was nearly killed less than a year ago and is still in pain and incapacitated from the crash. Because of my writings and ideas, an army of haters is eager to distort my words and my life and do me damage whenever and wherever they can. And yet I have so many blessings to count—a loving life-mate, amazing children, animals I adore, hundreds of thousands of supporters of my work, and friends to confound the haters. I see now that my father was right. I do lead a charmed life. To appreciate this, I needed only to embrace the good and bury the bad.

An Interlude at Sinai

On a bright afternoon in September, April and I drove to the Mount Sinai Cemetery Park in Simi Valley and bought two tombs for ourselves. The cemetery is situated in a nook of the Santa Susana Mountains, a green oasis at the opposite end of the valley from its most famous institution, the Ronald Reagan Presidential Library. The tombs we selected were located in a section called the Caves of Abraham, where vaults are available with stylish granite facings in greens and reds and sandstone colors, bordered in gold. In brochures and placards, discreetly placed, the park authorities convey their intention to memorialize the Holocaust and the six million who perished, as though this were a kind of eternal destiny of the Jews. I could not help visualizing a future in which Muslim *jihadists* came to dig up and desecrate the Hebrew dead, including April (who is not a Jew) and me.

We purchased these gravesites with no expectation of imminent demise, although in the context of this life the adjective "imminent," as we had recently learned, can be quite flexible. It had been only a year since April had come within a hair's breadth of the end of her life, and every time we stepped into a vehicle we were conscious that a split-second was all that might separate us from a terminal event. On the other hand, far from being morbid, we treated our tour of the gravesites as something of a lark, with April inducing me to photograph her clowning at her tomb site so she could send the photo to family for a laugh.

The primary factor that impelled us to close an uncertainty in our future was the desire to take care of details that could be overwhelming for the survivor when the day actually arrived. April, who was the likely candidate for this role, felt she would have to do something for my many supporters who would want to attend my funeral and honor my work. It would be trying enough for her without having to locate a final resting place, particularly one such as this that came with a large chapel. Since April wanted to be near me through this journey too, she was happy with the double tombs that we found.

But what started out as a convenience, a tying up of at least one loose end, turned out to be something else for both of us. The idea of knowing the conclusion of our stories proved comforting. Mount Sinai was a beautiful environment with a serenity that fit its purpose. As we walked the grounds of what we knew would be our last home, we felt unexpected relief.

The Time Is Now

For many years of our marriage one of my concerns was how to provide for April's future when I was gone, given the gap in our ages. Although I have a pension which has accumulated capital, there was not enough to provide her with an income that would allow her to keep the ranch for the years she could expect to outlast me, or to avoid living in severely reduced circumstances. To provide for her as best I could, I assumed the role of gatekeeper for our savings and tried to protect the pension capital any time she had a project that required us to draw on it.

I was unsuccessful in holding the line when Jon and Kathleen got married and April decided that we should have the wedding on our lawn. In her mind, this required substantial landscaping that included terracing the lawn and taming its wilder aspects, building a gazebo where the ceremony could take place, and paths that the bridal party and guests could navigate with ease. How could I oppose a mother's plans for the young man I looked on as a son? In the event, the wedding was a memorable one but it was also costly.

I had to admit that the benefits of her investment extended well beyond the wedding. The terraced lawn she created, with the plot of roses at the break and the little wooden bridge to cross over, affords me one of my great pleasures whenever I sit nestled on the rim of it in one of the rockers on our porch. Maybe it is just age, but taking in the ordinary glories of gardens and trees and the green of lawns is something I look forward to every day.

Nonetheless the ambitious project did reduce our savings and was a blow to my plans for her future. Moreover, it was only the beginning, as she moved on to remodeling the master bathroom. When the work on this project was completed, at just about the time my unfortunate encounter with the surgeon took place, April began to move into high gear in her beautification plans. She bought a saltwater tank with a magical coral reef to place in the sitting room, put elaborate cabinets in the guest room, shuttered the windows and painted the room white. Then she transformed the little office at the end of the hall with cabinetry and a desk, so for the first time I had a space that was organized for the household business. To this mix she added a sewing machine and sewing desk so that she could do quilting and work alongside me. Then she redid the little bathroom just off the office, taking out the bathtub and putting in a shower with small multi-colored stones for a floor.

When we settled on the date for the party that was going to celebrate our return to life, she moved outside and put a new face on the front entrance to the house with a glass-paneled front door and a porch and pathway refinished in bronze flagstones from Canada and Arizona; she ordered new classic carriage doors for the garage and started work on cabinetry and a laundry room in the interior. She re-landscaped the front yard, planting statues of children and horses and cutting away trees to open up the space. She hired a crew to construct a "rock garden" which looked more like an open-air temple, with the same beautiful flagstones and boulders, a water fountain, and a place to sit shaded from the sun. From this perch, one could look out on the house and horse arena and take in the towering trees on our property and the mountains beyond. Then she put in a fire pit and barbecue and acquired an elegant set of patio furniture on which we could dine in the country evenings. And not least or last, she had a garden designer plant hundreds of succulents and flowers and two flaming red crepe myrtles, re-composing the face of our house and its environs. And all this was only a preface to the remodel—really the reconstruction—of the half of the house where the kitchen and dining room were located, removing walls, raising ceilings, and installing fine cabinetry with horse head carvings to create an elegant new home.

All this capital-intensive activity was contrary to the long-held worries she had expressed about her financial security. It was not so much the amount of money we had to take out of our savings to finance the projects, although that was considerable. It was the principle, the discipline we had agreed to, which she was now throwing to the winds. Although I was duly concerned, I didn't put up any real opposition to the new projects. She was still in so much pain from the accident that I held back my concerns, and when each new tile and fixture and plot of greenery produced such looks of happiness, I could hardly say no.

It was only over time, as each transformation of our environment took place, that I began to see what she was doing and began to connect it to the accident and the new attitude that had emerged from it. She had apparently thought about those last things she always dreaded and refused to face but had come to an entirely different conclusion. Even as I was mulling these thoughts in my head, she embarked on yet another new project. Because my gate-keeping job was almost a reflex—despite what I knew, and all the other projects I had let pass—I tried to rein her in and get her to reconsider the course she was taking. She was using up the seed corn on which her future without me depended.

I will never forget the moment I said this, or the reaction that followed. We were standing in the hallway just outside our bedroom door. She took a step toward me and placed her arm on mine. Then she locked eyes with me, looked at me intently and said: "You think you're going to live forever, but a day will come when death puts its arms around you and grabs you, and bam you're gone. You're going to be dead one day. I'm going to be dead. So let's enjoy it while we're here. Let's be happy."

At first I wondered if this wasn't a euphoria born of despair. Perhaps she had come to the conclusion that she was going to die, or that she would want to die if I did. But then I reflected on the way she had justified these expenditures as investments in the value of the house, as though she were enhancing its sale price. I had dismissed these arguments out of hand because the housing market had been down for years and our house was well under water. From an investment standpoint her optimism didn't make sense. But then I received a call from a mortgage banker who wanted me to refinance the house because he thought it was ready to bring its original price. I had not paid much attention to the market recently because it had not changed significantly for so long. But this news put a whole new face on the matter. If the housing market was coming back, while we would not profit from the investment we were making in the house we might have a chance to recoup some of it and, if we were really lucky, call it a wash.

But there was also the possibility that the market would not come back, that it would crash as many were warning, and where would we be then? There was no way to know the future and where it would go. What I did know was that our home was looking dramatically different, more beautiful and inviting than ever. And it was this, not the monetary calculations, that lay behind it all—April's determination that we should make the years still before us as joyful as we could.

Life is a gamble, a series of plays; you win some and you lose others, and there are no guarantees of which way it will go. I liked what my wife had said, and all she had done to back it up. I liked her readiness to take a chance—a big chance—and to go with her dreams. Any way you looked at it, the time we were going to have together was diminishing. We were very much in love, and making the most of what we had left together was a good gamble. Carpe diem. It was a play I could certainly get behind, and I was grateful to my wife for the courage she showed in making it.

A Walk in the Sun

A walk is a basic human activity, an assertion of self. It is a matter of putting one foot in front of the other to say for the moment: *this piece of the earth is mine; mine to survey, mine to do my strut, mine to take my stand.*

Seven months have passed since I lost the use of my left foot and was confined to bed and wheelchair. The slow mending of the nerves has reached a point where I am walking with confidence and a positive attitude. The pain along the sciatic ridge of my foot is mainly gone, though each step carries some pain when I stretch the still-frozen muscles in my ankle and calf. I test myself to see how long I can walk without tiring or without my foot swelling to where the pressure becomes severe. I try to do a little more each day and can walk reasonable distances in the face of reasonable difficulties. For exercise I go up the driveway, which is a 20 percent incline about the length of a football field, along a row of shimmering olive trees which

April planted on one side, and towering palms on the other, until I reach the white mailbox and turn around.

I am still walking with a cane but see it now as adding style to my gait. I have exchanged the one I originally picked up in a medical supply shop for a wooden one with a fancy crook that I bought from a store that sells "Fashionable Canes and Walking Sticks." I have already danced on my beleaguered foot and will do so again at every chance that presents itself. As long as I have breath, nothing is going to stop me from being in the world and making the most of it.

Sometimes I will take the Chihuahuas with me. With only one free hand, I don't put them on leashes. But they are pretty obedient, for which I am grateful since I cannot chase after them. The auburn Lucy is the most headstrong of the three. Ignoring my commands, she runs off into the neighbor's yard. Lucky, the little white one with the missing front leg, hippity-hops beside me and is the most responsive of the lot, perking his head up when I call him, then bounding toward my outstretched arm. The black-and-white spot, Jake, and the deer Chihuahua, Abby, run on ahead but do so respectfully, allowing me to retrieve them at the top and turn them around. Then we all go down the driveway to catch up with Lucy near the bottom.

Often April and I take these walks together, bringing the boxer Merry along with us. These walks are pure happiness for me, and they encourage the thought that the more I push myself and the farther I go, the sooner I will be back to health. In seven months I have advanced from immobility to mobility and re-entered the world from which I was removed. As we walk, I take in the mountains around the house, and as we go higher the panoramic views of the valley below. I breathe the sea air that floats in from the Pacific and lift my face to the western sun. This is the pleasure of life, and I am part of it again.

Sometimes I grow misty in my walks when I think back over the years and remember the people I loved and the times I failed them. No regret is greater than these memories, salted by the wisdom of hindsight. I should have been a better husband and father and friend. I want to believe that the man I am now would have done better. But while my thoughts can travel back in time, I cannot. Consequently, there is little I can do with these regrets other than use them as an inspiration to be kinder and more understanding toward those I love in the days that remain.

All our journeys lead to diminishing returns, and there is no way to make it different. My desire now is that April and I will still have many years to enjoy the home she is re-making. If I should go before her, I hope its value will rise to the point where it becomes the nest-egg I failed to produce for her. The lesson I draw from all this is captured in a simple homily my daughter-in-law Felicia passed on to me: "The tragedy is not that we die. The tragedy is that we take so long to live."

I often wish I had April's readiness to relish the life in front of her. Yet with her example as inspiration, there is a sense in which I do. However skeptical I may be at first, I am drawn by her passions until, before I know it, I am in the moment and enjoying it to the full. Once I have nestled into the luxurious leather chair she bought for me, or taken a spin on the get-along scooter, I am ready to go, grateful to have had someone to push me over the edge.

When I look at the life receding behind me, I feel gratified to have composed a body of work reflecting what I have witnessed and learned; I take pride in the belief that it is good work and may be of some use to others. I am surrounded now by family and friends, and blessed in both. I have not forgotten those last thoughts that were the focus of my dour reflections at the start of this memoir. I accept that all I have loved and worked for may indeed vanish forever. But I am at a point in my passage where it no longer matters. What matters to me is this: I have lived as fully as I was able, I have produced wonderful children and am married to a woman with a zest for living and the heart of an angel, and I am looking forward to my next walk.

BOOK IV

Staying Alive

(2015–2017)

I

When we are young a day is long and a year can seem forever. Soon, however, a time comes when "forever" is no longer ahead of us but behind; no longer a wellspring of hope but a reservoir of irretrievable loss. "Forever" is what we have left behind, and can never get back.

When my mother was in her eighties, she suffered a series of strokes that removed her ability to recall almost anything that had ever happened to her. Even her husband, whom she had buried following more than fifty years of a joint life, was erased. Far from being the tragedy it may seem, this turned out to be an unforeseen blessing, burying her lifetime losses and providing her with a measure of peace to the end.

Images of my own youth are mostly irretrievable now. Among the ones I retain are the soft of my mother's skin and the worry in her eyes, and the rippling pleasure of my father's laughter, rare as it was. As I go about my routines, I am often brought up short by the wish that they both were here again and could reunite with me in the conversations we should have had but didn't, along with other opportunities that passed us by.

In age, we accumulate goodbyes and become accustomed to their permanence. If we are wise, we are reconciled to the losses; if we are lucky, as has been my good fortune, we may still find love sufficient to carry us on.

By April 2015 I had recovered enough from the botched hip surgery to embark on a two-week speaking tour across the country. Just before my departure I noticed that I was passing blood clots in my urine. At first I was merely annoyed by this encumbrance and how it might affect my plans to return to the campaign trail after a year of prolonged absences. To diminish their significance, I attributed the clots to a malfunction of the blood thinner I had been taking for the thrombosis that followed my surgical mishap the year before. This made it easy to put off attending to the problem until my speaking tour was over. On my return, I made an appointment with the urologist and underwent two exploratory operations, called cystoscopies, to see what was happening.

The tests revealed a more serious cause than I bargained for. The prostate cancer I had successfully lived with for 14 years had mutated, and appeared now in a virulent new form. A quick check of the Internet turned up this warning: "Aggressive neuroendocrine tumors are usually diagnosed at more advanced stages—a circumstance that generally results in a poor prognosis." In one study, 42 percent of patients with the disease were dead after six months, 85 percent after three years, and 94 percent after five.

While I mulled over this news, I was conscious of the fact that the problems with my leg had resulted from my failure to take such matters as seriously as I should have. In approaching the hip replacement two years before, I had treated the operation so casually that I picked a surgeon at random rather than seeking a referral. The result was the botched procedure that damaged my sciatic nerve and led to the clot. When I shared this sequence with my friend Ed Snider, he reproved my foolishness. It was this scolding that prompted me to turn to him now.

Eddie was six years older than I, and one of the more remarkable individuals it had ever been my good fortune to know. Nearly fifty years before I met him, he had created the Philadelphia Flyers, a National Hockey League expansion team, and then a multi-billion-dollar sports empire over which he still presided. For the last year, he had been suffering from a bladder cancer. I knew he was always connected to the best doctors available, which was a reason I should have consulted him about the hip replacement. The reason I hadn't was my reluctance to seek favors from him. But after the scolding, I knew he would be upset with me if I did not seek his counsel this time. When I told him about my condition he referred me to a UCLA urologist named Karim Chamie. It was Chamie who diagnosed the new cancer and persuaded me to schedule a surgery.

The operation was delayed for two months, however, because of a patient backlog at the hospital. This was a period of anxious concern for me because of the aggressive nature of the disease. If the cancer metastasized in this interim, there would be no stopping its progress. On August 14 I was able, finally, to check into the Ronald Reagan Medical Center and put myself in the hands of Chamie, who had engaged a colorectal surgeon to assist him. The cancer had invaded both my bladder and the lower end of my colon. Their plan was to remove the diseased organs and reconfigure my intestines to take their place. It was a complicated surgery, which lasted 12 hours— an ordeal from which I was mercifully shielded by the anesthesia but every minute of which April and my stepson Jon, who sat anxiously in the waiting room throughout the procedure, were forced to endure.

When I woke up battered and weak, it was to a new set of circumstances and worries. The old organs had been successfully removed, but now I had to wonder whether the ones my surgeons had contrived would actually work. As days passed, and the colostomy bag I was now supplied with remained empty, my concern level rose. Would I survive if my new tract failed to function? I tried to imagine what emergency measures my doctors could take to save me. While my anxieties rose, I found myself thinking of Dante's climb up the Mount of Purgatory where he visited souls in torment, suspended between heaven and hell.

My particular perch was the post-operative intensive care unit on the eighth floor of the Medical Center, where I was attended by nearly a dozen nurses and aides who had been recruited from every corner of the globe— Ghana and the Ivory Coast, India and the Philippines, Mexico and Los Angeles. Their presence was calming. This was partly because the circumstances that I found so unusual were obviously routine to them, but mainly because of the assurance with which they performed the tasks on which my recovery now depended. The nursing staff was managed by teams of young doctors and their apprentices who came daily to check on me and monitor my care. They were all part of the UCLA teaching hospital, which was rated among the five best in the nation. Nonetheless, all their professional efforts could not quite remove the anxiety that had become a new skin for me, marooned as I was, and pinned like Gulliver by the multiple IV tubes and monitor wires that lashed me to the hospital bed.

I was impatient to rescue myself, which I attempted to do by trying to eat normally and, as it turned out, imprudently. My body reacted by throwing up three liters of purple bile when I had barely finished the meal. When the mess was cleared, a young doctor appeared at my bedside, looking more pained than I felt as he inserted a plastic tube up my nose and down my esophagus. The tube was designed to suction bile accumulating in my body cavity and deposit it in a calibrated tank so it could be recorded before it was discarded. For the next two weeks, the bile continued to flow at the rate of more than a liter a day, while the tube left me with a punishing sore throat and a permanent flavor of the refuse on its way to the tank. The pressure of the swill on my diaphragm was also making it difficult for me to breathe. To relieve this distress, the nurses provided an oxygen tube laced around my ears and into my nostrils, adding to the many ties already locking me in place.

Another discomfort was the spike in my pain level, which the slightest movement triggered. I attempted to avoid these quakes by maintaining the same position for hours at a time. Maintaining a state of suspended animation was facilitated by the new organs, thankfully now working, which emptied into ostomy bags attached to my abdomen, eliminating the need for trips to the bathroom. An epidural in my back delivered a cocktail of narcotics at a controlled rate, providing me with the relief of a half-sleep. This peace was interrupted only by the regular ministrations of the staff, the hourly checks of my vital signs and the multiple blood draws that were purpling my arms and rendering them an increasing challenge to the nurses searching for a usable vein.

My efforts to remain motionless were also undermined by the insistence of my doctors that I get out of bed and walk. The purpose of the walks was to stimulate the new systems and prevent my limbs from atrophying further. An aide would come to assist me, unhooking the wires and reattaching them to the IV tower. I would then pause on the edge of the bed, shake off the dizziness, and rise slowly to push the IV tower down the hospital halls at an aching pace until I completed a round of the ward.

During these routines I was beset by hallucinations, a result of the opiates I had taken to suppress the pain. As I moved along the halls I saw the words "Abandon Hope All Ye Who Enter Here" emblazoned along them. This was the dire warning Dante had placed over the entrance to hell. One area of my brain knew it was a hallucination, insisting that, no, the hospital was actually a place of hope. But try as I might I could not erase the ominous message.

The pain in my core was so severe at the end of the first walk that I was unable to obey the nurse's instruction to repair to a chair and sit upright for an hour in order to extend the exercise. Within ten minutes I had reached my limit and was begging her to reconnect the wires and help me drag my exhausted body back to the bed. This provided relief, but not the rest my body was craving. Day and night I was unable to get in a real sleep, whether because of the drugs or the adjustments my body was making to the new systems. When evening set in, I tried to tire myself by watching the television; but the faces on the screen seemed to belong to inhabitants of a remote planet, and, try as I might, I was unable to maintain interest in what they were saying. When night arrived, I remained sleepless and adrift. Lying in the dark in my sea of wires, I felt I was in the trough of an endless wave, sweeping me towards destinations unknown. There was nothing to do but endure the journey, hoping that I would eventually wash up on a friendly shore.

A few days after the surgery, Chamie appeared at my bedside with unexpected good news. He had received the pathology report, and it showed that he had removed all the cancer. April, who had worried about my survival, was ecstatic. "You've got life!" she exclaimed. "They've given you a second chance!" When I was slow to respond, she admonished me: "You need to be grateful, and embrace it." Immobile in my bed and marinated in pain, I was having difficulty joining her happiness. As was her custom, she was attempting to lift the spirits in me that I was unable to raise myself, and on which my life had come to depend.

As the insomnia would not let up, I found a way to pass the seemingly interminable hours before dawn by monitoring the minute hand of the clock on the wall at the foot of my bed. My doctors had attached a booster to the epidural, which allowed me to get an extra dose of the drugs on the press of a button. But the button was programmed so that I could only get the dose at eleven-minute intervals. If I missed the appointed time I would not have a chance at that particular boost again. This provided me with an objective. From about 9 p.m. every night I lay in the semi-darkness, eyes fixed on the minute hand of the clock, and waited until it reached the mark. Then I pressed the button and released the drugs. In this way I was able to pass the night hours until the doctor teams showed up in the morning to review my case.

II

Proximity to death can lead one to consider its benefits. I had never before been in a place where my life seemed so tenuous and I had such intimacy with my mortal end. Consequently, I had never felt so comfortable with the idea of accepting what was going to be inevitable, and letting it all go. What was keeping me here? By any reasonable measure I had led a full existence. As my father said, life is a struggle—but suddenly it had become very hard, and I had no guarantee it was going to get much easier. Why not accept the unavoidable? Why not throw in the towel and embrace a last—and lasting—peace?

One reason was this: Every evening my wife would drive fifty miles to be with me in the hospital and spend the night on the couch in my room. Every time she stepped inside, I felt myself called back to the world I had almost left. A joyful aura filled the space around her and enveloped me. Despite these lifts her visits gave me, I tried to dissuade her from them because I knew her days were already burdened, looking after our little ranch, with its two horses and five canines. She was still suffering the effects of the car accident she had survived, and was in pain from a broken clavicle that had not healed. The hospital couch was not very comfortable and her sleep was constantly interrupted by the nurses' visits to my bedside. But she insisted, and even as I urged her not to come, I could not deny the exhilarating effects her visits were having on me. For more than twenty years we had been inseparable, and I could not imagine a world without her. I could not really entertain the idea of giving up and leaving her behind. It would be too great a betrayal, and if there was an afterlife, I would miss her too much.

In my second week in hospital, my executive assistant Elizabeth began showing up with her laptop to spend the afternoons doing her office work. This began a partial return to normalcy, reinforced by calls from my children and a warming visit from my son Ben and his wife Felicia, who made the trip down from northern California. There were also videos of the family dogs that April sent from her smart phone to inspire my return. Through the wires and pain and glacial walks, I was finally beginning to look ahead.

Two and a half weeks after I entered the hospital, my doctors decided I was ready to go. Weak as I was, and still on painkillers, I was elated to be free of the wires and tubes, to walk out into the sunlight and take in the open air. I was prepared for the fact that months of recovery lay ahead, but quickly learned that I had no idea of what that might mean. Although I was familiar with the term "dehydration," I was unaware how serious its consequences could be until I was taken off the IVs and their support. Soon after returning home, I woke up one morning so weak that I had to ask April to provide me a shoulder to lean on as I slid gingerly off the bed. With her support, I was able to manage a few steps before I felt my legs buckle and then my body collapse like an accordion, crumpling to the floor. For the next twenty minutes, I lay in our hallway unable to move while we waited for the arrival of a team of paramedics that April's 911 call had summoned to the house. After taking my vital signs, they hoisted me into an ambulance and drove me to the emergency room at Los Robles hospital, where I was hooked up to an IV and re-hydrated. When they released me later in the day, April drove me directly to my doctor who put me on a two-week regimen of daily IV hydrations, administered by a team of home nurses.

While Medicare provided a basic support system, these nurses were a gift from my friend Eddie, who hovered over us like a guardian angel. While April was suffering through the interminable wait for the outcome of my operation, Eddie called to reassure her that I was going to be all right, and that he would take care of anything she needed. "I felt so comforted by his calls," she told me later; "he was your friend, but when he said that, I felt he would be there for us—for me—and that brought me peace." When I was able to receive them, he made calls to me too. "I love you," he said. "You're going to get well, and when you get out of there we're going to tie one on and paint the town red."

A week or so after the operation he was on the phone again, asking me if I had round-the-clock nurses. When I told him that Medicare didn't provide for that, he said—and then insisted—that I get them and that he would pay the bill. When I resisted, he said I had to get them for April's sake if not for myself. It was hard for me to accept his gift, but he made it even harder to reject it. In the end, he was the last person I would want to feel badly because I couldn't handle the love he was showing me. So I relented and accepted his offer. When I did, I felt a great weight lifted, and a surge of energy pushing me along the path to health.

When I was back home, Eddie was my first visitor. He drove down from his Montecito estate and we sat out on the terrace April and I had built, with a ten-foot stone fireplace and a backdrop of three towering pine trees. Warmed by each other's company we sipped sodas, and talked about the sorry state of the world, and how we were foxhole buddies and would win our wars together. The glow of that afternoon is one of the fondest memories I have from this time in my life.

Bracing as it was, our friendship was fairly recent. We had met only eight years before, when he had already entered the coda of an incredibly full existence. He had created a professional hockey team in Philadelphia where there was none, and built a sports arena for it, and then an empire in sports media and arenas, and arena-suppliers, which extended across the nation. He had brought a championship home, inspiring the greatest public out-pouring of Philadelphians in the city's history. He had become one of its most famous and loved figures, and yet was also a major sponsor of such outliers as the philosopher Ayn Rand, and in the years I knew him, of my Freedom Center. These were acts that a man with his public presence but without his personal courage might not have ventured.

The first kindness I had received from Eddie was a choice seat at the seventh game of the eastern conference hockey quarterfinals, which his Fly-ers won with an overtime goal. Actually it was more of a proselytizing ges-ture than a gift, and succeeded in hooking me on the sport that was his passion. For the next eight years, with the help of a TV-season ticket, I almost never missed one. Whenever I had the opportunity to be on the East Coast I would take in a Flyers game in Eddie's box, where I got a close look at just how competitive he was. He had been attending these games for nearly 50 years, yet sat on the edge of his seat, high-fived every goal the Flyers scored, and became morose when the Flyers lost, as though he was a teenager and it was his first hockey season. Then, win or lose, he would stride down to the locker room to personally praise his players and staff, buck them up after a loss and talk strategy about tomorrow.

When Eddie appeared at my door I was saddened by the visible toll the cancer had taken on his elegant frame, and by the fact that he was in obvious pain. "We're tough," he said when the subject came up. "We're going to beat it." But the two of us knew this was bravado, and only one of us was going to survive. April had told him that my cancer had been removed, and I was about to be a somewhat free man again. He was not so lucky. His cancer had metastasized and spread to his bones. Before I left the hospital, I described Eddie's case to Dr. Chamie and asked him how much time he had left. "Four to six months," he said. That would be February or March I thought, over the knot in my gut. Eddie was not unaware of what the future held for him. He was too smart and had too many good doctors not to know. The romance of "We're going to beat it" was actually a pep talk—a gift—meant for me.

Soon after Eddie's visit my daughter-in-law Felicia organized a family gathering at our house. She made the trip down from northern California again with my son Ben, arranged to have her own large family come up from Carson, and also flew in her two children from New York and Florida. She contrived it as a party for my grandson Jules, whose birthday was close enough to make it plausible. They brought an opulent spread, which included homemade barbecued brisket, and topped it off with a cake and party hats. Their infectious good humor filled our home. To be surrounded by family and by all these youthful high spirits was bracing, and the afterglow lasted long after they had left.

I had been out of the hospital for three weeks and was still in the early stages of recovery. To prevent another dehydration episode, my doctor had instructed me to drink two liters of liquid a day and to eat well. Most common textures and tastes repelled me, and I could not handle anything but bland, liquid foods like cream of rice. It would be months before my appetite returned to normal. Along with managing the pain, these previously-taken-for-granted functions were now a principal focus of my waking hours. The most difficult parts of the day were the early mornings before the light returned. It was not just the thoughts of death that still hovered at the surface, but the kind of barely suppressed panic of one lost in a wilderness on a starless night. I had no idea what the future would bring, or whether I had a future, or if I did, how I would manage to find my way in it.

III

Fortunately, it was not too long before my recovery soon reached a point where I could look forward with some confidence. This new normal prompted me to savor my good fortune, and to reflect how I had reached this point. At the time the cancer was diagnosed, I had been presented with a choice of remedies. The team of doctors involved in my case recommended an eight-month course of chemotherapy followed by surgery, if that should prove necessary. The surgery seemed pretty drastic, and inclined me to take their advice and go with the chemo first.

I was days away from beginning the treatment when I received a call from Dr. Chamie, whom I had asked to review my options before the decision was irreversible. Chamie strongly advised me to do the surgery first. There was a chance it would remove the cancer, he said, while the chemotherapy would make me sick for months and my body might be so weakened as to render a surgery unfeasible. This eleventh-hour conversation persuaded me to change plans. I tried to imagine what the long months of chemotherapy would have done to my body and my state of mind if I had decided to stick with the original plan—whether I could have continued to fight for my survival. I was not sure I could have. My life had turned on a single decision that I had almost got wrong.

My friend Eddie had chosen to forego the surgery and pursue other therapies instead. They had failed, and now his cancer had spread to his bones, putting him in excruciating pain, and there was nothing his doctors could do to help him. As my own body repaired, slow as the progress was, my greatest distress was for my friend. He was such a good man, and so full of life, and I wanted to see him well again.

As Eddie's pain grew and his mobility declined, our date to get together became more and more remote. This was partly due to the slowness of my recovery but more to the fact that, as Eddie's health deteriorated, his schedule filled up with relatives and friends he had accumulated over a long lifetime before we met. He had six children and fifteen grandchildren who converged on his Montecito estate to see and stay with him. He had an even larger extended family from his business life as the head of two major franchises (along with the Flyers he owned the Seventy-Sixers, a professional basketball team). At one point the entire Flyers team visited him, as did movers and shakers of the sports world in which he had been a central figure for so long. I always understood that I was a very small piece of a very big life, a fact that only increased the gratitude I felt for the kindnesses he had done me, and the love he had shown.

Although we never saw each other again after our shared afternoon, we were in touch on an almost daily basis. Our exchanges were the continuation of a practice we had begun years before, when I started sending him comments after the Flyers' games. I was aware then that his message box was probably full of more informed and important observations from Flyers' coaches and executives. But I persisted because he always texted me back to wonder how I was doing whenever I missed a few games. I think he enjoyed the fact that I had the enthusiasm of a relative newcomer to the game, and that my excitement levels were close to his.

Encouraged by his son Jay, I now viewed these communications as weapons in the fight to keep him alive. I knew from my own trials how crucial the patient's attitude was. You had to keep looking ahead not to give in. As fate would have it, the Flyers gave Eddie an assist. After a poor first half of the season they were well behind in the race for a playoff spot. But now they had begun to make a run, and Eddie was thrilled. You could almost feel his passion to see them in the playoffs again. Even so, he never failed to defend his players on the occasions when they lost. I was so anxious for them to win for his sake that I would take out my frustration on individual players after a lost game, criticizing them for what I thought were poor performances. Eddie would then call me to point out the positive features of their play, encouraging me not to lose faith because our chances were still good. This told me he was still in the game, and so were the Flyers who continued to win.

Unfortunately, even as the team was gaining ground on its rivals, Eddie was slipping behind in his battle with the disease. The pain grew steadily worse, and there was little his doctors could do to stop it. In February we had an email exchange that went like this:

> DH: Terrible to lose a game on a bad call like that. I hope you're doing better than when we last talked. I think about you every day buddy.
> ES: Really miss you. Feeling rotten.
> DH: So sorry to hear this. Wish I were a believer so I could pray for your recovery. In my heart I am praying anyway.
> ES: can't think of anyone I'd rather have pray for me.

In the games that followed, the Flyers performed like Zenyatta, the queen of racehorses. They would often start a game slow and fall behind, playing catch-up until the final seconds or the overtime, when they would seize an unlikely victory. On March 28 there was a game like that against the Winnipeg Jets, in which the Flyers fell behind, caught up, and then, in the last 7 seconds of overtime our captain put the winning goal in the back of the net. I was exploding with excitement at the buzzer, and emailed Eddie:

> DH: Holy cow! I hope you got to see it. The heart attack kids did it again!
> ES: I did. Bad day.

My heart sank. Whether it was the brevity of his response or the failure to register even a hint of elation, I knew that it was over and this was the end. Two days later I sent what was to be my last text to him. I had talked to Jay and knew the kind of pain he was in—that he was mostly in bed, heavily medicated, and had told his son the end was near. A week or so before, he had repeated his desire to see me and said he would try to arrange it when he could. I didn't want him to worry about this. I began my email: "This disease is horrible and I understand why it won't be possible for me to come up. I am glad that your wonderful family is there. I want you to know that I love you and miss you. You are the classiest and most generous person I ever met. You have been an inspiration to me in fighting my own illness. Thank you for being such a great guy and for being my friend."

The Flyers loved "Mr. Snider" as they called him, defying his insistence that they call him simply "Ed," and told the press they were fighting for him. He was, as the hockey commissioner said, "the soul and spirit" of the team. On April 9, the final day of the season, the Flyers beat their archrivals to win a playoff spot. Two days later, their leader —my friend Eddie—was gone.

When you lose someone you love, you keep on losing them without end. To mourn Eddie's passing the Flyers put together an event at the hockey arena he had built, while the family organized more intimate memorials in Philadelphia and Montecito. Testimonials came from people high and low, from the hockey community, and from personal and business friends he had made over half a century. What they brought home to me was how common my experience with him had been—how he had reached out and touched people who neither expected nor asked for it, how he had come to them in their hours of need and put his arms around them the same way he had April and me. It caused me to wonder how a man who was such a world conqueror and visionary could be this kind of man as well—one who felt, and was able to take in, the needs of others who were not instrumental to his plans. Eddie had done so to such a degree that I felt shame when I thought about it, because I had tried all my life to be someone like that but had fallen so short of his mark.

He created many institutions, but the only one he put his name on was the Ed Snider Youth Hockey Foundation, a program to buy up local hockey rinks and create a training and education program for disadvantaged youngsters. Virlen Reyes, the first Snider hockey kid to go to college, gave one of the testimonials at the big memorial. Before she discovered the program, she said, "I was lost and quite frankly I did not see a reason in living." With the foundation's help Virlen became a hockey player and then captain of her college team, which won a national championship. When she was made captain, she called Eddie for advice. He said, "Virlen, don't be afraid, just be yourself. Accept the challenge and know that I'm very proud of you." On graduating, Virlen enrolled in an entrepreneurship program at Stanford University and reflected on her good fortune: "For the thousands of young people like myself who have been lucky enough to discover the Ed Snider Youth Hockey Foundation, we have a beautiful edge in life," she said. "We have been taught to understand our own potential and to know that there is no limit to what we can reach."

While Eddie did not have a traditional faith, he was nonetheless a believer. He told his children: "You have to produce something in this world or you'll never feel good about yourself." He created the Flyers and the Youth Hockey Foundation because they gave him pleasure and satisfaction. They were successful because they gave pleasure and satisfaction to others. This was the faith that connected the two sides of his life—his personal ambition and the love he felt for those who found a way to his heart. What defined him in the end was the gratitude that came with his achievements; his humility and graciousness. He had created the Flyers when there were no Flyers, and had made Philadelphia a hockey town when it was not a hockey town. He had treated his players and associates as family, and never forgot what he owed them.

When Eddie was breathing his last, his son Jay was at his bedside. Jay had once been the Flyers' president, and was a speaker at the memorial held in the Flyers' arena. Before twenty thousand Flyer fans he recalled those final moments: "Dad was very ill at the end of his life, to the point where even speaking was a great effort. He asked me to write a few things down, all of which came out in a single word or two. Except the final thing, the last full sentence he ever spoke to me. And this is what he said, not just for me or the family—he told me so I would tell you. 'I can't thank the Flyers enough for everything they've given to me and my family.'"

IV

Like other memories, both good and bad, the ordeals of my operation are receding into the past. This is the way of all our tribulations. At the time we encounter them, they appear overwhelming because the future lies ahead of us filled with unknown threats. But then the future becomes the present and the threats are no longer there. So it is with age, which steadily shrinks the distances in front of us, until all our uncertainties disappear.

My operation took place barely two months after the publication of the memoir I called, *You're Going to Be Dead One Day—A Love Story*. At one point it recorded my observation that "the world itself was passing me by. All around, others were stepping up. Swifter souls on the make, quicker minds addressing the tasks I once set for myself." I was no longer making the action but had become mostly a spectator. Or so I thought in this otherwise normal resignation of age, which was reinforced when the cancer struck. But as I clawed my way back to health, I found myself spurred on to an existence I had thought was pretty much past.

It began in the psychological abyss of the hospital stay, when I became aware of a move among some members of my board to retire me from the leadership of an organization I had created nearly 30 years before. They seemed to have been motivated by the thought that I was looking like a terminal case; and, that being so, it was better to replace me now than to wait until I actually dropped. The rebel board members were demanding a special meeting to vote on my removal while I was still in intensive care. When pressed, however, they agreed to postpone the day of reckoning until the beginnng of October, still only six weeks after the operation itself.

My longtime friend and longest serving board member, Wally Nunn, who was also one of my staunchest allies in the battle ahead, said to me later: "You asked for it by writing all those books about death, which caused people to assume that you were ready to go." And so I probably had. But that didn't alter my belief that if the plan to remove me succeeded, it would damage the organization and be personally devastating to me.

My fears might have been exaggerated. But they had a utility in steeling me for the fight. When the day of the meeting arrived, I was still shaky on my feet. I decided to come to the venue early and prop myself up in a chair at the head of the table. In this way I avoided having to shuffle to the seat when everybody was watching, which would have revealed how weak I was. When the others had arrived and the meeting begun, the verbal confrontation proved bitter and unpleasant, especially because these were all friends who had supported me until then. But the acrimony was inevitable, since I was fighting for my survival and defeat was not an option I felt I could live with.

When it was over, I was still standing. Unable to prevail, the rebels resigned from the board. But in the months that followed, they continued to support the Center and remain part of its community. We kept the board small, which made things a lot easier. I was supported by people—Wally, Peter and Mike Finch—to whom I owed my survival and who were like family to me. For my part, I had shown that I was still very much alive, and that was even more important to me than to everyone else.

It took me a while longer to recover my physical health, for the pains from the incisions to gradually calm down, and for my body to be restored to a reasonably normal state. One month after the board meeting, I summoned my strength and travelled with April to South Carolina to host the Freedom Center's Restoration Weekend, which was held on the battleship Yorktown in the Charleston harbor. In the months that followed I wrote many articles, edited two volumes of my collected writings, and oversaw their publication. This brought the total already published to seven of the nine I had planned. In the spring I spoke at San Diego State University and held a press conference attended by all the major media as part of one of our campus campaigns. I was back.

That same spring, April and I bought a red-haired poodle whom she named "Davey," causing a little confusion in the household. This brought our pack to six with the three Chihuahuas and the Boxer, Merry, and another addition whom we had adopted along the way. This was a German Shepherd mix who had been thrown away by his owners, found on the street by friends, and brought to us. He had no name so we called him "Buddy." A sweet and forbearing dog, his integration into the household was impressively seamless and peaceful. Davey, the youngest of the lot, brought a puppy's energy and enthusiasm, which was contagious even among the older dogs, Lucy and Jake, who were nearing their natural ends. But Davey's biggest impact was on me, taking years off my attitude and helping me look on each day as the beginning of something new, a feeling hard to hold onto at my age.

An equally invigorating event was the return of our horses, Alvin and Diddy, whom we had boarded at a nearby ranch. We had kept them there for nearly three years after April's near-fatal car accident because the injuries she sustained, which were long in mending, would have made it too dangerous to keep and work them. April was tending to them now and riding every day.

Exactly one year after the climactic board meeting, I received a phone call from Chris Ruddy, an old friend and the founder of the media complex

Newsmax. He wanted me to write a book about the upcoming presidential election, and asked if I could write it in six weeks so that it would be ready for publication in time for the inauguration. He wanted the book to be called Big Agenda, and said he was ready to put six figures into its promotion. Since I was feeling healthy and confident, I told him I could and would, and repeated that when he called me a week later to tell me the writing time had been cut in half.

I threw myself into the project and completed it on his deadline, which was November 9—the day after the election. The book appeared three days prior to the inauguration and, thanks to the hundreds of TV and online ads with which Ruddy promoted it, climbed quickly to the top of the bestseller lists and stayed there for weeks and months. It was the most commercially successful book I had published in thirty years, and resulted in invitations to speak all over the country. Thanks to the TV ads and interviews, my visibility was higher than ever. I was right in the thick of the action again. And it had all come to me unbidden.

For me, the new celebrity was more frisson than substance, though like every writer I was gratified to have so many people reading my work and, even better, expressing enthusiasm for it. But I had lived long enough to know that it is the life we encounter directly that sustains us, and the people we are close to. On this front, I could not have felt more fulfilled or happier.

Every morning begins with the same ritual. Before the sun rises there is a rustling at my bedside. It is Davey coming over to give me a morning kiss. He rears on his hind legs and scrambles with his outstretched paws to locate me. I reach over the side of the bed to joust with him, and then we embrace. When our canoodling is over, I roll back in quest of a few more winks, while he departs for other entertainments. In a few minutes I feel ready to rise, and unhook the night bag that collects my urine, and make my way to the bathroom where I can empty its contents. Then I proceed to the room that was once my office but is now my exercise space. It is furnished with a remarkable wall apparatus called Technogym, a gift from one of my supporters determined to keep me alive. My body is not yet ready for vigorous exertions, so I go over to the window where our doves, whom we have named Harriet and Maude, are waiting, and lift the night cover from their cage. In a squeaky voice, I sing them a wakeup song, and raise the blind that lets in the morning light, then make my way through the length of the house to the garage where I let out the big dogs, Merry and Buddy.

When these tasks are complete, I retrace my steps and return to the bedroom to dress. Sitting down, I pull on the therapeutic hose I must wear on my left leg to keep the clot from coming back, then my socks and sweats. When I am done, I walk to the dresser to prepare medicines for Jake and Lucy, who are now quite ancient and ailing. April has been roused by the sounds of these preparations, and is up and ahead of me, and out the front door to the horses. I follow her path to the hall closet, put on my warmest jacket and then my boots before I go to join her on the upper ranch, where she is pitching hay to Alvin and Diddy. My task is to muck the turnouts and stalls, working out the stiffness in my legs as I climb the steps to the ranch level, boosting my energy as I go. I enjoy these routines and the company of our horses who have become old friends, relishing their munching over the hay and the groans of pleasure that accompany it. I enjoy, too, the working partnership with my wife and the way these chores take me out of my head and into the world around me. By the time April and I return to the house, the sun is up, and I am ready for breakfast and the intellectual work of the day ahead. Life is good, and the latest turn in my fortunes is a reminder that the best way to insure this is not to be daunted by the darkness, but to press on.

What was always a certainty but now is one I cannot deny or deflect is that one day in the not too distant future a force greater than any I have ever experienced will descend on me and shut everything down, obliterating once and for all my presence on this earth. It may come in the form of a recurrence of the cancer, but it could also come as one of the many natural causes that are inscribed in our life scripts to bring them to a conclusion. I am at peace with this prospect. My only regret is the pain this will inflict on those who love and will miss me, most especially my wife April, and my children, and theirs.

I still hope to have many more years to savor the life that is mine and to reflect on its blessings. But my footprint is already set, and there is not much I can do to change or extend it. What is within my power is to embrace the people and animals I love and who love me, and not fail to appreciate how lucky I am to have them. When I look back over the setbacks and losses I have sustained, I am grateful for the toughness I was able to summon when to do so seemed quixotic. I am impressed by Eddie's advice that if you are productive for others you will feel good about yourself. I am blessed in a wife who insists that we engage the life before us, and whose love has lifted me through my ordeals. And I am blessed in my children and their children and the happiness that fills my heart whenever I think of them.

Having survived nearly eighty years, I can reflect on the fact that I have been alive longer than most of the people who have ever existed. Still, I would gladly go on for eighty more, which of course is impossible. Notwithstanding the many trials now fading behind me, I take this as a sign that I have lived a good life and done some things right. Given our mortal portion, I could not ask for more than that.